# Political communication today

**Politics Today**
Series Editor: Bill Jones

# Political communication today

Duncan Watts

**Manchester University Press**
Manchester and New York

*distributed exclusively in the USA by St. Martin's Press*

*Published by* Manchester University Press
Oxford Road, Manchester M13 9NR, UK
*and* Room 400, 175 Fifth Avenue, New York, NY10010, USA

*Distributed exclusively in the USA by*
St. Martin's Press, Inc., 175 Fifth Avenue, New York, NY10010, USA

*British Library Cataloguing-in-Publication Data*
A catalogue record for this book is available from the British Library

*Library of Congress Cataloging-in-Publication Data*
Watts, Duncan
    Political communication today / Duncan Watts.
        p.   cm. — (Politics today)
    Includes bibliographical references.
    ISBN 1-7190-4792-7. — ISBN 0-7190-4793-5
    1.  Communication in politics—Great Britain.   I.  Title.
II.  Series.
JA85.2.G7W38   1997
324'. 01'4—dc21                                      96-44005
                                                        CIP

ISBN 0–7190–4792–7 *hardback*
ISBN 0–7190–4793–5 *paperback*

First published 1997

01 00 99 98 97          10 9 8 7 6 5 4 3 2 1

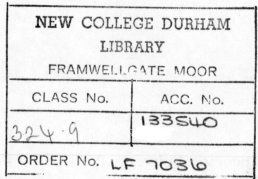
Typeset by Carnegie Publishing, Preston
Printed in Great Britain by Redwood Books, Trowbridge

# Contents

*To Jill, Peter and Ben*

# List of illustrations

# List of tables

# List of abbreviations

| | |
|---|---|
| AFP | Agence France-Presse |
| CCO | Conservative Central Office |
| GUMG | Glasgow University Media Group |
| IBA | Independent Broadcasting Authority |
| IRN | Independent Radio News |
| ITC | Independent Television Commission |
| ITN | Independent Television News |
| MORI | Market and Opinion Research International |
| NEC | National Executive Committee |
| NHS | National Health Service |
| PEB | Party Election Broadcast |
| PPB | Party Political Broadcast |
| RTV | Reuters Television |
| SDP | Shadow Communications Agency |
| SNP | Scottish Nationalist Party |
| UPI | United Press International |

# Acknowledgements

In compiling this book, much valuable information has been gained from various organisations and individuals who answered my (numerous) queries. A number of Peers and rather more MPs were willing to take the time to fill in a questionnaire (or explain why they would not do so), and several Embassies were helpful in providing data on the use of the cameras in their countries' legislative assemblies.

The BBC and ITC gave me access to a series of useful documents and members of their staffs (and those of Channel 4, Sky and The Parliamentary Channel) answered particular points and mentioned possible contacts for me to pursue, as also did the Managing Director of NTC Publications, David Roberts. Several press editors also were kind enough to ensure that I received articles contained in their newspapers from some years ago.

Many individuals made material available or offered thought-provoking observations, and, in particular, Dr Bill Jones made several initial suggestions on the framework of the book. Others have helped in a variety of ways, not least my wife, Jill, who gave constant support and encouragement even when the task of sifting through a vast amount of information was daunting.

To all, listed or unlisted, who have helped me in writing *Political communication today*, I express my sincere thanks. Of course, any errors of fact which have gone unnoticed are my own responsibility, and if by mistake any material has been used without appropriate attribution, then this too is something for which I accept the blame and offer apologies.

# Introduction

The theme of political communication is a relatively new area of study. Over several years it has been customary to include a section on the media in textbooks on British government and politics, but today television and news-papers are the most important topics in what has become a wider field of academic concern. Here, we are using the term 'political communication' to include all those means by which information is conveyed from those who rule or aspire to do so, to those over whom they have influence, the governed. This covers such items as the blatant manipulation of that information, as well as the more subtle means of persuasion, which embrace various forms of publicity and propaganda.

## Mass communications and their importance

One of the main criteria of a democratic system of government is the extent to which the means of mass communication are allowed to operate without restraint upon them. Britain scores well by this standard of judgement. The press is privately owned, and largely free from governmental restriction, save only for considerations of national security. The broadcasting authorities, the ITC and BBC, are able to wade into the waters of political controversy, as long as they maintain a balance between representatives of the main parties.

Since its inception, the BBC has jealously guarded its reputation, and although before the war it was determined to eschew political controversy this self-imposed gag was relaxed after 1945, and disappeared in the Suez Crisis before it was finally dropped in 1957. Since then, Ministers have not been spared from criticism at times of national difficulty.

In any system of parliamentary democracy, there needs to be a means of communication between government and the governed. This ensures that the former is responsive to the latter. Electors are required to choose between various alternatives on offer, and need information before they can express choices. If government is to continue to govern by consent, it requires inform-ation about the electors and how they feel. The media, then, act as intermediaries in the process of political communication, enabling the govern-ment and its opponents to speak to the electorate and the electorate to communicate with its leaders.

Today, this communication is unlikely to be direct, for in most cases people do not see their politicians other than at election time, and even then in most cases they are more likely to see someone canvassing on their behalf rather than the person who seeks office. They may happen to live in a town or city where they get a Ministerial visit, but in the nature of things most voters have to be content with seeing or hearing those who aspire to rule over them second-hand. This is where the media perform such an invaluable function, and television in particular makes it possible to address more people in one evening than a politician could hope to meet in a prolonged series of mass meetings up and down the country.

Diverse forms of communication exist, including a number of ways by which local communities can exercise some political muscle. In the United States, these may range from the familiar to the uncommon. In New Jersey, those who opposed a tax increase organised a mass phone-in to a radio station to attract attention to their grievances, as part of a general revolt against their growing burden of taxation. By contrast, landlords in California who objected to the introduction of rent control decided to circulate video-tapes which depicted pro-control members of the Santa Monica city council in an unflattering light.

In Poland, members of Solidarity helped to sustain the momentum of their movement by recording video messages which could then be played back on machines shared by sizeable groups of people. Elsewhere in Eastern Europe, under the former Communist regimes, some people made their own satellite dishes to enable them to receive foreign programming, and shun the highly-controlled service which the state administered.

In less advanced countries, low-power radio stations have been widely used in South America to win the backing of the people for revolutionary movements, in places ranging from Cuba in the 1950s to Guatemala and Nicaragua more recently. In China, in 1989, student rebels used fax machines owned by private businesses to convey information to the outside world about what was happening in the struggle for democracy.

In whatever society we are discussing, there is a need for those in power or aspiring to attain it to have some means of political communication. Many members of the public wish to know what is happening. To distribute their views, people who are politically motivated will use the means of technology available. On the one hand, we have the fragmented means of political involvement at the local level, which are likely to develop in the future as interactive information technologies allow people to participate directly in decision-making; on the other, we have the world of the major news organisations, increasingly dominated by a diminishing number of ever-larger business corporations. Fragmentation and concentration, local and national activity, go hand in hand; mass communication is the means by which those who would rule over us or influence political decisions operate in the modern world.

## Our primary concerns

The term 'mass media' is a catch-all phrase which denotes all the popular communication outlets such as television, radio, newspapers, periodicals and magazines, and posters, as well as others to which we have alluded. All are concerned with the dissemination of ideas in the form of information, entertainment and persuasion; but although the term is all-embracing, in popular usage it refers primarily to broadcasting and the press.

We are especially concerned with the impact of the two major mass media, the press and television, on political life, so that news and current affairs rather than entertainment are our main area of interest. Although from time to time the cinema, popular music stations or magazines may merit a brief mention, this is not our main purpose and they occur only as much as they affect our political arrangements.

## The formation of public opinion

For most people, their political information and guidance derive from personal experience, gossip and hearsay, and the media. Few have any contact with their MPs, or with political parties, so that primarily, they obtain their information from television and the newspapers, and reach their judgements and conclusions on what they hear on radio, see on television and read in the press.

A study of the 1959 election by Trenaman and McQuail[1] showed that for most people television was the medium which had done most to increase awareness of political issues and personalities, and since that study it has been commonly assumed that broadcasting is now the main medium of communication for the mass of people, having superseded the press in its universality and appeal. Television is now widely accepted and relied upon as a primary source of information and comment on public affairs.

## The growth of the media: newspapers

A combination of technological developments and an enlarged electorate seeking information have been the mainspring of the development of the mass media in Britain and elsewhere. New forms of communication have appeared, and political parties and politicians have adapted to the new possibilities and adjusted their campaigning methods appropriately. The growth of the popular press illustrates the way in which pioneers with available money have seen the potential of technological innovations, and in so doing have provided a means of acquiring influence for themselves and have also opened the way for those in power to achieve the same.

Newspapers in their modern form date back to the early nineteenth century. The invention of the steam-driven printing press in 1814 led to a growth in the circulation of papers, and at the end of the Napoleonic Wars there were some 250 available throughout the country, though most were only concerned with local affairs. However, the London papers and those of the northern industrial towns often provided extensive coverage of political events and commented upon them. The laws of libel and the sense of public propriety were less strict than they are today, and *The Times* wrote most outspokenly on the death of George IV in 1830; no twentieth-century proprietor would dare to publish the scathing caricatures of Gillray and Cruikshank which were then so popular.

Despite prosecutions for seditious and blasphemous libel and the imposition of a heavy stamp duty, it proved difficult to suppress the activities of those who produced radical news-sheets, and governments of the day found it difficult to secure convictions in the courts. Such press freedom was much envied by European liberals who enjoyed no such liberty under their reactionary regimes. It allowed many people – beyond the tiny minority who had the vote – to be informed of and involved in political affairs.

The increase in the franchise in 1832 and again in 1867 provided a powerful impulse for the development of newspapers, as did the progressive elimination of widespread illiteracy with the gradual spread of mass education. The development of the electric telegraph meant that stories could be gathered and communicated more quickly, and after 1860, when the telegraph cable was laid across the Atlantic, it was possible to gain items from America as well. The new rotary presses enabled papers to be printed on both sides at a prolific rate, and faster means of transport meant that they could be available in many areas within a few hours of publication. Cuts in newspaper duty and then their elimination by more liberal politicians such as Gladstone encouraged the growth of the industry, and by the 1870s there was a flourishing provincial daily press as well as that operating in London.

Penny morning papers abounded, and over them all stood *The Times*, selling at three times as much. Still, however, many of the penny dailies catered for the upper and middle classes, providing a very detailed political coverage. Their staple diet was political speeches, and proceedings in Parliament were reported fully and read with much enthusiasm. Journalists were initially banned from the Members' Lobby, but after 1885 the elite on the 'lobby list' were allowed to stand in the hallowed territory and address MPs as they moved around the Palace of Westminster.

It was in the last decade of the century that a real breakthrough occurred, for by then the effects of popular education and the new working-class voters were making themselves felt. The *Daily Mail* was published in 1896 by Alfred Harmsworth, later Lord Northcliffe, who was inspired by the earlier success of *Titbits*. The *Mail* may have been 'written by office boys for office boys' in the view of Lord Salisbury, but it meant wider dissemination of political gossip and opinion, and within four years it sold nearly a million copies. Other popular dailies quickly followed, such as the *Daily Express* in 1900, as proprietors 'cashed in' on the buying potential of the newly literate.

A trend only too familiar today was also in evidence: Northcliffe bought *The Times*, the *Observer*, the *Daily Mirror* and the *Evening News*, as well as many provincial papers. He became a force in the land, and used his influence to hound Cabinet Ministers who fell foul of his outlook. Press barons had become a source of political influence, and politicians such as Lloyd George could recognise their potential and the need to keep it in check.

## Newspapers and their influence today

Newspapers have less impact than they once did. Their readership is not what it was in the great days and television has replaced the press as the main means of communication. Party leaders of the past treated the Press Barons with respect, although when they made life uncomfortable for Stanley Baldwin in 1929–31 he responded with a devastating put-down: in a fine phrase, he said that they wanted 'power without responsibility – the prerogative of the harlot throughout the ages'.

In the early 1950s, there was a prolonged assault by the Tory *Daily Telegraph* on Eden, and he was forced to issue a denial or any intention to resign. A decade later, the editor of *The Times* wrote 'Why Home Must Go', and this is often depicted as an influential part of the pressure on him to step down. Mrs Thatcher escaped such criticism, but John Major's government has been less well served, and erstwhile friendly papers ranging from the *Sunday Times* and the *Sun*, both from the Murdoch stable, have shown only muted enthusiasm for the survival of his government.

Today, it is the tabloids which are seen as presenting the greater problem, for they are the papers (with large circulations) which, as part of their menu of salacious and saucy stories, delve into people's private lives, exposing scandals of public interest but also details of their personal idiosyncrasies and sexual preferences in which there is no legitimate public concern. It is also the tabloids which have made life difficult for the Labour Party in recent years, for although Labour was able to develop as a major political party in the face of a hostile press, the degree of hostility, not to say venom, has markedly intensified in the last two decades.

## The rise of broadcasting and moving pictures: radio, films and television

Today, although politicians on the left might rail against the behaviour of the press and in particular its overwhelmingly pro-Conservative bias, greater attention is concentrated on the content of programmes on radio and television. Owners and editors of newspapers count for less than they once did, and it is BBC management, editors and journalists and those working in commercial radio and television who are of more concern – if only because these media, especially television, are the ones which command so much public attention.

Radio was the first significant rival to the newspaper industry, and it was slow to develop as an important form of communication. The first broadcast occurred in 1901, but regular broadcasting only began in the United States in 1920 and in Britain, in 1923. Some politicians quickly became adept in handling the new medium which had a popular reach well beyond anything that was formerly available to them. In Britain, Stanley Baldwin, and in America, Franklin Roosevelt, soon saw its potential, and Roosevelt was able to address the American people from his rooms in the White House as though they were his intimate friends. Brendan Bruce has written of his skills as a performer, noting that:

> What he said was personal, both in terms of content and style. He spoke slowly as if to a friend on the telephone . . . informally and warmly, calming their fears of economic hardship . . . He spoke of his family and his home life . . . the effect was electrifying on the people. The President was speaking to them, them personally.[2]

Roosevelt was a master of more than one form of communication, for as the microphones were turned off, 'in would troop the newsreel cameramen with their noisy equipment. For the cinema was just as powerful a medium for his New Deal policies as radio, and, in a wider context, even more important.'[3] In its early years, Hollywood, the home of the movie industry, was a willing accomplice in government propaganda, conveying images of German atrocities in World War One.

If Roosevelt was a master of radio and skilled in sensing the new significance of moving pictures, he was also the politician who first appeared on television – in a little-noticed gathering at the New York World's Fair, in 1939. The British television service had started broadcasting three years earlier, and an outside broadcast team was present when Neville Chamberlain returned from his meeting with Hitler at Munich in 1938. After the war, it was some time before the new medium was allowed to cover political affairs, for any subject likely to be debated in the House of Commons during the following fortnight was not considered suitable for discussion (the Fourteen-Day Rule).

Radio was still the major means of communication in the 1950s, though the first head of broadcasting at Conservative Central Office, John Profumo, had studied the way in which the US Presidential election had been handled and saw that there was potential for the use of television by British politicians. Churchill and others were uneasy with the medium, and it was not until the arrival in Downing Street of 'Supermac', Harold Macmillan, that Britain produced a political communicator who was at ease with the cameras. He was a true professional, and as was once said of one of his Tory predecessors, George Canning, he was 'an actor: a first-rate one, no doubt – but still an actor'.

1959 was a turning-point in the history of British electioneering. It was in the election of that year that what David Butler has referred to as the 'professionalisation' of the British campaign[4] really began. Ever since, television has dominated our political life, not just at polling time but throughout the duration of a Parliamentary term.

Broadcasting is a less opinionated and better medium for conveying information than newspapers. Television has been a counter to the overt political bias of a right-wing press. Moreover, the constant exposure of the public to politicians of another or no party serves to show people that those who govern them are not totally unreasonable, that they have a case that can be stated and therefore that denunciation of the other side as mere blackguards is implausible. Its merits and limitations are a subject requiring much greater analysis than this brief review can allow, and we will return to the impact of television on our political life later in this study.

## The scale of the mass media today

The mass media are certainly massive, for the vast majority of homes (around 96 per cent) have a television, some two or even three, and almost three-quarters also have a video.[5] BBC1 and BBC2 transmit around 17,000 hours of programmes a year for their national and regional audiences, and viewers spend an average of nearly four hours a day watching television or video playbacks. Coverage of political issues is always a key feature of programming, and as we have seen, at election times it is particularly extensive and achieves saturation levels. Between them, news, current affairs, documentaries and features can occupy nearly a third of the viewing time.

In 1992, there had already been heavy political programming in the pre-election period, and all organisations made a major commitment of resources for the campaign itself. According to the calculations of Martin Harrison,[6] the total number of hours devoted to political coverage on the terrestrial channels was modestly up on the figure for 1987, and reached about 200 in all. Each of the 300 news bulletins through to polling day offered election coverage, and on days when there was little news (primarily Sundays) it was possible to provide a rehash of earlier stories, or a stocktaking survey of the state of play so far. Sixty-five per cent of BBC bulletins and 59 per cent of those on commercial television were devoted to election issues. Those who had Sky receivers could view political programmes all around the clock, should they have so wished!

An ITC survey[7] showed that 83 per cent of respondents viewed at least one news bulletin a day, and 63 per cent claimed to have read a newspaper. Television news audiences declined during the campaign, but there were still some 14.6 million viewers on BBC on an average weeknight, and 12.3 on ITV. It was therefore unlikely that many could have been immune from such a heavy political diet, and the average person is said to have watched election programmes for about four hours.

Network radio serves around 27 million people in Britain, broadcasting around 35,000 hours of programmes each year on five channels. In addition, in many homes a newspaper is taken or people have access to one. More daily newspapers, national and regional, are sold for every person than in most other developed countries. On an average day, 62 per cent of people over the age of fifteen read a morning newspaper, and 71 per cent a Sunday one.

The universality of the media is evident, and given such a vast audience they must be seen as fundamental to our democracy. Their relevance to public opinion is central. They reflect public opinion, as well as being a major influence upon it.

## Governments, politicians and the media

Ministers will seek to exploit the mass media for their own purposes, and the Prime Minister is in a position to control the public relations of the government through the press aides at Downing Street. As Crossman put it in *Inside View*,[8] the press are 'fed with the Prime Minister's own interpretation of government policy and . . . present him as the champion and spokesman of the whole cabinet'.

The press accepts this relationship. Because of the value of Number 10 as a source of news, many newspapermen wish to remain in good favour with the Prime Minister and his supporting public relations staff. The foreign trips of Prime Ministers usually draw considerable press and TV coverage, as do receptions for statesmen visiting Britain. Mrs Thatcher's unannounced visit to the Falkland Islands in 1983 was extensively covered by a BBC Television team which happened to be there when she arrived, and Downing Street then subjected the BBC to some pressure to make its film available to ITV and thus ensure that the commercial channels would not be deprived of the sight of the Prime Minister's activity.

Such manipulation of publicity helped to make Mrs Thatcher seem increasingly important, whilst others in government declined relatively in popularity. One of her predecessors, Harold Wilson, was also very conscious of the techniques of manipulation, and the Conservatives came to suspect him of regularly contriving some exciting news release on the opening day of their annual conference in order to blot them out of headlines. Whereas the Leader of the Opposition can only react to events, the political initiative lies with the Prime Minister.

A common complaint is that those who control the mass media also determine the agenda for discussion and the editors of a popular programme have an enormous opportunity to influence day-to-day political conversation. In making their decisions over what to include, they may be reflecting the concerns of the electorate, but this is only one consideration in their professional judgement of what is 'newsworthy'.

Politicians often resent the influence of broadcasters and envy their ability to control communications. The Falklands War in 1982 was an occasion when many right-wing politicians, particularly those in government, were irritated by the unwillingness of the media to wave the patriotic banner as much as they would have liked, and Mrs Thatcher wondered why they could not speak of 'our boys down in the South Atlantic'.

Non-elected as they are, the influence of broadcasters is viewed by some politicians as potentially undemocratic. What they choose to show and the way in which they choose to show it can have a significant impact on the standing of the parties and the politicians. Hence the parties are always on the lookout for any signs of a breach of the guidelines on impartiality with which they have a statutory duty to abide. Whether or not an interview with the Prime Minister will actually affect the outcome of a local election, it is the thought that a free platform might be made available which causes so much anxiety to party managers.

If elected politicians had exclusive rights of conduct over political argument, important and controversial areas might be excluded and inconvenient ones ignored. The media at their best can act as a watchdog for the electorate, and hold those who rule over us to account for their actions. Interviewers put MPs on the spot, and in so doing perform a public service.

Each side needs the other. The politicians want publicity: they need an outlet for their viewpoint, and are sensitive to the way in which they are allowed to put their ideas across. Broadcasters are interested in entertainment as well as political education. They know what is likely to be popular with the viewers, and that lengthy and uninterrupted political expositions may not make good viewing. They seek to make politics exciting, and look for ways of presenting material in a way which heightens public fascination; sometimes, this means failing to take politicians seriously.

Making fun of politicians is a national sport from the days of *That Was The Week That Was* (TW3) in the early 1960s, down to *Spitting Image* today. With the decline of deference, those in high places were regarded with less respect and interviews by early interrogators such as Robin Day could be searching and sometimes hostile in tone. Senior Labour figures were incensed by the treatment accorded to them in *Yesterday's Men* (1971), a sometimes irreverent programme which discussed how former Cabinet Ministers were using their time.

In days past, politicians were able to advance their career without having to watch for the searching lens of the cameraman. Today, they need to do so under the glare of the television lights, not just in interviews but in the House of Commons as well, since the voters have been able to see Westminster at work. They have had to respond to the television age.

## Politicians, parties and television

Television has indeed changed the way we perceive politicians, and if our survey dwells heavily on the American experience this is because its impact first became apparent across the Atlantic. However, as in so many areas of culture, what happens in the United States happens in Britain a few years later. Though first developed in the United States, new political propaganda techniques and the use of professional advisers who specialise in their use subsequently appeared elsewhere. British politicians now lean heavily on advisers for advice on their appearance.

It was in America during the Presidential election of 1956 that, for the first time, the mass electorate of a democratic country could regularly see the competing nominees for the Presidency on their screen. As a result, one of the great concerns that Adlai Stevenson's and General Eisenhower's advisers shared during the campaign was that 'when tilting their heads to read their speeches over television, the candidates's hairless scalps were elongated, suggesting giant eggs'. In the words of Kathleen Jamieson, 'For the first time baldness became an issue of concern in a presidential campaign.'[9]

The shape of people's bodies is largely irrelevant to the shape of their ideas when they are addressing the public in writing or on the radio. But it is quite relevant on television. Television has made the 'look' of a politician vital, and Professor Postman argues that the extent to which a President is remembered for his appearance rather than his political acumen has been underestimated. Thinking of Nixon, Carter or Reagan, it is their image, how they looked on television, which is the main memory. Before the development of photography, anyone thinking of Madison, Jefferson or Monroe would have thought of the words they uttered; 'Now we think of their images.'[10]

Laurence Rees makes the point that in an age of television, George Washington or Abraham Lincoln may not have fared so well under the gaze of the camera, for it can play 'cruel tricks' upon some of those who are recorded. He quotes Raymond Strother (a veteran Democratic Consultant) as saying that some people are 'not electable' on grounds of their appearance.[11] In his view, Lincoln 'could never have been elected today', for some of his unattractive facial features (protruding nose, fleshy lips and sharp chin) would have lessened his appeal. For Strother, Gary Hart was the ideal of what a candidate should be like. He was his political consultant in the 1984 Presidential campaign, and observing him at close quarters remarked:

> I thought he was the perfect man. You want them to represent sort of a Mid-western accent and style. They can't be too regional. They can't be too southern. They can't be too western . . . he was a handsome, striking man and people were drawn to him physically. Gary Hart looked like a President. He looked like a candidate should look.[12]

Unfortunately, in the eyes of many Americans, he was unable to act in the way that they thought a President should do. His failure to discipline his private life meant that his personal assets were never put to the disposal of the American people via the White House.

Strother notes a fundamental change in the appearance of politicians since the invention of television: 'If you had a yearbook of the US Senate from thirty or forty years ago, you'd find a lot of unappealing, unattractive people. If you had a yearbook of people elected in the last ten years, you'd find a whole group of attractive people.'[13] Conventional good looks are seen as an advantage, and fatness or baldness as quite the opposite. Writing of Strother and other consultants, Rees remarks that: 'They realise that the candidate has to compete for attention on television amongst a variety of other TV performers who are themselves, to a varying degree, chosen for their looks.'[14] Postman agrees with this view, and claims that the early twentieth-century President, William Howard Taft, would never have been chosen today, for a 327lb image 'would, in all likelihood, overwhelm any articulate sentences that would issue forth from the image's mouth'.[15] Particularly in the United States, with their thirty-second commercials, politicians are trying to sell themselves. 'Physical attraction helps . . . [as] other socially desirable human attributes are associated with it.'[16] Television is a medium in which attractive people flourish.

Propagandists on both sides of the Atlantic have great influence, and only a naive politician would not listen to the advice of a television expert. The same is true of Britain. Harold Wilson, on becoming leader, had his teeth fixed, and a make-up man from Hammer Horror films was brought in to advise on make-up, for as the campaign progressed in February 1974 great bags were known to form under his eyes and make a bad picture.

In the 1970s Sir Gordon Reece examined the photo opportunity in the United States, and Labour has recently employed American Democratic consultants, Doak & Schrum. Before the 1992 election, Rees records a meeting between the former Conservative Director of Communications, Shaun Woodward, and Roger Ailes, who did much propaganda work for the Republicans in the 1980s.

What Marshal McLuhan and Postman have concluded is that television is not just another medium 'through which thoughts, opinions and personalities can be transmitted. Television has changed the very way it has become necessary to communicate, and thus the very way it has become necessary to formulate political discourse.'[17]

The mass media are a vital part of the political system, and parties and politicians have had to adjust to their changing form. In Britain, the Conservatives have long been in the forefront in the use of new forms of communication, but in recent years Labour has realised the potency of the media and the danger of seeking to operate without them. Successful media presentation and manipulation requires careful planning by expert advisers, and this is the route which both parties have increasingly taken.

There has been a growing professionalism in the conduct of British election campaigns. The parties have attempted to concentrate their key forms of communication around their agenda, be it via party election broadcasts, press conferences, speeches or paid adverts. As the authors of *Political Communication* have noted, election campaigns have become agenda-setting games: 'The object is to concentrate the attention of television and newspapers on your strengths (and their weaknesses), thereby deflecting attention from your weaknesses (and their strengths).'[18]

They show how in 1987 Labour scored well on agenda-setting, around the social themes of health and education, but in so doing the party 'detached itself from the election-winning economic issues'. In Norman (now Lord) Tebbit's words, 'perceptions of economic well-being are the master-card in all this'.[19] Labour had learnt enough to ensure that its level of professionalism was far superior to any of its previous efforts, but that election showed that – even with the most effective use of new forms of communication – it was difficult to sell a product which was widely perceived as being faulty and not yet ready for marketing.

### Themes and perspectives

In order to provide a theme for our study, it is necessary to examine the main theories of the mass media, for an examination of the different perspectives, be they Marxist or liberal, influences the view taken of matters of ownership and of the effects of the media. Entirely differing approaches to the nature of power and its distribution in society are held by pluralists and Marxists.

The approach adopted here has been to review the competing theories before we proceed to examine key areas of the mass media. The form and structure of mass communications, the relationship between ownership and control are then analysed, as are questions of impartiality and the attempted manipulation of information by the government. The influence of the media on politicians and people, especially that of television, is then assessed, so that a judgement can be reached on the extent to which they both shape political opinion and reflect it.

Fundamental to the study is an attempt to ascertain the way in which parties and politicians – both in Britain and the United States – have sought to come to terms with the available means of mass communication, especially in the age of television. Austin Mitchell, MP, has observed that

> instead of being grateful for the opportunity to reach constituents, politicians began to realise that they had power to insist on conditions, interviewers Jimmy Young and Wogan being preferred to Dimbleby, Walden and Paxman. 'No go' areas came into interviews. Politicians dodged and weaved as always but also developed the technique, displayed then more frequently in sticky situations, of rounding on the interviewer, the messenger bearing the bad news and the organisation which backed both. The worst situations produced the worst bullying.[20]

Some politicians have admirably mastered the media and how best to exploit its potential. Most of them realise that today they need the broadcasters and are concerned to ensure that they use the opportunities presented most effectively. Their party managers have come to appreciate that a concern with communication skills is as important, if not more so, than the message being communicated. Mitchell remarks that

> Policy-making became part of an image-building process, rather than the ideological obsession it had been. Labour learned [in the 1980s] what the Conservatives already knew; the art of the sound bite, the quotable quote rather than the long ramble which could be edited; the happy phrase which conveys the useful half-truth; the art of spin doctoring; the photo opportunity as a substitute for interviews, information, or even sense; the methods of mood creation.[21]

The nature of party propaganda has changed, and all involved can see the need to woo the voters, by appealing to their emotions as much as to their intellect. Parties began to train their spokespeople in the techniques of present-ation and image-building, and began to see how they could use the media: 'The ratio between hard information and mood creation tilted in favour of the latter.'[22]

By so concentrating on the image rather than the reality, there is a danger to the traditional concept of democracy which places the emphasis upon reason and judgement rather than upon the values of those who are today's 'hidden persuaders'. Our study will conclude by assessing the extent to which present and future trends pose an insidious threat to the workings of our democratic system.

## Notes

1  J. Trenaman and D. McQuail, *Television and the Political Image* (Methuen: London, 1961).
2  B. Bruce, *Images of Power* (Kogan Page: London, 1992), pp. 18–19.
3  *Ibid.*, p. 19.
4  D. Butler in I. Crewe and M. Harrop (eds), *Political Communications: The General Election Campaign of 1987* (Cambridge University Press: Cambridge, 1989), p. xiii.
5  *Britain 1995: a Handbook* (COI for HMSO, 1995), p. 479. (Same source for number of radio listeners and newspaper readers, below).
6  M. Harrison in *The British General Election of 1992* (Macmillan: London, 1992), p. 156.
7  J. Wober, *Televising the Election, Preliminary Report*, ITC Research Paper (London, May 1992).
8  R. Crossman, *Inside View: Three Lectures on Prime Ministerial Government* (Jonathan Cape: London, 1972), p. 67.
9  K. Jamieson, *Packaging the Presidency* (Oxford University Press: Oxford, 1984), quoted in L. Rees, *Selling Politics* (BBC Books: London, 1992), p. 52.
10  N. Postman, *Amusing Ourselves to Death* (Viking Penguin: New York, 1985), quoted in L. Rees, *Selling Politics*, p. 52.
11  R. Strother, quoted in L. Rees, *Selling Politics*, pp. 52–3.
12  L. Rees, *Selling Politics*, p. 55.
13  *Ibid.*
14  *Ibid.*
15  N. Postman, quoted in L. Rees, *Selling Politics*, p. 53.
16  M. Cook and R. McHenry, *Sexual Attraction*, quoted in L. Rees, *Selling Politics*, pp. 53–4.
17  M. McLuhan, quoted in L. Rees, *Selling Politics*, p. 13.
18  I. Crewe and M. Harrop, *Political Communications*, p. xiii.
19  N. (now Lord) Tebbit, quoted in *ibid.*, p. xiii.
20  A. Mitchell MP, *The Media*, Wroxton Papers in Politics (Phillip Charles Media: Barnstaple, 1990), pp. 13–14.
21  *Ibid.*, p. 13.
22  *Ibid.*

Part I

# Theories, organisation, partisanship and effects

# 1

# Theoretical approaches

Studies of the media in recent years have attempted to place them in a broader social context. The main preoccupation has been the interrelationship between ownership, control and output, and the influence which each of these have upon attitudes. Three main theories have been put forward in analysing these themes, and we will examine each in turn.

### The pluralist model

This is the one which conforms to the principles of a liberal-democratic society with a market economy. In this model, the audience is paramount, for the owners (controllers and producers) of journals, newspapers and broadcasting compete for readers, listeners and viewers, and therefore respond to market demand. The consumer influences the end-product, for the owners need public approval, if they are to sell their goods, gain a good market share and make a worthwhile profit.

Owners and producers decide on the content of their output on a professional basis. They exclude the illegal and unsellable, but otherwise choose material on the basis of its suitability for the target audience and in the light of its inherent importance and interest. News is viewed as a neutral description of real events, which have an objective reality.

Pluralists will concede that there is bias in the media. Most newspapers are pro-Conservative, and the tabloids in particular concentrate on the sensational, trivialise more serious issues, and tend to treat women as sex-objects. The broadcasters tend to take a moderate, pro-establishment view in their political and current affairs programmes. However, such tendencies derive not from the deliberate attempts of those in the media to manipulate the recipients, but because they are responding to audience choice – what the market wants. Many people like to read about sex and violence, they like to see girls on page three of the *Sun*, and on more important matters may themselves take a pro-establishment view.

Furthermore, by virtue of the diversity of ownership in a market economy, a range of opinions will emerge. There are many media outlets, and they adopt a different bias to meet the demands of their differing audiences. Moreover, for those who wish to hear or read a different point of view, there are organs which cater primarily for minority tastes. *Spare Rib* meets the need of radical feminists, the *Morning Star* puts forward a pro-communist message and on television there are two channels which are designed to provide less popular programmes. Series such as *Ebony* are designed for the interests of ethnic minorities.

In other words, it is up to the consumer to choose those parts of the media which best suit his or her interests. Because the consumer is king, then any influence on public attitudes will be primarily to reinforce them. We watch or read what we wish to find out, and inasmuch as we are exposed to information which challenges our assumptions then we 'turn off', either literally or meta-phorically. We remember only that which conforms to our own beliefs, and ignore or regard as misinformed that which is not attuned to our ideas.

In this model, the consuming public is not a passive body which, when injected with a hypodermic syringe, absorbs its content (the 'hypodermic' model). By contrast, it is a heterogeneous group of consumers who use the media in the way that suits their needs; they take from it what they wish to (the 'uses and gratifications' model). John Whale is an exponent of this approach and his *The Politics of the Media* provides a useful account of his thinking, as the extract in the box on p. 24 indicates.

To those on the left, such a theory is inadequate, misconceived and mis-leading. The issue of control is central to their criticism and Marxists in particular believe that the content of the media is manipulated by those who own the press and broadcasting organs.

### The mass manipulative model

This offers an entirely different approach to the pluralist one. Far from the consumer being an influence upon the media, it is the other way round. Consumers are the gullible recipients of the message which the media impart. They constitute a homogeneous body which, when it is indoctrinated with a single viewpoint, soaks it up. This is often referred to as the 'hypodermic model' of media influence. A patient is injected with an antibiotic, and as a result changes occur to his or her body. So with an audience; it is dosed with a message which produces changes in behaviour or in attitude.

On the religious right (the so-called moral majority in the United States and assorted fundamentalist Christians in Britain), supporters detect elements in the media who seek to undermine conventional moral standards. Editors and producers do this by depicting an excess of sex and violence on television and in the press, which is seen as corruptive of decent standards of behaviour. Mrs Mary Whitehouse, and the National Viewers' and Listeners' Association which she founded, articulate this approach.

Among media theorists who support this model, it is the Marxist version which is much more common. Marx believed that 'the ideas of the ruling class are in every epoch the ruling ideas'. Members of that class, wishing to perpet-uate their survival as the dominant order, would endeavour to persuade the rest of society that a continuation of the status quo was in their interest as well. They would do this by numbing any radical instincts, so that their own values could prevail.

There are several interpretations of Marxist thinking, and although many sociologists have been inspired by his distinctive approach, they have deviated from it in particular respects. For this reason, they are often regarded as neo-Marxists rather than as strict adherents of the creed.

Among these neo-Marxists was the Italian, Antonio Gramsci (1891–1937), who was an early exponent of the notion of hegemony in society. Like several others whose thinking and writing came under the Marxist umbrella, he was wary of the exclusive emphasis on material or economic factors as a determinant of historical change. For Gramsci, ownership of the means of production would not alone enable the ruling class to monopolise power; it needed the support or at least the acquiescence of the rest of society, if it was to retain its hegemony or leadership.

In common with other neo-Marxists, he stressed the importance of ideas in helping to preserve the present state, and felt that institutions such as the educational system, the church and the mass media all had a more significant role than Marx ever allowed. If popular approval and consent were achieved, then the ruling class had achieved hegemony.

He argued that within society there are ruling elites, unrepresentative in their membership, and that these run institutions of which the mass media is one. The media were in Gramsci's view a powerful means of retaining class dominance. Owned by the ruling class, they were the more potent as they could convey the message of their proprietors across the nation and into every home. They denied access to those who would peddle challenging ideas, and kept the rest in a state of bemused satisfaction by feeding them on a menu largely composed of entertainment. As a result of what is presented over the air and on screen, the beliefs and tenets of these elites are so widely held that they are not seriously discussed at all.

Also in this neo-Marxist category were members of the Frankfurt School of sociologists. It was originally based at the Institute of Social Research which was founded at Frankfurt University in 1923. Its members were also concerned with the influence of the media on mass culture. Many of them fled from Germany in the 1930s during the era of Nazi rule, and took with them the unforgettable experience of a people ruthlessly manipulated by those in control of propaganda. They sought safe haven in the United States where their theories of culture and society were developed and elaborated.

Social theorists of this radical left variety departed from conventional Marxist beliefs in a number of ways. Marx saw the inevitability of the fall of capitalism because it would be brought down by economic crisis, whereas Jürgen Habermas, in *Legitimation Crisis*, argued that the collapse could be indefinitely delayed. Whereas Marx believed that there was potential for class conflict to go on increasing, Habermas felt that the possibilities of 'class compromise' might make this unlikely; the workers could be won over and bought off. One way in which this might happen is via the use of the media.

Whilst deeply critical of capitalism, Habermas, Adorno and others argued that it keeps the workers in a state of contentment by providing (via the media) a diet of entertainment which blunts the critical senses. Something of the flavour of these sentiments was encapsulated in the lyrics of a song by Dire Straits in 1982, 'Industrial Disease':

> They're pointing out the enemy to keep you deaf and blind
> They wanna sap your energy, incarcerate your mind
> They give you Rule Britannia, gassy beer, page 3,
> Two weeks in España and Sunday Striptease.[1]

This 'pap' has the effect of encouraging people to think that they have a choice between soap operas, pop music, quiz shows and other light amusements. In reality, they are being exploited and manipulated, despite the illusion of freedom. Marcuse was a member of this Frankfurt School of thought, and he summed up the effects of media trivia: 'The hypnotic power of the mass media deprive us of the capacity for critical thought which is essential if we are to change the world.'[2]

More recently than these social thinkers, others have written in similar vein. Instrumentalists such as Miliband speak and write of direct control over the production of the communications industry by the ruling class. Structuralists (such as Althusser and Marcuse, among others) offer a different emphasis, and see editors and journalists as being willing tools of the ruling class and its ideology, only too happy to conform to the interests of capitalists.

All in this school agree that the owners use the media to put forward their own outlook and foist it upon those who hear or read. They consciously seek to influence the public response, by ensuring that the contents of their organs conform to their ideas and purposes. Their ownership allows them to become ever richer and more powerful.

They point to the domination of the press in many countries by major business tycoons, and the Murdochs, Maxwells and Rowlands of this world are said to be interested in perpetuating their own position rather than seeking to provide people with a balanced account of what is happening. On occasion, they may even purchase papers which register a loss (e.g. Murdoch and *The Times*), for it gives them the chance to advance their own beliefs, as well as a sense of personal satisfaction.

Theorists of this school would suggest that advertisers contribute to this manipulative effect, for they provide the income on which newspapers depend. If advertisers do not provide advertising copy to papers of which they disapprove, then those papers might fail; indirectly, therefore, they help to influence press content.

The broadcasting authorities are also included in this model. Although the BBC is a public corporation, and commercial television and radio are controlled by the ITC and subject to the regulation of Parliament, the people who inhabit the world of broadcasting are seen as pro-establishment. There may not be capitalist ownership, but those who are appointed to key positions are, in the words of Stuart Hood, 'men and women drawn from the list of the "good" and the "great".' [3]

These are people who are likely to be amenable to the views of those in power, their natural inclination being to support the status quo in society and shun any radical assault on accepted values. If necessary, they can be 'leaned on' by those in power, and if they show signs of resistance, they can be replaced. Those in power represent the interests of the capitalist class, and through this control over the two institutions which regulate broadcasting, they can ensure that any challenge to their outlook is fended off. In 1985, it was claimed that the internal security service, MI5, had an office in the BBC, and its representatives sat in on key appointments to ensure that 'safe' choices were made.

Such a Marxist view concentrates on ownership of production and bias in output, and tends to assume that to demonstrate that these exist is enough to prove particular effects on the often-uncritical consumer whose hearts and minds have been manipulated.

## The hegemonic model

A less extreme position between the other two models is that represented by the interactionists or hegemonics. Those who articulate this position see the media as on the one hand reflecting the existing views of the audience, and on the other as helping to create and reinforce a consensus outlook. Their claims are more modest than those who take a mass manipulative line, although they accept some aspects of their case. They do not see bias in newspapers and on television as being consciously introduced, and argue that it derives from the attitudes of those who inhabit the world of the media. They suggest that the dominant class in the media propagate the dominant or hegemonic value-system in society. But if 'those who produce media output may be conditioned by powerful forces . . . they are not totally determined by them'.[4]

In Britain, the media are seen as being dominated by the comfortable middle classes, for those who work within the newspaper business or broadcasting tend to represent a narrow and often privileged section of British society. They take a generally safe stance on political, social and economic issues, putting forward views which many people might consider to be 'reasonable' or 'common-sense' ones, which command the agreement of the majority of people of moderate persuasion. This stance encompasses the outlook of the Labour right, the 'wet' Conservative left and the centre ground of the Liberal Democrats and their forebears.

The selection and presentation of news is seen as all-important, and Cohen *et al.* talk of the 'manufacturing of news' and 'agenda-setting'.[5] Agenda-setting is the idea that the media have an important influence over what people think about, because the agenda for discussion is laid down by those who produce programmes and those who edit and write for newspapers.

Instead of events in the news having an objective reality, the news is what broadcasters and journalists say it is. In their choice of items and their use and interpretation of the material, journalists and broadcasters reflect the existing consensus. In this sense, news is seen as socially constructed rather than a neutral description of what happened.

The consensus approach eschews extremism of the right or left. It was at ease with the rise of the Social Democrats in the early 1980s, hence the allegation that the party was a 'media creation'. On many issues, the middle-of-the-road supporters of this approach will take an establishment line, and typical attitudes might include support for parliamentary democracy and the monarchy, criticism of 'excessive' trade-union power and approval of 'big business' and its role in the creation of wealth. They may be unsympathetic to 'odd' or minority causes. Striking trade unionists and pressure-group activists, such as gays and anti-nuclear campaigners, are likely to arouse their disdain, and the behaviour of radicals, coloured people and the industrial working class might not meet with their approval.

The natural leanings of those who adopt this cautious middle ground are certain to be confirmed as they adapt to the prevailing ethos of the media world. They learn to appreciate what the controllers in television and the editorial office will expect of them, and to convey their stories in the light of this safe approach. Alternative viewpoints, especially those which are more radical or challenging, are less likely to get an airing. The media's refusal to tackle some issues is sometimes referred to as 'gate-keeping'; whereas a strike may be reported, probably unfavourably from the workers' point of view, industrial injuries and diseases (more damaging to the management image) hardly merit a mention.

As the existing consensus is seen by leftish students of the media as pro-capitalist, sexist and racist ('white, male, middle-class and middle-aged') then it follows that the output reflects these prevailing attitudes. It reflects the perspective of the leading personnel in the media, which therefore reinforces their hegemony or dominance.

The most well-known exponents of this view (sometimes referred to as the Qualified Left Critique) are to be found in the Glasgow University Media Group (GUMG), whose research has had a very significant influence on study of the media in recent years. Their work, quoted in the box on p. 25 and examined in more detail later in this book, stresses that

the world view of journalists will pre-structure what is to be taken as important or significant. It will do this in two ways. First, it will affect the character and content of specific inferential frames used in the news. Second, it will set general boundaries on where news is looked for, and on who are the significant individuals, the 'important' people to be interviewed.[6]

Hegemonists such as members of the GUMG share a number of similar assumptions to Marxist critics. They both lament the lack of real diversity in news, believing respectively that this springs from either the influence of a small number of capitalist proprietors or from the editors and journalists who produce the coverage of news and current affairs. Whether or not these safe opinions are put forward consciously or unconsciously, the effect is to ensure that only a limited variety of viewpoints can emerge. By stressing the interests of the owners of wealth and property, this helps to ensure that conservative values and ideas are advanced, and that the dominant ideology of society is preserved and strengthened.

They are echoing the views of a long line of Marxist thinkers and writers, not all of them British, who argued that society is divided between capitalists and the proletariat, and that the ruling class will seek to advance their class interests. Their case rests on the view that in every age those who control the means of production, distribution and exchange strive to preserve and safe-guard their own private position, and ensure that their values are the ones which prevail. Subversive voices which challenge their beliefs – be they strikers or Greenham activists in the 1980s – do not get an airing, and if they are shown at all they are presented in a hostile way.

The Establishment knows how to preserve itself, and proprietors, editors and journalists angle the portrayal of current affairs in such a way as to ensure that dissenting voices will be characterised as deriving from irrational people bent on destruction of society as we know it.

It is easier to describe the views of those who espouse the positions outlined than to assess the merits of these interpretations and come down on one side. Elements of truth can be recognised in all of the theories. For instance, it is certainly true that ownership of the media is concentrated in ever-fewer hands, and many would agree that television often shuns the views of those at the margin and presents a consensual image. Yet this is not to say that this concentration of ownership necessarily has an impact on the content of the paper or other medium which is owned. Even if it does have an impact, this does not demonstrate an effect on the readership. Similarly, the GUMG may well be right in pointing to the way in which the message conveyed is per-meated with the ideas and attitudes of those who inhabit the world of the consensus. Again, this does not indicate that the views of the journalists and editors involved make a deep impression on the consumers who listen to, watch or read the material on offer.

Pluralists may point to the diversity of views on offer through the various media and stress the importance of consumer choice. However, it is undeniable that the effect of market competition and trends in ownership has not been to widen choice but to reduce it. A theoretical increase in the number of organs available, be they newspapers or television channels, does not in itself amount to an increase in the range of opinions transmitted. Moreover, if there is a narrowing of views presented, then this may be very significant if it can be

## The three viewpoints: some key extracts

*The pluralist approach*

From John Whale, *The Politics of the Media* (Fontana: London, 1977), pp. 84–5: how readers determine the type of content in newspapers.

It is readers who determine the character of newspapers. The *Sun* illustrates the point in its simplest and saddest form. Until 1964, the *Daily Herald*, and between 1964 and 1969 the broadsheet *Sun* had struggled to interest working people principally through their intellect. The paper had declined inexorably. Murdoch gave up the attempt and went for the baser instincts. Sales soared . . . At the *Express*, the message was received . . . The new Chairman, Victor Matthews, launched . . . a paper called the *Daily Star* which extended the *Sun* formula even further downmarket. At the *London Evening Standard* (another Beaverbrook paper) Matthews' dismissal of a cultivated editor, Simon Jenkins, in the same month, presaged a similar approach there. These were owners' decisions, certainly; but they would have meant nothing without the ratification of readers . . . [Where] proprietorial influence survives at all, it must still defer to the influence of readers . . . The press is . . . predominantly conservative in tone because its readers are.

*The mass manipulative approach*

From Ralph Miliband, *The State in Capitalist Society* (Quartet: London, 1972), pp. 203–10: the media's way of propagating a conservative view of society.

The nature of the contribution which the mass media make to [the] political climate is determined by the influences which weigh most heavily upon them . . . they all work in the same conservative and conformist direction . . . The first . . . derives from the ownership and control . . . Rather obviously, those who own and control the capitalist mass media are most likely to be men whose ideological dispositions run from soundly conservative to utterly reactionary; and in many instances, most notably in the case of newspapers, the impact of their views and prejudices is immediate and direct, in the straightforward sense that newspaper proprietors have often not only owned their newspapers but closely controlled their editorial and political line as well, and turned them . . . into vehicles of their personal views . . .

Quite commonly, editors, journalists, producers, managers etc. are accorded a considerable degree of independence, and are even given a free hand. Even so, ideas do tend to 'seep downwards', and provide an ideological and political framework which may well be broad, but whose existence cannot be ignored by those who work for the commercial media . . .to the financial viability, which means the existence of newspapers and, in some but not all instances, of magazines, commercial radio and television . . .

A third element of pressure upon the mass media stems from government and various other parts of the state system generally. That pressure . . . does not generally amount to dictation. But it is nevertheless real, in a number of ways . . . [including the supply of] explanations of official policy which naturally have an apologetic and tendentious character. The state . . . now goes in more and more for 'news management', particularly in times of stress and crisis . . . the greater the crisis, the more purposeful the management, the evasions, the half-truths and the plain lies . . .

### The hegemonic approach: agenda-setting

From Glasgow University Media Group, *War and Peace News* (Open University Press: Milton Keynes, 1985), pp. 198–201: an item on Greenham Common, the United States Military Base, near Newbury, Berkshire, where Cruise missiles were stored, and where women set up a peace camp in the 1980s.

We analysed the coverage of six women's peace demonstrations that appeared on the news between December 1982 and December 1983, in a total of thirty-eight bulletins; and compared it with other reports including some from the women who participated. We found that many features central to the camp were not covered in the news. First, why is the camp all-women? This is a fairly obvious question, asked by many visitors to the camp except apparently TV journalists; it does not seem to be prevalent in news reports and was not explained or raised in any of the coverage in our sample. How is the camp run? The women's peace movement has developed its own form of organising, based on collective decision-making and individual responsibility, run without leaders or any formal structure of bureaucracy. It's an exceptional method, quite distinct from the way CND, for example, or any political party works; but again the TV did not tell us about it . . .

A second source of conformist and conservative pressure upon newspapers and other media is that exercised, directly or indirectly, by capitalist interests, not as owners, but as advertisers . . . their custom is . . . of crucial importance . . .

A further question is, what exactly is the political protest the camp is making? The broadcasters have grasped the fundamental idea that the camp is opposed to Cruise missiles – although even this is not always clear. Coverage on the two ITV evening bulletins . . . avoided giving any reason at all for the women's action . . .

On ITN, the newscaster began: 'At Greenham Common, police broke up an attempted blockade by women peace protesters' (ITN, 17.45, 4.7.83); and the correspondent concentrated on how the women were dragged away rather than why they were there . . .

demonstrated that the media do have a real impact on the attitudes of those who use them.

At this stage, it is important to be aware of the schools of thought which exist for they provide a perspective to assist us in sifting through the evidence which follows. It is, perhaps, best to allow spokespersons of the different models to present their own case, as is done in the extracts on pp. 24–5.

## Notes

1  As quoted by P. Trowler, *Investigating the Media* (Unwin Hyman: London, 1988), p. 50.
2  Marcuse, *The Hypnotic*, quoted in *ibid.*, p. 50.
3  S. Hood, On Television (Pluto: London, 1983).
4  GUMG, *War and Peace News* (Open University Press: Milton Keynes, 1985).
5  Cohen *et al.*, *The Manufacture of the News* (Constable: London, 1973).
6  GUMG, *More Bad News* (Routledge and Kegan Paul: London, 1980).

# 2

# Radio and television

## Growth and development

From 1922 to 1954 broadcasting was a monopoly of the BBC, and since December 1926 the BBC has been run as a public corporation. Its Charter underlines its responsibility as a medium of public service, and states its functions as being 'to inform, to educate and to entertain'. The first Director-General, Sir John Reith, imparted a tradition of high morality, propriety and political impartiality, though in the 1926 General Strike he saw his duty as clearly to support the views of the Government, under attack as it was from the miners and others: 'Assuming that the BBC is for the people and that the Government is for the people, it follows that the BBC must be for the Government in this crisis too.'[1] Though his standards could be austerely high, and there was sometimes a pompous and narrow moral tone to broadcasting in those days, Reith laid down the foundations of a widely-admired service of great educational and cultural value.

The BBC became the sole provider of television programmes once they were regularly transmitted in 1936. For many years it was allowed to operate without competition for it was felt that this would lower the quality of programming. Broadcasting was viewed firmly as a public service provided for the nation as a whole by the body best fitted for this purpose.

Eventually, Conservative legislation in 1955 permitted the establishment of a commercial alternative (ITV), in which substantial shareholdings could be held by the business interests of large corporations. Thus from the beginning, Granada (a company with widespread media and leisure interests) was the largest shareholder in Granada Television.

When the new commercial companies arrived on the scene competition for viewers developed, though the BBC is less bound by the requirement to get high figures than ITV which needs to appease its advertisers. BBC traditions did not crumble under the impact of the new rivalry, though inevitably its attitudes changed, reflecting changes in society's outlook. In the 1960s, critics on the right began to lament the arrival at the BBC of a new 'cultural radicalism', which was a way of objecting to too many plays on sex and violence, and the more liberal use of 'obscene' words; Lord Reith would not have approved of satire and other innovations.

The BBC prided itself on its coverage of current affairs, but the ITV channels took up the challenge admirably. In the report of the Annan Committee on Broadcasting in 1977,[2] it was found that some BBC programmes in that area were 'dull'. By contrast, those on commercial television were commended.

The BBC gained a second channel in 1964, and in 1982 another commercial one was established, Channel 4, which was also funded by advertising. For many years, this duopoly of the BBC and ITV continued in British television, their position unchallenged. One network was financed by the licence fee, the other by all the advertising revenue, and the competition between them was based on the quality of what they produced. Both organisations had one popular and one minority channel, and each was able to command a fair share of the viewing audience. Both sought to do what the BBC Charter had said it should – 'inform, educate and entertain'. ITV always placed rather more emphasis on popular programming (with plenty of American series and situation comedies) to capture a wide audience, but the BBC also saw the widespread appeal of such programmes and put on many of its own.

### Recent developments in television: the Major approach

In the last few years, there have been dramatic changes in the range of broadcast material available and in the running of television and radio. Far more services are available as a result of the increase in radio frequencies, and the development of satellite and cable television. These changes in technology and the rising demand of consumers to have access to them meant that legislation was necessary to provide a new regulatory framework in which the media could operate.

The Broadcasting Act of 1990 overhauled the regulation of television and radio, and was designed to offer viewers and listeners access to the range of programmes available whilst at the same time maintaining standards of taste and quality. Among the changes:

1   The IBA was replaced by a new Independent Television Commission (ITC) and a Radio Authority, and cable was brought under their jurisdiction. The ITC lacked the powers of the old IBA over scheduling of programmes, though over licensing and ownership its rules were stricter.

2   These bodies awarded licences to the highest bidders in a competitive tendering procedure (subject to certain quality controls), though for local radio the awarding of a licence was determined by audience demand and the increasing choice which any new entrant in the field could provide.

3   Provision was made for a new independent television channel, Channel 5, and three national commercial radio stations, as well as for new local radio stations.

Much concern was expressed at the time about the Government's commitment to the existing high standard of public service broadcasting, though Ministers stressed that the BBC's role was a 'cornerstone' of the new arrangements for it offered diversity and quality, its programmes covering a range of public tastes. Channel 4 retained its brief to be innovative and to cater for those interests not covered by ITV (or Channel 3 as it was to be officially known). Altogether, therefore, three out of the four channels were to operate under the same obligations as before.

Furthermore, a limit was placed on the output of non-European programmes put out by the BBC and ITV, and the controls demanded by the ITC in awarding licences were a check upon the quality of scheduling. Both channels were charged with ensuring that at least 25 per cent of their programmes derived from independent producers.

The controls offered limited reassurance to critics of the new Act who felt that the Government was inspired by an obsession with a free-market philosophy in which competition was all-important, even if standards were sacrificed in the process. The Act was the most important legacy of the Thatcher era in the field of the mass media, and its results are still with us today.

## Ownership and control

The British Broadcasting Corporation (BBC) was actually established as a public corporation in 1927. By its Charter, it was made responsible for public service broadcasting in the United Kingdom, and its task is to provide high-quality programmes of broad appeal. The Charter lays down its constitution and financial arrangements. It has a Chairman, Vice-Chairman and ten other governors appointed by the Crown on the advice of the government of the day. The Governors oversee the work of the organisation, but day-to-day running is in the hands of the Board of Management under the leadership of the Director-General (currently John Birt). The home services of the BBC are financed by revenue from the licence fee (£86.50 for colour) which is paid by every household with a television receiver– or should be! Almost 21 million licences are issued per annum, all but a million for colour sets. For external services, Parliament votes a grant-in-aid.

The licence fee has long been a source of controversy, unloved by some on the political right. They dislike the way in which a public corporation is granted a bounty denied to commercial television, and feel that it makes the BBC feel too secure and certain of its survival in the harsh financial world of the 1990s. When the Peacock Committee reported in 1986,[3] some Conservatives were hoping that free-market views would predominate and that as a result of its findings the BBC might be broken up or at least lose its dependence on the licence. However, although some concessions to the commercial lobby were made, Peacock rejected any advertising on the BBC and wanted to see the annual fee indexed to inflation.

The Independent Broadcasting Authority (IBA) was created in 1954 to oversee the provision of commercial television services by the ITV companies and ensure that they fulfilled their role of information, education and entertainment. The Chairman and members of the IBA were appointed by the Home Secretary. The IBA has now been replaced by the Independent Television

Commission (ITC), which has a Chairman, Vice-Chairman and eight other members, all of whom are now appointed by the Secretary of State for National Heritage.

These ten people are responsible for licensing and regulating all non-BBC television services operating in or from Britain, including Channel 3 (ITV), Channel 4, cable and satellite services. They distribute and monitor the licences, but are not involved in the detailed scheduling of programmes. That is the responsibility of the ITV Network Centre, which is wholly owned by the ITV companies; it undertakes the commissioning and scheduling of programmes shown throughout the ITV network, and provides a range of services to the companies when a common approach is needed – in such fields as the development of training and new technology.

Commercial television comprises fifteen of these companies, independent programme contractors such as Anglia and Granada which are licensed to supply programmes in the regions. A common news service is provided by ITN. The licensees derive most of their revenue from the sale of advertising time on television, and some have sufficient resources to produce their own programmes and sell them to other regional companies; others 'buy in' most of their programmes.

The companies operate on the basis of a franchise. Each one plans the programme schedule for its region, and has to withstand competition for the franchise when it comes up for auction, as they do every ten years. Newspaper proprietors may acquire an interest in television companies, although safeguards are built in to ensure that they do not have more than a 20 per cent share – thus allegedly curbing a concentration of media ownership.

The last franchise renewal was conducted under the terms of the 1990 Broadcasting Act. It was carried out in October 1991, and those who were victorious won the right to run programmes from January 1993. Twelve existing and four new companies were successful bidders. To gain the award of a licence, companies had to pass a quality threshold (with diverse programmes, including regional and national news and current affairs programmes, and children's and religious ones), though generally the successful ones were those who were able to make the largest bids; if a company offered a significantly better quality of service, then a lower bid could be accepted.

The fear of shoddy, unimpressive standards on commercial television has been to some extent justified, and in its report on the performance of companies in their first year of operation since the 1991 auction the ITC was critical of the ITV Network Centre's schedule, which it described as cautious, predictable and lacking in innovation. Its current affairs performance was 'better than some of its eager critics asserted and there was no significant narrowing of the agenda compared with the recent past'.[4]

Channel 4 was previously owned by the ITC and financed by the regional companies. Under the 1990 Act, it is now run as a public corporation, licensed and regulated by the ITC, selling its own advertising time and retaining the

proceeds. Its brief is to present a suitable proportion of educational programmes and to encourage innovation and experiment, and roughly half of
its viewing time is devoted to informative items. To fulfil the criteria it has
been set, it commissions programmes from the ITV companies and buys others
from overseas. It makes no programmes of its own.

Both the BBC and the independent television companies have a considerable
degree of freedom in the programmes they produce. When matters are raised in
Parliament, the responsible Minister is the Secretary of State for National
Heritage.

Local commercial radio was permitted by Conservative legislation in 1973
and is run by several large companies. It is not a vast money-spinner, so that
larger conglomerates are less involved than in television, but some commercial
chains are international in scope.

### The duty of impartiality

Under their respective charters, both the BBC and commercial television have
a duty to be impartial in their political coverage, and both aim to achieve a
high degree of balance and impartiality. The wording in Chapter Three of the
Producer's Guidelines could not be clearer: 'The notion of impartiality lies at
the heart of the BBC. No area of programming is exempt from it.' The ITC
adopts a similar approach.

The BBC jealously guards a reputation for fair reporting and aims to present
a range of opinions. Inevitably, it errs from time to time, and both parties have
at times criticised its alleged bias – the Labour Party in the 1970s was very
suspicious of the BBC, as have been the Tories since the mid-1980s. Politicians
are sensitive to a rough handling in interviews. However, as a former Chairman of the BBC, Lord Hill, put it 'impartiality remains our duty and our
objective . . . the BBC espouses no causes; it tries to hold the ring in argument'.[5]

The obligation of impartiality is interpreted by both organisations as a duty
to present a span of views, left, right and centre, of groups which operate
within the democratic framework. As one of the Directors General of the
BBC, Sir Charles Curran, remarked: 'We are biased in favour of parliamentary democracy.'[6] Similarly, the BBC shuns extremism and his predecessor,
Sir Hugh Greene, felt that neutrality about racism was undesirable; it must
be opposed.

However, even if within the limits it sets itself, the BBC (and ITV) might
claim impartiality, as we shall see, there are many politicians who doubt the
validity of its case. If there is no overt bias, then other critics might point to
the existence of a hidden bias in favour of certain 'consensus' (and often
conservative) values.

All of the main political parties believe that they get unfair treatment at
times. As a third party, the Liberal Democrats fear that they suffer from neglect
and are therefore particularly sensitive about their coverage during election
campaigns. Labour is wary of a bias in reporting on issues such as industrial

relations and the existence of 'extremists' in their midst. The Conservatives, now long in office, believe that that the BBC is over-keen to expose the less successful and more gloomy aspects of life in Tory Britain – hence their depiction of the 'Beeb' as the 'Bolshevik Broadcasting Corporation' at a Tory Conference (Kenneth Baker, Party Chairman, 1990).

Channel 4 has a different view about balance. Its responsibility is to be innovative, and rather than producing programmes of the traditional format in which a spokesperson of the left, right and centre is each given two or three minutes in any discussion, it aims to achieve balance over a longer period. Therefore, a programme might start from the assumption that all participants are committed on the left or right, and develop the arguments at greater length and in greater depth because all agree about fundamentals. The other side can have a similar programme later in the schedule.

### Party political broadcasts

Both bodies consult with the Government and Opposition parties in the Committee on Party Political Broadcasts over the allocation of party political broadcasts (PPBs). Under the terms of the 1990 Broadcasting Act, airtime is normally made available to the UK parties represented in the House of Commons and to the SNP in Scotland and Plaid Cymru in Wales. Channel 4 does not transmit the annual series of PPBs, but does put out election ones.

The number of annual broadcasts is normally settled twelve months in advance. The maximum number permitted is five, and there is a long-standing convention of equality of time between the government and the official opposition. All parties are entitled to a broadcast for every 2 million votes polled at the previous general election, subject to the limit of five.

In addition, at general, European or local election time, parties are entitled to broadcasts. The allocation is related to the level of support gained in previous elections and to the number of candidates nominated. The charters of the BBC and ITV compel both sides to screen these broadcasts at peak time at a length to be negotiated with the parties.

In the European election of 1994, the number of candidates fielded permitted not only the three established parties to show broadcasts, but also the Greens, the Liberal Party, the Natural Law Party and the UK Independence Party.

### Current plans

It is still premature to pass a judgement on the long-term prospects of our commercial channels, faced as they are by competition for advertising revenue from BSkyB, the satellite services operated on a subscription basis by Rupert Murdoch's organisation. By 1992, boosted by some sporting successes, Sky appeared to be covering its operating costs and moving towards viability as more people bought satellite dishes to gain access to its programming. Since then, its profitability has increased and it is now an established player on the media scene.

Cable television has yet to make a significant impact, for most households do not have access to its products in 1996 – though by the end of the century, it should be much more widely in use.

An issue of greater relevance to most people is the future of the BBC. In November 1992 the Major Government produced a discussion paper which established a framework for debate on the structure and role of the Corporation.[7] It responded with its own document, *Extending Choice*, on the way forward for the organisation.

This is an issue of political importance, for the present Charter of the BBC expires in 1996. At stake is the whole question of the commitment to public service broadcasting which has come to be associated with a broader remit than that of the original Charter, 'to inform, educate and entertain'. It involves a commitment to put on minority programmes and ones which challenge the viewer's intellect and imagination, rather than to opt for material which helps it in the 'ratings war', to news and documentaries rather than showbiz entertainment.

In the new era of multi-channel broadcasting it is unlikely that the BBC can retain its traditional share of the audience, and as its share declines then the justification for a compulsory licence fee comes into question. Does this make advertising inevitable? Is there likely to be a reduced emphasis on current affairs to boost viewing figures? Should the BBC cease to employ its own orchestras and run popular music of the Radio One type? Such issues are all going to be debated – if not finally resolved – in the mid-1990s.

Some of the questions posed were answered by the publication of a White Paper by the Heritage Secretary, Peter Brooke, from which it was apparent that the BBC had staved off the threat to its dominant role as the country's dominant public service broadcaster. It endorsed the changes made by the present Director-General, John Birt, and showed that the plans of some on the Tory right to break up the BBC and privatise the organisation had been thwarted.

The main points of the White Paper were:

1   The Charter was to be renewed for ten years from 1997.

2   The licence fee was to be retained until 2001; the inflation-linking formula would be re-examined in 1996–97, and the whole licence system reviewed before 2001.

3   The BBC was to retain all its TV and radio services.

4   The BBC was to develop its commercial activities, so that in theory it could join a consortium to bid for Channel 5 or commercial radio licences – though these activities would not be cross-subsidised by the licence fee.

5   The Broadcasting Standards Council and the Broadcasting Complaints Commission were to be merged, in a move to simplify regulation.[8]

In some ways against the odds, the proposals mean that the BBC has been preserved. This is a victory for the Birtian revolution, under which the Director-General has sought to inject market forces and rigorous business practices into a conservative and traditional organisation. It has been a skilful political exercise, but critics of the new regime say that his 'reforms' have dismantled the old-style BBC at the behest of Ministers; they accuse him of running a 'fear and sycophancy' regime, and strongly dislike his managerial style. Without his changes, the BBC may not have survived as a licence-funded public service broadcaster into the next century.

According to Colin Seymour-Ure, the broad lines of Tory policy as it developed under Mrs Thatcher have continued during the Major premiership. These include:

1   The inevitable incidents of political pressure on the media; politicians of any colour wish to use the media to best advantage and see that they get a 'friendly' coverage of their performance – or at least avoid too many hostile references.

2   The application of free-market principles to the development of television, a policy already laid down by the time that Mrs Thatcher left office and which was put to the test in the first ITV auction in 1991.

3   A 'benign indifference' to the concentration of ownership in the media which means that the Government seems to be unworried by the cross-ownership of the press and other media, which allows the Murdoch empire to control Sky television and other newspaper groups to have a stake in ITV companies. Under the Major administration, ITV companies have shown an interest in merging, and no objection was registered to the takeover of Central by Carlton in 1994.[9]

This issue of television ownership is a controversial one to which we must return, though it is best considered in tandem with the question of ownership of the media as a whole.

## Notes

1   Lord Reith, as quoted in A. Briggs, *The Golden Age of Wireless* (Oxford University Press: Oxford, 1965), p. 365.
2   Report of the Committee on the Future of Broadcasting, 1977, HMSO, Cmnd 6753.
3   Report of the Committee on Financing the BBC, 1986, HMSO, Cmnd 9824.
4   ITC, Performance Review, 1993.
5   Lord Hill, as quoted in I. Gilmour, *The Body Politic* (Hutchinson: London, 1969).
6   Lord Curran, as quoted in I. Gilmour, *The Body Politic*.
7   Report of the Committee on the The Future of the BBC, A Consultation Document, 1992, HMSO, Cmnd 2098.
8   Report on The Future of the BBC; Serving the Nation, Competing Worldwide, 1994, HMSO.
9   C. Seymour-Ure, *Politics Review*, vol. 2, no. 3 (February 1993), p. 13.

# 3

# The press

In 1900 there were twenty-one national daily newspapers; now there are ten. However, although circulation figures are now higher than they were nearly 100 years ago, there has been a slow but steady decline in the sale of newspapers in the post-1945 era. In 1970 the overall circulation of nationals and dailies was 37 million, in 1980 33.5 million and by 1995 the figure was down to around 30 million.[1] Several papers have ceased production around the country and the long-established *Times* still runs at a heavy loss.

The atmosphere in the 1970s was one of contraction, but this later changed. The move of the Murdoch papers from Fleet Street to Wapping in 1986, with the opportunities to use labour-saving machinery and cut production costs, gave the press a new lease of life, and led to the establishment of additional newspapers by other proprietors. Founding a new broadsheet or tabloid was cheaper and easier than before, and a paper could survive with a much smaller circulation. Among others, the *Post*, the *News on Sunday*, the *London Daily News* and the *European* made their appearance. When Eddie Shah launched *Today*, it was seen as the harbinger of a new era which would open up a pluralist newspaper market with more choice for all. New titles, new ideas, new journalism would follow.

Despite the transformation in production techniques, a launch was still an expensive business. But titles such as the *Independent* (pioneered at a cost of £20 million in 1986) have since found a niche in the market and it continues its battle for survival. The *Sport*, if its diet of sex and sport can be counted as a newspaper, was in daily production by 1992 and remains strong. On Sundays the *Independent on Sunday* has kept going (with difficulty), unlike the *Sunday Correspondent*, which had a brief life during 1988–89. *Today* later became part of the Murdoch stable and for a while looked more viable than in its early days, but it has subsequently disappeared. The revolution of the mid-1980s now looks a less clear-cut triumph.

New and less labour-intensive techniques have made some revival of the national press possible, and helped to resolve the long-running problems of poor industrial relations in Fleet Street. Yet the decline of daily sales has continued in the last ten years, and even if more papers are available than they were in 1984 the tendency to concentration of ownership has intensified.

Despite the declining sales, newspaper reading in Britain is a well-established habit and far more people read than buy a copy. Because the country is geographically small and has a good network of communications, it is feasible to distribute daily papers on a national scale. Because of this, national dailies have a dominant position, whereas in the much vaster United States almost all papers are local and regional. Britain has 1,400 such papers, but the politically significant ones are the national dailies and those published on Sunday.

### Ownership and political leanings

Ownership in the western world is concentrated mainly in the hands of a comparatively small number of large organisations which tend to be very wealthy and right-wing in their political viewpoint. This is particularly true in Britain, and a few proprietors have a monopoly of the papers sold. News International, the Murdoch empire, produces about a third of all the papers read, and with the Mirror Group it accounts for nearly 50 per cent of sales. Like most commercial enterprises, newspaper companies exist to make a profit and given the costs of production in newsprint and labour they need a good circulation.

In 1994–95, a ferocious price-war was waged between the Murdoch empire and its rivals. The viability of the _Independent_ has been threatened by such cut-throat competition. If initially the reader benefits from lower expense in buying a newspaper, in the long term the cost of these cuts may be that some papers cease publication. Rupert Murdoch has speculated that in the long run, only three papers will exist; _The Times_ as a quality broadsheet, the _Sun_ as a mass-readership tabloid, with maybe the _Daily Mail_ left as an up-market popular read.

Advertising heavily subsidises the revenue of papers, and enables them to be sold at much less than their real costs of production. In the late 1980s, a quarter of the _Sun_'s income came from its advertisements, and in the case of the the quality papers the amount was around 60 per cent. Pleasing the advertisers is therefore another limitation. They can be upset by hostile articles in the paper and withdraw their advertisements (for example, the Wills tobacco company withdrew its material from _The Times_ in the 1980s after the publication of an item critical of the effects of smoking). Moreover, to keep advertisers happy, editors need to cater for popular tastes and give the public what it wants – to boost circulation.

### Political content

The political leanings of most newspapers are Conservative, though papers are financially independent of the main parties and do not follow strict party lines. The _Telegraph, Express, Mail_ and _Sun_ are unwaveringly pro-Tory, as is _The Times_ which can, however, adopt a more critical and independent line. The _Mirror_ is pro-Labour, though it also can show a rebellious spirit whenever the party moves too far to the left. The _Independent_ claims to be neutral between parties (though in economic thinking it inclines to the right), whilst the _Guardian_ is by tradition more leftish in tone; as originally a Liberal newspaper,

Table 3.1. *National newspapers*

| Title | Date founded | Owner | Circulation (Oct. 1995) | % of market |
|---|---|---|---|---|
| **Dailies** | | | | |
| Popular tabloids | | | | |
| Daily Mirror | 1903 | Mirror Group | 2,552,501 | 18.4 |
| Daily Star | 1978 | United Newspapers | 748,363 | 5.5 |
| Sun | 1964 | News International | 4,055,746 | 29.6 |
| Mid-market (tabloids) | | | | |
| Daily Mail | 1896 | Associated Newspapers | 1,853,236 | 13.5 |
| Daily Express | 1900 | United Newspapers | 1,251,431 | 9.1 |
| Today | 1986 | News International | 573,680 | 4.2 |
| Qualities (broadsheets) | | | | |
| Financial Times | 1888 | Pearson | 297,382 | 2.2 |
| Daily Telegraph | 1855 | The Daily Telegraph | 1,052592 | 7.7 |
| Guardian | 1821 | Guardian Newspapers | 405,716 | 3.0 |
| Independent | 1986 | Mirror Group | 296,869 | 2.2 |
| The Times | 1785 | News International | 675,032 | 4.9 |
| **Sundays** | | | | |
| Populars | | | | |
| News of the World | 1843 | News International | 4,473,405 | 29.4 |
| Sunday Mirror | 1963 | Mirror Group | 2,508,590 | 16.5 |
| People | 1881 | Mirror Group | 2,102,269 | 13.8 |
| Mid-market | | | | |
| Mail on Sunday | 1982 | Associated Newspapers | 2,033,832 | 13.4 |
| Sunday Express | 1918 | United Newspapers | 1,350,559 | 8.9 |
| Qualities | | | | |
| Sunday Telegraph | 1961 | The Daily Telegraph | 673,540 | 4.4 |
| Independent on Sunday | 1990 | Mirror Group | 330,991 | 2.2 |
| Observer | 1791 | Guardian Newspapers | 484,236 | 3.2 |
| Sunday Times | 1822 | News International | 1,270,402 | 8.3 |
| | | **Total** | 15,227,764 | |

Notes

1. For our purposes the *Daily Sport* and *Sunday Sport* are irrelevant: their interest is almost exclusively titillation, not information.

2. Circulation figures based on those provided by the Audit Bureau of Circulations (ABC). Other details adapted from *Britain 1996: a Handbook* (COI for HMSO, 1996).

3. *Today*, then losing £10 million a year, closed in November 1995, a victim of intense competition and a sharp increase in the price of newsprint.

it is now willing to show sympathy to Labour though without endorsing many party attitudes.

The extent of right-wing dominance has increased in recent years, for in 1945 35 per cent of the market favoured the Labour Party, whereas by 1995 the figure was down to just over 20 per cent as represented by the *Mirror* and the *Guardian*. However, to point out a sharp bias to the right in newspaper coverage is not to say that newspapers therefore necessarily influence readers to that point of view.

Particularly with the 'quality' or 'broadsheet' papers, people tend to choose one which is in line with their general outlook; for example, the progressive middle classes favour the *Guardian* or the *Independent*, and businessmen prefer *The Times* or the *Telegraph*. In other words, rather than it being the case that the *Telegraph* influences its readers to Conservatism, it is Conservative diehards who are likely to read it in the first place.

Table 3.2. *Social class and political leanings of newspaper readership, 1992*[2]

| Paper | Party backed | % of readers in social class | | | | Party backed by readers | | |
|---|---|---|---|---|---|---|---|---|
| | | AB | C1 | C2 | DE | Con. | Lab. | Lib. Dem. |
| Daily Mirror | Lab. | 6 | 18 | 36 | 40 | 20 | 64 | 14 |
| Daily Star | pro-Con. | 4 | 14 | 38 | 44 | 31 | 54 | 12 |
| The Sun | Con. | 5 | 17 | 35 | 43 | 45 | 36 | 14 |
| Daily Mail | Con. | 24 | 32 | 25 | 19 | 65 | 15 | 18 |
| Daily Express | Con. | 20 | 34 | 26 | 20 | 67 | 15 | 14 |
| Today | Con. | 12 | 26 | 37 | 25 | 43 | 32 | 23 |
| Financial Times | No endorsement | 57 | 30 | 8 | 5 | 65 | 17 | 6 |
| Daily Telegraph | Con. | 49 | 32 | 11 | 7 | 72 | 11 | 16 |
| Guardian | Lab./LD | 52 | 27 | 11 | 11 | 15 | 55 | 24 |
| Independent | none | 52 | 29 | 11 | 7 | 25 | 37 | 34 |
| The Times | Con | 61 | 26 | 8 | 6 | 64 | 16 | 19 |

Source: Adapted from M. Harrop and M. Scammell, *A Tabloid War: The British Election of 1992*, tables 9.1 and 9.4.

### The concentration of ownership and the diversity of viewpoints

The postwar reduction in the number of national newspapers and the tendency towards monopolistic ownership have reduced the number of range of viewpoints available to readers. Concentrated ownership means that left-wing parties get an unfair deal. Moreover, the fewer the number of papers, the less likely it is that any one of them will be able to risk an unpopular view, if it carries the possibility of a loss of readership and advertising revenue. Diverse opinions may not be possible.

The Tory governments of recent years have allowed such a concentration to continue. The law provides a safeguard against the risks inherent in such a narrowing of ownership, and government consent is necessary before a newspaper or group of papers can be transferred to a proprietor whose circulation will, with the newly acquired ones, exceed sales of more than 500,000 daily. Except in certain cases, the President of the Board of Trade is expected to refer any such proposals to the Monopolies and Mergers Commission. Yet this anti-monopoly legislation has not curbed the trend, and in 1981 and 1987, when Rupert Murdoch acquired *The Times* and *Today* respectively, no such referral was made; the Government allowed the deals to go through unchallenged.

Private ownership of newspapers, rather than any form of state control, is widely seen as a guarantee of freedom of choice and a bulwark against state tyranny. But is it healthy if a few proprietors can dominate the dissemination of ideas?

### Bias in the press

In any system of private ownership, the likelihood of bias becomes a probability for proprietors and the editors whom they appoint are likely to reflect a particular line. Some proprietors have notoriously directed editorial policy, whilst others have not. Whereas under the proprietorship of Lord Thompson, the previous owner of *The Times*, the editor had considerable discretion, in the Murdoch era today there is said to be more interference. Harold Evans, the former editor of the *Sunday Times*, claims to have been dismissed because he withstood attempts at such influence. The paper has continued to have a forthright editor with his own views, but Andrew Neill – who has now moved on – was probably selected for this and other tasks in the Murdoch empire precisely because he shared a number of Murdochian ideas.

Owners tend to be wealthy persons whose background and views incline them sharply to the political right, and we have seen that British papers lean clearly in this direction. It may be true that most individuals do not buy newspapers because of their political slant, and indeed in several surveys *Sun* readers have often identified the sympathies of their paper inaccurately. It may also be the case that of those who are informed before reading a paper, the effect of the papers is to confirm their existing view rather than to mould their opinion.

However, for many people the fact that papers tend to be overwhelmingly anti-Labour, a bias that has become more marked since 1974 when Murdoch bought the *Sun*, means that pro-Conservative views unhealthily abound. To some people this matters less now that the advent of television has provided another means of mass communication, and if Labour has come to expect the worse from newspapers they are understandably more touchy about receiving a fair deal from television companies.

The standard of political coverage varies enormously. The 'qualities' allocate to news and current affairs a treatment in some depth, whereas in the tabloids events are treated more briefly and dramatically. At election time, there is more focus on political events, and the best of the press can be usefully informative. But the tabloids display partisan bias and are sometimes guilty of gross distortion. Bilton and Himelfarb's study of the role of the press in 1979 concluded that 'the strongest impression of Fleet Street's role during the campaign was the extent of bias among the popular dailies'.[3] In 1992, Butler and Kavanagh could write similarly, making the point that though 'the Conservative tabloids were relatively muted for most of the campaign', there was nonetheless a 'final blitz' even if 'it was not self-evidently stronger than in 1987'.[4]

This anti-Labour bias has long been discerned. The Royal Commission of 1967 noted that some papers display persistent anti-Labour bias, an anti-union stance and unfair treatment of individuals in the Labour Movement. It remarked that 'some newspapers on the right seek discreditable material which can be used to damage the reputation of Labour ministers'.[5] In 1992, similar complaints were heard by those on the left about the attempts to 'dig for dirt' on Neil Kinnock.

It has been an established trend in the elections of the 1980s and 1990s for the tabloids to become even more partisan, and critics have pointed to the extent of distortion and outright lies. Attempts have been made to smear people's private lives and to ascertain information injurious to leading figures. David Steel, the victim of such attempts in 1987, could write of his contempt for 'the gutter press who are debasing this whole election',[6] and Neil Kinnock found 'a press which in sections is more irresponsible, more prone to slander, more filthy than we have had in this country before'.[7]

In 1987 readers of the *Sun* were urged not to let 'Kinnock's crackpots wreck Maggie's revolution'. He suffered again from media attention in 1992, an election in which the Labour message was subjected to sustained bias, which became ever more desperate the nearer it seemed that the country was to getting a Labour government.

### The tabloids in 1992

In the 1992 election, there was sustained denigration of the Labour Party in the popular press, with the *Sun* being the leading exponent. Its election-day headline ran: 'If Kinnock wins today will the last person to leave Britain please turn out the lights'. Earlier onslaughts had been of a similar nature, and in focusing on the personality of the leader and on the threat of Labour's tax plans the right-wing press in general exposed a weak link in the party's armoury.

The *Sun* was in no doubt about its triumphant role in the narrow Conservative victory, and blazoned the view that 'It's the Sun wot won it.' Several commentators shared this assessment. A former treasurer of the Conservative

Party, Lord McAlpine, soon expressed the gratitude of many Tories for the role of the tabloids in the 1992 election: 'The heroes of this campaign were Sir David English (editor of the *Daily Mail*), Sir Nicholas Lloyd (editor of the *Daily Express*), Kelvin MacKenzie (editor of the *Sun*) and the other editors of the grander Tory press.'[8]

Labour was quick to endorse his judgement, and Neil Kinnock elaborated in this way: 'Never in the past nine elections have they (the Conservative press) come out so strongly in favour of the Conservatives. Never has their attack on the Labour party been so comprehensive . . . This was how the election was won.'[9] It noted that working-class voters in the South had swung sharply to the Conservatives in the last few days of the campaign, and that the *Sun* sells strongly in the region; indeed, Basildon, a notable Conservative success on polling day, has the highest proportion of *Sun* readers in the country.

The evidence is less clear-cut than this would suggest, for it does not explain why (according to a MORI/*Times* survey) readers of the non-aligned *Independent* swung by almost as large a percentage as *Sun* ones in that same period, as indeed did readers of the staunchly pro-Labour *Daily Mirror*. The *Express* and *Mail* also provided a very partisan – if less strident – coverage in favour of the Tories, but their readership was less moved.

Maybe followers of the *Sun* were more susceptible to blatant propaganda than were those of these more up-market tabloids, but it would be misleading to exaggerate the Labour claim that they were defeated because of the machinations of the press. For Ivor Crewe the impact of the *Sun* campaigning was worth no more than six highly marginal seats at most, all areas of high *Sun* popularity.[10]

### Subsequent developments

The Conservative victory in 1992 and the Berlusconi one in Italy in 1994 may well have been influenced to some degree by the power of media moguls. In the light of this, Tony Blair has given a high priority to improving relations with proprietors such as Rupert Murdoch, and if he cannot win their active approval he hopes at least to modify their opposition. This has led him to meet press owners and explain his position and goals. The aim is to try and reduce hostility to the party in the tabloid editorials, and to plant as many articles as possible in traditionally anti-Labour papers.

Both sides have something to gain from the conciliatory moves. Mr Blair wishes to get an easier ride than did his predecessors, but for a proprietor such as Rupert Murdoch there may also be an advantage in toning down his previous opposition and offering flattering observations about the new leader. In the event of a Labour general election victory, he would be hoping for a softer line on media ownership than Labour has adopted in the past.

In contrast to Labour's less strained relations with some elements in the press, the Conservatives have had a difficult time – particularly with the tabloids. Tory divisions over Europe are a key reason why John Major can no longer rely on editors and journalists to give their traditionally slavish support to the party. The *Daily Express* was the only one of the four pro-Tory flagships – the *Mail*, the *Sun* and the *Telegraph* being the others – to endorse the Prime Minister as he fought off John Redwood's challenge for the leadership. By early 1996, even its loyalty was stretched, and it urged a tougher stand against Britain's European partners in its 'stop the Euro-rot campaign'. The *Telegraph* was much more direct in its call for leadership, describing the government as a 'disaster'. Traditional Tory allies were being unusually nasty, but the prospect of an election might be the catalyst to bring some of them more enthusiastically back into the fold.

## Notes

1  *Britain 1995: Handbook* (COI for HMSO, 1995), p. 492.
2  M. Harrop and M. Scammell, *A Tabloid War: The British General Election of 1992* (Macmillan: London, 1992), pp. 181–2, 190.
3  M. Bilton and S. Himelfarb, *The British General Election of 1979* (Macmillan: London, 1980), p. 259.
4  M. Harrop and M. Scammell, *A Tabloid War*, p. 208.
5  Report of the Royal Commission on the Press, 1977, HMSO, Cmnd 6810 addendum to chapter 10, paras. 5–11.
6  M. Harrop, *Press: The British General Election of 1987* (Macmillan: London, 1988), p. 168.
7  *Ibid.*
8  M. Harrop and M. Scammell, *A Tabloid War*, p. 208.
9  *Ibid.*
10 I. Crewe, 'Why did Labour lose (yet) again?', *Politics Review* (September 1992).

# 4

# The media overall: ownership and regulation

## The debate on ownership and control

Much of the academic debate about the mass media relates to consideration of its ownership and control, though the second is not necessarily a consequence of the first. The Conservative Government has been committed to a policy of deregulation and market forces, and has not until recently shown much concern about the tendencies towards monopoly implied by the increasing concentration of ownership.

That such a concentration exists is hard to challenge, as we have seen in the world of newspaper proprietorship. However, it extends more widely, for conglomerates have a finger in several pies, as Table 4.1 illustrates. Apart from his ownership of several British newspapers and others in countries ranging from Australia to the United States, Rupert Murdoch also owns Sky television (which took over its rival, BRB, in 1992 and relays programmes to European audiences); his interests extend to ownership of Twentieth Century Fox, the film/TV studio, as well as to many other international holdings.

Cross-ownership between the press and other forms of communication has been allowed. The law permits newspaper proprietors to have a 20 per cent stake in one ITV station and companies become involved in not just television and radio, but also in fields such as book publishing and the theatre (see Table 4.1). The Conservatives have permitted the extension of the Murdoch empire in this country, and according to their critics they have placed greater emphasis upon the freedom of business corporations than upon the interests of the consumer. Cable and satellite services such as Sky do not operate under the same public service obligation that affects domestic broadcasters, and the *laissez-faire* policy involves a theoretical widening of choice but a narrowing of real diversity in programme content.

Radical writers on the left lament the trends in the ownership of the communications industry, and Murdock and Golding[1] have documented the tendency for multinational companies to extend and strengthen their holdings in several areas of the media – carefully avoiding the pitfalls of anti-monopoly legislation by ensuring that they do not acquire outright control of any one medium. They have noted that the dominance of a few corporations has affected every sector of the media. In some cases, the domination is one of individuals – Murdoch, Maxwell (until his mysterious death), the Bernstein family (Granada) and others – whereas in other fields the large corporations are more remote from the day-to-day running of the businesses they control.

Many pluralist commentators are less alarmed by this analysis, and suggest that if ownership mattered so much in the world of commercial television one might expect the product of ITV companies to be very different from the BBC. They may express more concern over the concentration of ownership in the press. John Whale[2] has taken such a view, but notes that ultimately people have the freedom to shun the papers of those who put forward biased propaganda and to look elsewhere. For him, the real threat to press freedom comes not from a narrowing of ownership, but from any threat of state control over the industry. The freedom of the press is seen as something which rests on secure grounds in Britain, and it is in those countries which have authoritarian regimes that the real threat to journalistic freedom derives.

### Recent developments

There has been much anxiety in the last few years about the extent and growth of cross-media ownership in the expanding media market-place, as revealed in Table 4.1). In the discussion, there has been broad agreement that any media policy needs to secure a number of objectives:

1   Guarantee protection against the creation of monopolies, ensuring an effective plurality of editorial voices across the media and fair competition for advertising revenue.

2   Maintain a diverse supply and range of programmes, underpinning an extension of viewer choice and value.

3   Offer proper and effective access to new media players.

4   Secure adequate investment in the industry, and stimulate creative talent.

*Government proposals on cross-media ownership, 1995:*
*The Broadcasting Bill, 1996*

The long-awaited Government proposals on cross-media ownership were finally published in May 1995. They were designed to ensure genuine competition and diversity, whilst at the same time enabling the media companies to remain strong, viable and able to compete in a rapidly-evolving media world.

In the short run, the main provision was that newspapers with less than 20 per cent of the market would be able to buy control of television companies as long as they did not breach 15 per cent of the total TV market. Commercial television companies would be able to buy newspapers for the first time, subject to certain restrictions.

In the longer term, the proposals remained embryonic, but they sought to break down the old barriers of print and screen. They envisaged that there would be a new concept, the total media market, based on some kind of points

Table 4.1 *Media ownership*

| | National press | Regional press | Publications | Television interests | Radio interests |
|---|---|---|---|---|---|
| 1. United Newspapers | *Daily Express, Sunday Express, Daily Star* | 106 regional titles – e.g. *Yorkshire Post* | Regional magazines and periodicals | | |
| 2. D.C. Thomson | | *Dundee Courier, Evening Telegraph, Sunday Post* | Sporting Post, Beano, etc. | Carlton/ Central | Transworld Communications, Piccadilly Radio, etc. |
| 3. Guardian Media Group | *Guardian, Observer* | *Manchester Evening News, Reading Evening Post, etc.* | Auto Trade, etc. | GMTV | |
| 4. Hollinger Inc. | *Daily Telegraph, Sunday Telegraph* | | *The Spectator* | Carlton | |
| 5. International Thomson Corporation | *Scotsman, Scotland on Sunday* | *Belfast Telegraph* and other dailies | | | Belfast Community Radio |
| 6. News Corporation | *Sun, Today, Times, Sunday Times, News of the World* | | Harper Collins | BSkyB | |
| 7. Pearson | *Financial Times* | North of England Newspapers, Westminster Press | *The Economist,* Longman Group | Independent TV facilities | Essex Radio |
| 8. Newspaper publishing | *Independent, Independent on Sunday* | | | | |
| 9. Mirror Group (stake in 8, above) | *Daily and Sunday Mirror, Daily Record, People* | | | | |
| 10. Daily Mail and General Trust | *Daily Mail, Mail on Sunday, London Evening Standard, Standard* | Northcliffe Newspapers, Bristol United Press | | West Country Broadcasting, ITN, Teletext, Reuter | GWR Group, Classic FM |

Source: Based on *Britain's Media* (Campaign for Press and Broadcasting Freedom), and adapted to show only those groups owning national newspapers at December 1995.

system reflecting the different contributions of radio, television and news-papers, with no company being able to control more than 10 per cent of the total. This arrangement would be policed by a regulator with wide powers to accept or reject mergers even above the 10 per cent ceiling. These would be based on a notion of the 'public interest', involving the promotion of diversity and the maintenance of a strong industry which can compete globally.

Most newspaper companies welcomed the proposals which would enable them to own an ITV station for the first time; they saw this as a much-needed liberalisation of the rules. By contrast, News International and Mirror News-papers were noticeably cool in their reactions; their expansion would be capped, although nothing in the proposals would make them immediately give up anything they now own.

Some voices were more critical, for the National Union of Journalists sees the settlement as one designed to appease the large media companies; it would, in the view of its spokesperson, lead to a reduction in titles. However, the general reaction on the opposition benches was more favourable, perhaps because there was a chance that the Murdoch empire would be shackled. The proposals echoed Labour's own plans to introduce a public-interest criterion in its approach to large takeovers in all industries.

When the resulting Broadcasting Bill was published in December 1995, its terms suggested a further relaxation of the rules of ownership of ITV com-panies. The two-licence limit is to be removed and replaced with an ownership limit of 15 per cent of the television audience (e.g. Carlton and Central, which then had a 9.4 per cent share, would not be able to take over Yorkshire–Tyne Tees (5.9 per cent). During its passage, the Labour position was notably more sympathetic to further liberalisation of existing media restrictions. The Oppo-sition was prepared to allow the larger newspaper groups to buy into commercial television as well as cable, satellite and digital television. Its spo-kespersons were aware that any attempt to curtail News International would also prevent the Mirror Group from diversifying into terrestrial television.

The question of media ownership is a controversial area of policy. Britain is not alone in seeking to regulate a fast-changing sector, for technological advance, cross-media alliances and global networks make it hard to balance public-policy objectives and market imperatives.

It has been a problem for Italy whose former Prime Minister, Silvio Berlus-coni, has ownership of three television stations. Aware that he would never win the right to broadcast in competition with the state-owned television monopoly, he set up an operation in Monte Carlo, close enough to the Italian border, and beamed in his programmes until a compliant government – aware of the difficulties of controlling the situation – gave him legitimacy.

Britain and Italy have much in common in the development of the media scene, for in both cases an all-powerful baron has been able to flourish in a regulatory vacuum in which any rules have been vague and easily evaded.

Rupert Murdoch has been able to avoid the strict percentages concerning ownership laid down in the 1990 Act, for they were not applicable to non-domestic satellites; his seven BSkyB channels are non-domestic, for the satellite owner is based in Luxembourg.

The fundamental issues of who owns what, and which companies should be free to operate in which sectors, are a concern of most governments. In Canada, government has tried to limit cross-media ownership, but it too suffers from a high degree of dominance from a small number of media players. The United States has tried to limit the concentration market by market, prohibiting local papers from dominating the local television network as well. The European Union is in the early stages of consultation on how to proceed, and may eventually put forward proposals affecting the fifteen-nation community.

Most countries have experienced the same difficulty in effecting any measure of regulation. The tendency towards concentration is widespread, but rules are difficult to apply and too easy to evade. In Britain, there have been some interesting changes of attitude on the issue of cross-ownership in recent years, for many politicians on the left have accepted that the Opposition should no longer be so concerned with 'shibboleths which have dominated Labour thinking for the past forty years'.[3] Nor should they be concerned about 'monopolistic control' of news, information and entertainment. Indeed, the notion has become increasingly meaningless with the 'multiplicity of entertainment channels, and a growing range of interactive services' replacing a limited number of channels. The old boundaries between newspapers, television, computers and telephones are breaking down; Labour policy needed to recognise the new situation.

Well-funded and sustained lobbying by big media companies has taken a similar line, urging the lifting of cross-media ownership restrictions, and the adoption of commercially advantageous media policies by governments. The European Publishers Council (EPC) has been typical of this kind of thinking, and the tone of its report is illustrated by comments such as the following:

> cross-media activity is not only inevitable, but essential if newspapers and magazine publishers are not to lose competitive advantage and so atrophy . . . Large-scale deregulation of national cross-media ownership restrictions is a prerequisite for economic growth in order that European media companies can compete in the world market.[4]

The EPC contains most of the key media companies in Europe, and they share the concern that the European scene will become dominated by larger-scale American and Japanese competitors without deregulation. The *Guardian* Chairman, Harry Roche, has suggested that there is too much regulation in Britain, and claims that 'as publishers, we have a right to be active in every area of the media'.[5]

Most of the powerful media voices are arguing for change, and in the light of this it is important to bear in mind that their position is influenced by the prospect of their becoming ever-larger global players. This is a legitimate aspiration which may serve the public good, but the issue of ownership is one which does have wide-ranging implications for journalistic standards, as well as for programme variety and quality.

In any democratic society, the aim of policy in this field must be to ensure that there is the widest range of news, views and programming available. Commercially-oriented media corporations do not have that goal in the forefront of their thinking, and the danger is that, far from greater diversity, we end up with a narrowing of choice.

## Regulation of the media

The freedom which the media enjoy also carries with it certain obligations concerning the content of what is communicated, and because of this some regulation is considered desirable and necessary.

### Newspapers

The press enjoys the same right, as does any individual, to comment on issues of public concern, but this general freedom is subject to certain laws. There is no law specifically governing the operation of newspapers, but several statutes have elements which affect their operation. These govern such matters as ownership in television and radio companies (see p. 44), and laws on contempt of court, official secrecy, obscenity, blasphemy, sedition and defamation may also be applicable (see box below). Similarly, publications have to be wary of any breach of the race relations legislation.

---

### Legal limitations on media freedom: a summary

**The Official Secrets Act**: this makes it a criminal offence to disclose information which the government defines as secret.

**Defence or D-Notices**: these are issued as requests to journalists not to report items believed to be injurious to the national interest; they may involve military secrets or other information of use to a potential enemy.

**Contempt of court**: this forbids the reporting and discussion of cases currently under discussion in a court of law.

**The laws of libel**: these forbid the publication of untrue statements which are liable to bring a person into contempt, ridicule or hostility.

**The Race Relations Acts**: these forbid the expression of opinions which encourage hatred or discrimination against people because of their colour or race.

**The Obscene Publications Act**: this forbids the publication of anything likely to 'deprave and corrupt' members of the public.

---

Apart from these legal controls, there are those restrictions designed to promote standards of accuracy and fairness on the part of journalists. From 1953 newspapers were regulated by a Press Council which was established to:

1 Preserve the freedom of the press.

2 Maintain the character of the press in accordance with the highest professional and commercial standards.

3 Consider complaints about the conduct of the press or the conduct of persons and organisations towards the press; to deal with these complaints in whatever manner might seem appropriate.

The Press Council was widely seen as a toothless bulldog, and its ineffectuality led to the establishment of a new body, the Press Complaints Commission (PCC), in 1991. This followed the recommendations of the Committee on Privacy and Related Matters, chaired by Mr (now Sir) David Calcutt, an enquiry established by the newspaper industry to see if it could make self-regulation of the press work more effectively. Concern had been growing for some time that the journalistic standards were too low, and that invasions of privacy, and inaccurate and biased reporting, were all too frequent. Some commentators were calling for government regulation of the press, and if this was to be fended off it was felt that the industry must put its house in order.

The PCC comprises newspaper and magazine editors, as well as people from outside the industry. It deals with complaints from members of the public about the contents and conduct of newspapers and magazines, and advises journalists on how they should respond under the Code of Practice which has been created.

In 1991, the Government asked Sir David Calcutt to review the process of self-regulation, and the report of his enquiry was published in January 1993. It favoured the introduction of a statutory complaints tribunal, but Ministers were reluctant to depart from the traditional belief that the press should regulate itself. A series of revelations about the intrusive activities of journalists, particularly those concerning the Royal Family, led many people to believe that firmer action was needed to control the excesses of over-zealous reporters, and a law on privacy has been mooted and much discussed. In their White Paper (1995) *Privacy and Media Intrusion; the Government's Response*, the Government stuck to its earlier attitude and continued to reject the notion of state regulation and legislation to protect privacy.

*Television and radio*

Television is similarly subjected to controls, and broadcasters have to comply with legislation on issues such as obscenity and incitement to racial hatred. Moreover, programmes are expected to display accuracy and impartiality in matters of political and social controversy, and to provide a proper balance and wide range of subject matter. The BBC, ITC and Radio Authority have codes covering matters of decency and taste, and the Broadcasting Standards

Council (BSC) was set up in 1988 to meet public anxiety about the scheduling of programmes containing portrayals of sex and violence. It monitors programmes, undertakes research and receives public complaints (2,032 in 1994–95, of which 303 were upheld).

The Broadcasting Complaints Commission (BCC) deals with complaints which relate to unfair treatment of individuals or groups, such as the unwarranted infringement of their privacy or the inference of wrong or unlawful behaviour on their part. In 1994–95, it received 1,135 such protests.

Many people in the media would argue that British television is over-restricted, and that this regulation is motivated not by a concern to ensure diversity but rather, more negatively, to curb what may be shown and narrow consumer choice. In other words, it is excessively patrician and protective. We have the BBC Board of Governors, the ITC, the Radio Authority, the BSC and the BCC all protecting us from the dangers of exposure to material considered unsuitable for our eyes and ears. In several cases, critics of the Government have noted that the men and women put in charge of this regulation tend to be sympathetic to the viewpoint of Ministers. The appointments of Lord Rees-Mogg at the BSC and Sir Marmaduke Hussey as Chairman of the Board of Governors at the BBC have been obvious examples of the Government making politically-inspired choices.

Despite the existence of such formal restrictions and controls, some people are still sufficiently concerned about the influence of the media that they see a need for further controls. Tony Benn has argued that 'broadcasting is too important to be left to the broadcasters',[6] and has on occasion suggested that the state might consider taking over and operating a newspaper of its own to provide information which is free from the usual right-wing bias of affluent proprietors. Many people would find any such notion of government ownership or regulation perturbing, and would doubt if the state could be trusted as much as present owners, who at least have other preoccupations to stop them from spending too much time on influencing their editors.

Others demand stricter censorship on matters such as sex and violence on screen, or to prevent the expression of views which are anathema to the majority of people. The Government has already temporarily banned Sinn Fein spokesmen from speaking their own words on television, and some found it objectionable that those words should still be spoken (accompanied by a picture) by actors whose mouth movements were often cleverly synchronised with the script. They might also be alarmed about copycat crimes, in which behaviour such as rioting in one part of the country is portrayed on screen and imitated by rioting elsewhere.

There is a balance to be struck between responsible reporting of crime and encouragement to criminal behaviour on the part of others. To give people the detailed information on how to manufacture weapons of deadly potential may invite emulation, but the stories of what is happening in our democracy and the analysis of why such things occur is important information to us all and should be in the public domain. We have a right to know, and journalists on television or in the press have an obligation to seek out and present the truth as they see it.

## Notes

1 G. Murdock and K. Golding, *For a Political Economy of Mass Communications* (Socialist Register: London, 1973).
2 J. Whale, *The Politics of the Media* (Fontana: London, 1977).
3 G. Kaufman MP (Chairman of National Heritage Select Committee), as quoted in G. Williams, 'Do Leopards Change Their Spots?', *Free Press* (March/April 1995).
4 European Publishers Council Report, *The Emergence of a Multimedia Industry in Europe*, 1995.
5 Speaking on behalf of British Media Industry group, quoted in G. Williams, 'Do Leopards Change Their Spots?'
6 A. Benn MP, public speech in October 1968.

# The news and current affairs

## Approaches to studying the news and current affairs

There is at first sight much evidence to substantiate the manipulative model of bias in the media which, as we have seen, suggests that their owners use them to ridicule and suppress challenging ideas and preserve the status quo. Partly this is done by ignoring or lampooning their targets for attack, partly by opting instead for an unvarying gruel of sex and scandal – trivial stories about television personalities, titillating pictures, opportunities to win prize draws and special offers.

Whilst attempts at social control in totalitarian countries are overt, in the privately-owned British press they are made by press moguls such as Rupert Murdoch. Some of his predecessors have been keen to testify to their desire to mould the views of their readership. In Lord Northcliffe's words: 'God made people read so that I could fill their brains with facts, facts, facts . . . and later tell them whom to love, whom to have and what to think.' On television and in other broadcasting media, manipulation is less obvious, for they are only indirectly run by the state through public corporations or regulatory bodies which control the franchise of the commercial network.

In support of the manipulative view, our study of the concentration of ownership provides examples of a few people who own large empires, not just in one medium but, for example, across broadcasting, films and publishing. These moguls and their editors are usually members of the Establishment in Britain, examples ranging from Lord Rothermere of Associated Newspapers to today's figures such as Lord Stevens, the owner of United Newspapers – though the Murdoch papers take a notably anti-establishment line on the behaviour and value of members of the Royal Family. They openly seek to control content, and their editors are loyal and act in a way of which their proprietor would approve. At the very least, they know the mind of that proprietor and can interpret his or her thoughts.

In the case of newspapers, they are distributed by wholesale companies, two or three of which control the bulk of circulation. The tendency to monopoly is seen in the narrow range of news agencies which feed stories to the news bulletins on television. Much information derives from a few of them, particularly Reuter, AFP and UPI, and it is provided by only a few outlets, BBC Radio News, BBC TV News and ITN and IRN. There is a similar monopoly in the poster industry. The bulk of the 100,000-plus sites in Britain are owned by four firms, whereas ten years ago at least five times more were in the business.

The material available in newspapers and in news and current affairs programming is, then, according to the manipulative viewpoint, narrow in range and similar in purpose. Far from merely reacting to people's preferences and at most reinforcing their judgements, these media help to shape them. They do have an influence and the nature of that influence is discussed elsewhere.

The hegemonic model, as we have seen in Chapter 1, goes some way along the same road without endorsing the Marxist view of the propagandising role of those who belong to the manipulative school. Hegemonists do not accuse the state of directly dictating the contents of the media, nor do they claim that the media is the tool of the ruling class, but they do believe that the media is biased and that this derives from the type of person who operates in the media world. According to this school, the range of views given any weight or credence is not as large as it could be, for one view of the world emerges most strongly. It is the dominant (hegemonic) consensus, pro-establishment outlook. Ideas which fit into that consensus will be put across as normal and desirable, and others depicted as deviant, wild, perverse or just woolly and unworkable.

Greenham or black activists, striking miners or gay parliamentary candidates are outside the consensus, whereas the views of moderates of the left or right of centre are portrayed as normal. Among the media professionals who perpetuate these views, journalists are often youngish, and editors male and white, and in the words of the Glasgow University Media Group, 'the world view of journalists will pre-structure what is to be taken as important or significant . . . it will affect the character and content of . . . the news'.[1]

Whatever the natural leanings of the new entrants to the profession, they soon learn how their papers or programme editors expect a topic to be presented, and what should be given an airing. They learn to anticipate the mind and judgement of their superiors in the hierarchy. According to this view, they decide the media agenda, and that agenda tends to be the same on ITN and the BBC, which although they often differ in the stories in bulletins, nonetheless usually reflect the same type of media view of what constitutes the day's news.

In contrast, Pluralists believe that there is a range of opinions on offer which cover various viewpoints – from Channel 4 and BBC2 with their minority tastes to BBC1 and ITV with their more popular approach, and from the *New Statesman* and *Private Eye* to the *Spectator* and the right-wing journal, the *Salisbury Review*. They concede that among newspapers there is a bias to the right, but inasmuch as this occurs, it is because those who produce them are giving readers and listeners what they want, catering for a mass audience. If we have a conservative press, it is because, in John Whale's words, 'its readers are conservative . . . If any substantial number of people seriously wanted the structure of society rebuilt from the bottom, the *Morning Star* would sell more copies than it does.'[2] In this view, the reason for the *Sun*'s pre-eminence is that is is particularly successful in attuning its contents to the demands of those who buy it. The media corroborate and strengthen existing views rather than alter them.

## News in the media: three standpoints

|  | *Pluralist* | *Manipulative* | *Hegemonic* |
|---|---|---|---|
| **1. Sources of news** | | | |
|  | Several sources, so that content of news is diverse. Even if some have a message to impart, this is balanced by others who take a different view. | Most news stories derive from capitalist press agencies such as Reuter, and from official sources. Little serious news derives from ordinary people. | As with manipulative model – official sources mainly. Few ordinary people, stories are London-based. |
| **2. Selection and use of news stories** | | | |
|  | Stories assessed for suitability to viewers, listeners and readers; TV wants visual stories, tabloids sensational ones and qualities serious ones to probe in depth. Aspects selected are those deemed to be newsworthy for target audience. | Presentation will be slanted according to line taken by proprietors. Journalists expected to write stories appropriate for the official editorial line. The emphasis is pro-establishment, and hostile to dissident minorities (strikers, protesters, etc.). | Stories chosen for topicality and news interest, but judgement made by programme editors and journalists who reflect middle-class (and often metropolitan) priorities. Their perspective emerges in presentation of new items, through settings, camera-work and loaded vocabulary. |
| **3. Impact of news on listeners/viewers** | | | |
|  | Believe that a good range of views is proffered, with more national news than in many countries. Little indication that media change views; tend to reinforce existing ones (see, L. Festinger *A Theory of Cognitive Dissonance* (Peter Row: Evansten, IL, 1957). | Viewers/readers get little real choice; papers are mainly right-wing, and television news bulletins very similar in style. Audience accepts and absorbs much of what they get – 'hypodermic effect'. | Choice is wide enough in theory, but all media run by a similar type of person and propound similar values. By choice and presentation of stories ('agenda setting'), they perpetuate dominant 'hegemonic' perspective of society. |

## The news and current affairs: their meaning and scope

In discussing the way in which the media handle the news and current affairs, the first problem is to decide what constitutes news. Herbert Gans has provided a detailed explanation of the processes involved. In *Deciding What's News*, he writes:

News is information which is transmitted from sources to audiences, with

journalists – who are both employees of bureaucratic commercial organisations and members of a profession – summarising, refining and altering
what becomes available to them from sources in order to make the information suitable for their audiences.[3]

It is a complex definition which dwells more on the processes involved in
selecting and compiling the news, rather than on the content which is on
offer. There are, however, immense difficulties in deciding on the basis of
content what counts as news. Different people have very different perceptions
in deciding what is news and what is really important news. If we include the
occurrences relating to government and public affairs happening every day
in every country, the volume is clearly immense and the supply is never-
ending. Severe pruning is inevitable, and it is really in the selection of items
from the mass of material available that the preferences of individuals and
groups become important.

Broadcasters and editors have to decide what is important and 'newsworthy', and in deciding what to include and exclude they are concerned
with obvious factors such as the regularity with which an event or sequence of events occurs, the scale of the occurrence (a minor tremor or a
major earthquake) and the size of its impact on those affected. However,
there are other factors which are also significant. Where did the event occur?
Did it involve the rich and famous? Did it have a personal story or human
drama?

Sometimes an event which is unpredictable and a rarity will still be covered,
simply because the magnitude of what happened is such that there is likely
to be great interest, even if the event happens in a non-fashionable area.
Ethiopia and Mexico do not normally rate much attention in British news
coverage, but a famine in the one or an earthquake in the other are of such
a scale that they arouse interest; they are great human dramas, which arouse a
full range of emotions in the reader, listener or viewer.

The former editor of the *Guardian*, Alastair Hetherington, has provided a
list of factors which he rates as important in the choice of items. After stressing
the social, political, economic and human significance of particular stories, he
suggests drama, surprise, personalities, sex, and numbers affected as relevant
considerations.[4]

Inevitably, most stories are about domestic events with which people can
identify more easily. Matters which affect their personal well-being (the performance of the economy, government spending plans) are likely to rate
highly, as are issues which pose a potential or actual threat to the stability of
the community (an IRA bombing campaign or the activities of protesting
groups such as animal rights, black or gay activists).

For reasons we have given, editors and journalists tend to have similar
views about what constitutes news, and this ensures that similar types of
events are picked out on each bulletin on any channel. The actual stories

might differ however, for there is no agreement about which particular stories are news (see box below).

It comes down to a matter of professional judgement, and what counts as news will reflect the 'feel' of the news editor for the newsworthiness of a particular story. In general, there tends to be a concentration on the good

---

**What is the news? An evening's viewing**

On one night in February 1995, the following stories were included within the two main evening bulletins on BBC and ITN:

| *BBC 9 p.m.* | *ITN 10 p.m.* |
|---|---|
| 1 Baring's Bank takeover | Baring's Bank takeover |
| 2 Currency fluctuations | Resignation of junior minister |
| 3 Resignation of junior minister | Currency fluctuations; Europe |
| 4 Croatia; fears of new war | Clause Four of the Labour Party |
| 5 Clause Four of the Labour Party | New venues for weddings |
| 6 China; economic reforms | Australian yacht-race problems |
| 7 Sinking of ship (*Derbyshire*) enquiry | China; succession/economic prob- |
| 8 World Poverty Conference, Bolivian example | lems/Animal rights |
| 9 Anglican–Methodist Conference | Tagging offenders |
| 10 Baring's update/recap | Sinking of ship (*Derbyshire*) enquiry |
| 11 | World Poverty Conference, contrast of Mozambique and South Dakota |
| 12 | Headlines repeat, Barings and junior minister |
| 13 | New MG |

Of the BBC stories (apart from the recap), five were on domestic issues, two related to Europe, none to the United States and two to global questions.

Of the ITN ones, eight were on domestic issues, one related to Europe, none to the United States specifically and three to global questions.

In both cases, there was a fairly similar balance of domestic and international material used by the newsroom editors. Four of the top five stories were same, although they rated differing levels of priority. After that, some of their choices were the same, but different domestic stories aroused their interest. Both sets of material were 'news', but not the same news.

A study of bulletins throughout the evening revealed that Channel 4 and ITV included more 'world' coverage. The proportion of domestic items was as follows:

| ITN 5.40 | BBC 6.00 | Channel 4 7.00 | BBC 9.00 | ITN 10.00 |
|---|---|---|---|---|
| 77.7% | 75.0% | 60.0% | 66.6% | 55.5% |

and the mighty, for personal stories are seen as likely to arouse the curiosity of the viewer or listener. Elite countries predominate over those which are less fashionable (unless there happens to be an international conference at the time, as in our example), so that in recent years the fate of the ex-Cold War nations carries more weight than African states such as Chad or South American ones such as Peru. Stories are more likely to rate as news if they reflect domestic rather than international issues, for it is assumed that people prefer incidents which may have a bearing on their own lives. Journalists also realise the importance of using material which is clear and intelligible, and if it can be supported by good visual material, its appeal is likely to be all the greater.

In devising the agenda, the instincts of journalists are all-important, and it is because of this that although people tend to think in terms of news as 'truth' ('I saw it on television news, it must be right') there may well be a bias in the coverage offered, a bias which reflects the values and attitudes of those involved in the processing of gathering and compiling the news. This is not usually intentional within television, although in the newspapers distortion is often deliberate and designed to influence opinion.

## Bias in the news

Moving from who determines the agenda and the criteria on which decisions are made, controversy abounds over the actual content of the news. Is it as impartial as it is supposed to be? People assume that in getting the news from television they are getting the truth, for the Charter requires broadcasters to act with 'due impartiality', which involves the need to avoid taking sides in any dispute and ensuring that the case of all parties involved is given due attention. Golding and Elliott describe impartiality as 'a disinterested approach to news, lacking in motivation to shape or select material according to a particular view or opinion. Objectivity [requires] a complete and unrefracted capture of the world.'[5]

It is this claim for objectivity which is often dismissed by some critics of the media, for they believe that partiality does exist, even if it is not usually of the obvious kind. The wording outlined in the annex to the BBC's Licence refers to a duty to 'treat controversial subjects with due impartiality . . . both in the Corporation's news services and in the more general field of programmes dealing with matters of public policy'. Some would argue that the BBC, in particular, is not as 'rigorously impartial' or 'balanced' as its spokespersons would claim – a viewpoint to which we must return.

Television neither acts as a government spokesperson nor does it assume a completely neutral position on various issues and problems. We have seen how the BBC has not felt that it could be neutral about racism or alternatives to parliamentary democracy (see p. 31), but on most issues it endeavours to assume an explanatory and sometimes more critical role, presenting programmes in which all shades of opinion can be discussed. A completely unbiased approach is difficult to achieve, and listeners and viewers are capable of observing the intonation or emphasis of a newsreader, interviewer or commentator.

In assessing bias, there is a difference between the news as it is presented in a 25- or 30-minute bulletin, in which selection is necessary and live reporting from special correspondents is sometimes included, and the more reflective approach of programmes which can devote more time to covering issues of current topicality. *Channel 4 News* or *Newsnight* devote more time to background analysis of the day's events, and in probing interviews they can seek to establish a fuller representation of what actually occurred and of its significance. Many of the people who work on such programmes as editors or presenters have a background of working experience on other news programmes, and it is fair to assume that the same people who once curtailed events in such a way as may have given a misleading impression are therefore capable of examining an issue in depth and with greater objectivity in a format which enables them to explore the topic in more thoroughness.

In either case, of course, broadcasters are likely victims of news management of the type which we have explored in Chapter 8. Information can be released at certain times to steal the headlines and ensure that good news is highlighted, and that bad news loses its impact. The timing of a press release can make all the difference to the headline attention it receives in the bulletins.

It is with the world of politics and business that we are primarily concerned, as we seek to explore the prevalence and nature of television bias. However, we must firstly examine our own approach when confronted with material 'on the news'.

### Whose bias?

It is difficult to be objective about issues and to decide what represents a biased opinion. Much depends on where you, the listener or viewer, personally stand, as to whether you will consider a programme to be partisan. This was well-illustrated by an advertisement which appeared soon after the launch of the *Independent* newspaper in the 1980s. On large hoardings, it asked (in very large, bold lettering) 'It is; are you?' Below was a reference to the name of the paper which prided itself on its freedom of political leanings in either direction.

The point is a fair one, namely that bias often lies in the eye of the beholder. If you are a strong Conservative and see your party's performance over many years being subjected to detailed and critical scrutiny, the programme may well seem unfair; yet in reality it may be an objective and analytical survey of what has happened. Because the Conservatives have been long in power, it is necessarily their policies which are reviewed and open to examination. Similarly, a programme exposing the strike-prone nature of a particular group of workers might seem to be anti-union and anti-Labour to someone on the left, but others further to their right may see it as a fair assessment of the issues.

## Overt bias?

At various times in recent decades politicians and others have accused the media of bias. In the 1960s, the suggestion from the right was that 'cultural radicalism' was undermining the accepted standards of British life, and that satire programmes were harmful to the status and reputation of politicians whose word was undermined. In the 1970s, Labour was concerned that when in opposition in 1970–74, its performance was being unfairly attacked and this precipitated a long-running duel betwen Harold Wilson and the BBC; in the 1974 election, he would only allow himself to be interviewed by ITV reporters as he travelled the country because he thought he was being unreasonably treated.

Labour is very sensitive about securing a fair deal on television, given its treatment by the tabloid press in the last two decades, and some of its supporters have been particularly suspicious of signs of bias that can creep into reports – not necessarily overtly, but nonetheless there by implication. This sensitivity is still in evidence today, and some left-wing politicians are notably prickly when being interviewed, suspecting that the BBC is giving them a hard time and seeking to denigrate their party. They feel that through the language of presenters and commentators a pro-establishment view of society emerges, and that the BBC is sometimes very concerned to opt for the safe 'consensus' middle ground.

Liberal Democrats, and their predecessors, have often felt that they were the victims of a different form of bias, not one of content but of neglect. As a third force, they felt that they have suffered from a lack of media exposure, and that sometimes they have fared badly in the allocation of party political broadcasts – particularly at election time. Like the other parties, they carefully monitor media coverage of elections; in their case, it is as much to ensure that they get their fair share of airtime as it is to check that references to them are free of bias.

Since 1979, Conservative Ministers have often been dissatisfied with the BBC which, as a public corporation funded from a licence fee, is doctrinally displeasing to a number of them. Some have felt that the party has been given a rough ride from hostile interviewers, and a number of well-publicised disputes have arisen. Mrs Thatcher was upset by media coverage of the Falklands War in which she felt that there was insufficient support shown for 'our boys down in the South Atlantic' and too much scrutiny to British policy before and during the fighting. Norman Tebbit, as Party Chairman, accused the BBC, and particularly Kate Adie, of 'slanted reporting' at the time of the raid (by American jets based in the United Kingdom) on Libya. He compiled a dossier of BBC 'partiality' to the Libyan cause, and felt that there were too many episodes in which the BBC showed itself to be aligning itself with the Labour attack on the Government.

The difficulty is clearly the greater when one party has been in office for so long, for inevitably, in examining any issue, from homelessness to Northern

Ireland, from race relations to the performance of the economy, it is the Tory Government's record which is under critical scrutiny. Tory Ministers were there when the decisions were made.

In the mid-1990s, it is not only Conservatives such as Jonathan Aitken (see p. 99) who attack the BBC. Labour claims that the Corporation has been too conscious of political pressure from the Government in the Birt regime. In the spring of 1995, it argued that the BBC was allowing itself to become the accomplice of a media blitz by the Prime Minister, part of which was an interview with *Panorama* three days before the Scottish local elections. It seemed that balance was being eroded, the more so as a programme on Westminster Council had been withdrawn at a similar time the previous year. The Court of Sessions upheld the argument of the opposition parties and stopped the programme being transmitted in Scotland, on the grounds that it could give the Conservatives an unfair advantage at the polls by the providing the Premier with an unopposed platform.

Labour was keen to flex its muscles to ensure that the BBC did not bend in the face of a spate of recent Conservative attacks.

The broadcasters strenuously insist that there is no conscious bias, and stress their duty to provide programmes which are balanced and content which is impartial. They also point out that when criticism comes from left and right, then this might suggest that they are succeeding in their task.

Some research conducted over many years has suggested that there is a bias to the centre in television coverage. Blumler and McQuail (*Television in Politics, its Uses and Influence*) found that in the 1964 election TV coverage, the news more than PPBs tended to incline people to the moderate position as represented by the Liberal Party. They saw this as happening not because of a pro-liberal influence with television, but more because television reaches the type of voters who would not attend political meetings directly; it rallies the uncommitted voter.

In contrast, the GUMG, which also believes that broadcasting is overly sympathetic to the middle ground, has a different explanation. It has claimed that coverage of politics eschews the extremes of left and right, and favours 'wet' Conservatives and rightist socialists. It believes that these leanings derive from the attitudes and values of those in the media.

### Hidden bias?

Many factors come into play where visual images are concerned, for, in the words of the GUMG, news on television is influenced by the 'dominant assumptions of our society. From the accents of the newscasters to the vocabulary of camera angles . . . the news is a highly mediated product.'[6] Its studies imply that such things as choice of pictures and language, and the intonation with which words are delivered, the setting in which they are offered, can affect the objectivity of the outcome. It may well be that the BBC and ITV are pledged to balance and freedom from bias, and in their avoidance of open partisanship of one party and its spokespersons over another this can be fulfilled. But the hidden factors mean that there is a latent bias which is the more difficult to detect.

The broadcasters have enormous influence, and this is not always readily apparent. Newscasters who present the news might seem to be reading from a neutral script which eschews any favouritism to one side or other. But of course before the news gets to that stage the question arises as to 'What is the news?'

As we have seen, according to television it is what the producers of the *Nine O'Clock News* or *News At Ten* say it is; in other words, they determine the agenda, and say which stories get reported and which ones can be ignored or placed lower down the ranking order of 'newsworthiness'. Often the top five topics on either bulletin may be quite different and some stories only appear on one channel, yet both sets of broadcasts claim to be 'the news'. Politicians, particularly in minor or third parties, often feel that their speeches get unreported because they are not deemed to be so headline-catching and relevant, so that they are placed at a disadvantage in getting their views across.

In the words of Moyra Grant, 'rather than getting what they want, viewers and readers get to want what they are given'.[7] She notes how certain types of story become fashionable, such as satanic child abuse and 'male rape' cases; as the topic of the moment, they attract undue attention and create the impression that such incidents are becoming ever more common. Also, stories which are easily reported and photographed because they happen in London can get undue prominence.

Those who point to biased reporting often point to the remarks of those who comment on the news. When the BBC or ITV go across to their special correspondent, perhaps one who speaks on industrial relations, references to 'militants', 'extremists' and 'wreckers' may creep in. The choice of language, or indeed of location for photographs and interviews, may well be relevant.

The Glasgow Media Group has often observed this tendency to 'hidden bias' in the media, a bias which is the more dangerous as people believe they are getting impartial news. In several studies, ranging from *Bad News* and *Trade Unions in the Media* to *More Bad News* and *War and Peace News*, its researchers have examined the way television handles matters such as industrial relations, general economic coverage and topics such as defence and disarmament. Much of their work has focused on the alleged pro-management, or more specifically anti-union attitude, to which we must shortly turn in more detail.

Critics of hidden bias have long noted how in reporting industrial relations issues, the management representative is often interviewed calmly seated at his desk, talking 'reasonably' and 'persuasively' about his endeavours to achieve a fair settlement, whereas union leaders are often photographed at an outdoor meeting, haranguing an audience in language designed to whip up support for strike action. The viewer is left with the impression of the sense of responsibility of the one, and the waywardness and unreliability of the other.

In *The Media and Political Violence*, Richard Clutterbuck also notes an inadequate coverage of the union viewpoint, a reflection of the antagonism to strikes often displayed by journalists and TV viewers. Not surprisingly, he found that this 'bias' towards management was not a matter of anxiety to members of the public who were interviewed, for people were not conscious of any leaning in the presentation. He distinguished between the quality papers and current affairs/documentary programmes which in his view give a good background analysis, and the two-minute news extracts which concentrate on the 'highlights' of a day's picketing in any industrial confrontation – and do not give a fair picture of what actually occurs.

Industrial relations correspondents on the media have come in for particular criticism. In discussing the year-long confrontation in 1983–84, they and other journalists constantly alluded not to 'the coal dispute', but to the 'miners' strike'. The impression created was that the blame for the problem could be laid at the door of the workforce.

In that strike, there were frequent allegations from the left about the unfair way in which NUM spokesmen were depicted. A Channel 4 programme after its conclusion illustrated just how events can be portrayed in different ways. *The Battle for Orgreave* was made by someone committed to the miners' cause, and it showed scenes of violence used by the police against strikers who were seemingly peacefully picketing. The use of a zoom lens picked out incidents in which there was clear evidence of police brutality.

Critics of the programme pointed out that the use of a wide-angle lens would have shown that the situation looked more threatening to the police as a column of strikers was advancing in a way that could be seen as menacing. Both views were in a sense correct, in that the camera was depicting what was happening; but the impression given varied according to what the photographer chose to show.

The issue of hidden bias has been a contentious one, and not all academics have been convinced by the sort of analysis conducted by the GUMG, which has been criticised for its selective use of evidence to substantiate the viewpoint of its team.

### The coverage of industrial relations: the GUMG and its critics

Using 'content analysis', the GUMG has conducted a number of studies of aspects of the media, *Bad News* on industrial relations, *More Bad News* on the same theme, *Really Bad News* on political coverage and *War and Peace News*, which dealt especially with the Falklands War and the Greenham protesters. All of their studies have been based on research which attempts to measure some aspects of the content of particular programmes or types.

*Bad News* was based on a detailed study of news broadcasting on all channels in the first five months of 1975. Items were classified according to type and they were timed. The circumstances were also noted (e.g. interview, studio or outside broadcast, etc.), and this statistical data was then run through the computer for analysis, so that very detailed information was available on which to base the researcher's conclusions.

They concluded, *inter alia*, that the effects of strikes were more likely to be reported than the reasons for their occurrence and that undue emphasis was placed on the tactics of the strikers at the expense of explanation of their attitude and thinking. The suggestion was that by the use of 'loaded' language such as 'incited', 'trouble-makers', 'radical' and 'extremist', and by the use of film to reinforce the message of the dangers of strike action and the resultant near-anarchy, that the news gave a one-sided and simplistic view of disputes.

In the first survey, they concentrated on the reporting of a strike at British Leyland in 1975, and even more specifically on the way in which the media handled Harold Wilson's speech of 3 January. Among other issues he tackled the issue of poor industrial relations, and made reference to the motor industry with its 'manifestly avoidable stoppages of production'. It was this part of the speech which was reported on television, and it made it seem as though strikes were the main problem facing car firms. In his remarks, the Prime Minister focused on the reactions of management as well as the unions, but the part which was emphasised in television news bulletins was the reference to the behaviour of the unions involved.

According to the GUMG the account given of that speech was a classic example of misreporting, for it selectively picked out that part which dwelt with conflict and the union role in promoting unrest. The same allegation was later made about the miners' strike, where it was said that the issue of pit closures and the future of the industry received far less attention than the references to violence on the picket line, and secondary and violent picketing. Was this deliberate or unconscious bias, or merely because the more dramatic aspects of the daily events were newsworthy and therefore made the news, whilst the more reflective aspects of the dispute could be covered in detail elsewhere?

The broadcasters decide on the most important issues of the day. They do so in the light of their own beliefs about what is important and significant, and as we have seen, Hegemonics argue that this is itself a reflection of the middle-of-the-road consensual view which eschews extremism and casts a more critical glance at picket-line violence than police intimidation. In setting the agenda, the media men and women are gatekeepers for some stories are included, others rejected. They tend to favour ones about strikers more than ones about the behaviour of businessmen.

*More Bad News* enlarged upon the earlier study and elaborated on the thinking of the GUMG. It stressed the importance of journalistic views in defining news and on the locations in which media men and women chose to locate their interviews.

Such research has been the subject of academic disputation, much of it led by Professor Harrison of Keele University. He concentrated on the Leyland issue, and his findings differed from those of the GUMG in several important respects.[8] He studied the ITN transcripts for the five-month period. He noted that this was a period in which industrial relations were poor and there was much discussion of industrial unrest and the strike-prone nature of British industry. He denied the group's contention that undue emphasis was placed by the broadcasters on the problems of some industries, especially Leyland, and made the point that the newsworthiness of the topic reflected the significant 'knock-on' effect of strike action on other industrial sites. He also stressed that the emphasis placed upon inconvenience to the public was a reflection of the fact that there were vastly more adversely-affected customers than there were striking car workers.

Harrison was convinced that news values are not regularly hostile to trade unions, nor does film material always depict a critical image. Rather than the media, the GUMG itself was displaying a slanted approach. It looked for a detailed bias against unions and, on the basis of narrow evidence, found what it was seeking. In the relevant period, it did not study management which also claims to be the victim of media discrimination. Overall, he felt that to place great emphasis upon one particular episode was a misguided way of approaching the subject. There may well be truth in the general allegations of the GUMG, but if the case is a contentious one it is bound to cast doubt on the validity of the argument.

This is not the place for a point-by-point assessment of the claim and counter-claims, but it is fair to point out that Greg Philo of the GUMG rebutted the rebuttal and suggested that the backing and finance of ITN were behind Harrison's work, and that his critique was perfunctory and not based on all available evidence – only on that selective material which ITN had chosen to make available to him. This was said to have omitted key passages and was an inaccurate account of what had actually gone out over the air.

Others have contributed to the different interpretations of the GUMG and Harrison. The Labour Correspondent of BBC Radio News, Nicholas Jones, has suggested that the bias is not within the news media, but reflects the fact that spokespeople for management have generally been more adept at representing their case.[9] In any dispute, there is a battle for propaganda, and for a long while unions were less skilled at getting their message across and feeding information to the broadcasters in a way which was likely to be well received.

Of course, his area of concern was radio news, where there is a likelihood of more detailed background coverage and explanation than on television. On television the image is more important, and time is more precious, and so Jones's contribution to the debate is not a convincing rejoinder (by itself) to the GUMG's arguments about the nature of television. Moreover, his work reveals a preference for the activities of moderate trade union leaders over those who could be seen to be more militant, and it could be that his whole approach to the subject serves to confirm the Group's case about the dominant values of people who work in the media.

## Other criticisms

Some critics of television news attack it from a different standpoint. They suggest that the whole agenda covered by editors and journalists has moved to the political right, so that views which would have been considered to be moderate, centrist ones in the past are now seen as leftist today. Newsmen and women are said to have downplayed industrial unrest and environmental concerns as too dull and boring, whilst issues that are covered with more regularity, such as financial affairs, are handled in such a way that they sound too much like Treasury handouts. This may reflect the skill with which the Government handles aspects of news management, and the fact that many presenters and special correspondents have a close relationship with Tory politicians and tend to accept the information they are fed uncritically. There is also no lack of City pundits to consult to convey a rightist interpretation of such questions.

A particularly strong indictment of the quality of news output emerged in *J'Accuse; The News*[10] in which the speaker, Allison Pearson, suggested that 'the news has gone quietly bonkers'. She argued that BBC and ITN are 'working to agendas and subject to pressures that we at home simply can't see', and suggested that a combination of the 'mania for ratings' and BBC concern for the renewal of its licence 'has produced an entire new branch of pornography – the Human Interest story'.

She went on to suggest that both organisations were excessively conscious of the competition from Sky, Ceefax and Teletext, and were overly concerned with selling the news in an acceptable and painless manner. The result is that the form of coverage has become more important than the content, so that news bulletins are beset by gimmickry. Pictures change every few seconds, and at worst it seems as though the broadcasters are busily packaging and selling a product, by making it painless and anodyne. It looks good, and the settings can be fine; the BBC refurbished its studios for the *Nine O'Clock News* in 1993. The result is that the news has a 'magnificent ersatz authority', and she felt that she was the victim of an extremely effective and slick 'con-trick'.

The charge is that the medium is dictating the message, that increasingly, stories are written to wrap around dramatic pictures, and if the camera wasn't there then there is no story; it isn't news. Sometimes the camera intrudes into places which seem inappropriate, so that a funeral can be accompanied with close-ups of grieving relatives. The funeral of James Bulger and the embarrassing way it dwelt on details of the child's belongings illustrate the preoccupation with stories for which there is plenty of film, too much of which is being used. It was a very sad event which merited coverage, but as the lead story on both channels, the personal tragedy received an elaborate and prurient treatment.

Entertainment and information have become blurred and what is lacking is 'real NEWS, something genuinely NEW, something others won't necessarily want you to know'. The lament is for good investigative journalism, which is prepared to tackle difficult issues and ones which might unearth wrong doing. On 'sleaze', an area where Ministers were vulnerable to criticism in 1994–95, it was the press which delved deeply and did much of the searching investigation. The initiative in portraying big stories these days comes from the newspapers more often than from television news, especially over the 'cash-for-questions' scandal.

There is less coverage by experienced foreign correspondents of events abroad for cost-cutting has led to a decline in their numbers. The danger is that important events abroad are not placed in context, starving people look like starving people and they could be desperate people anywhere. But the analysis of why they are in such a position and what could be done to change the situation and prevent another disaster is often missing. Much of the concern is with the pictures and any accompanying soundbites, but 'other people's tragedies are shamelessly rigged and presented as stirring mini-dramas for our catharsis'.

Much of the coverage of Africa especially is from Western aid experts, and little is heard from Africans themselves. Not surprisingly, we are given a distorted view of the continent which, as we have already explained, is a very underreported one except at times of war or famine.

Television plays into the hands of the politicians who are adroit at news management. Often they are allowed to deliver a carefully prepared and selective message to the audience. For whereas on radio a brief interview can still be rigorous, on television the question can be evaded by the use of a satisfying soundbite:

> Television news is an instrument of democracy. If it persists in treating the trivial and the serious with the same thumping sense of significance, if this is the style to which we are to become accustomed, then how will anything seem new, how will anything surprise us or make us think?

### The public view of television's impartiality in news coverage

Impartiality or otherwise can be measured in different ways. One method is that of 'content analysis' adopted by the GUMG. This is also the method adopted by the political parties who are understandably sensitive about ensuring that they receive equal coverage at election time. Such an approach does not allow for the effect of the coverage in influencing public attitudes; it may be that one party or politician receives fewer minutes of airtime, but that does not necessarily mean that his or her impact is proportionally diminished. Research conducted annually for the ITC uses the assessment of public opinion as a means of reaching a judgement about the fairness of its coverage.[11]

Respondents who claim partiality in any area of programming (such as current affairs) are asked to indicate the nature of this bias. They are then invited to consider the fairness of the treatment meted out to particular groups in society, the categories ranging from public-sector employees such as teachers and health workers to the disabled, from religious groups to the police force. A further set of core questions relate to the treatment accorded to the political parties.

In 1993, the majority (71 per cent and 65 per cent, respectively) thought that coverage of 'News' and 'Current Affairs' was 'fair and unbiased'. The proportions differed when the information was broken down according to the degree of interest in and commitment to politics shown by the respondent. Of those who were 'fairly or very interested' a smaller percentage (67 per cent) felt that there was a lack of bias in the news, whereas of those who showed 'little or no interest' 75 per cent detected no partiality to one side. The same was true of attitudes to current affairs programmes.

Support for one or other of the political parties tended to be a relevant factor in determining attitudes to alleged bias. Labour supporters were more likely to see factual programmes as fair than Conservatives in the area of news and current affairs. Committed people were also more likely to detect bias in favour of or against the various listed categories among the population.

The researcher found that of all of those surveyed, 29 per cent felt that news and current affairs programmes were biased against single parents, 26 per cent against the unemployed, 18 per cent against the disabled, 19 per cent against women and 14 per cent against ethnic minorities. Of all of those interviewed who were interested in politics, 25 per cent felt there was a bias in favour of management whereas 17 per cent felt that unions were better treated.[12]

The most significant aspect of the findings from our point of view concerns the measurement of bias in the treatment of the main political parties. Over the years in which some form of question has been asked on this aspect, ITV has usually been regarded as more unbiased than the BBC, often by as many as 10–15 per cent (e.g., in 1992, 66 per cent felt that ITV did not favour any party whereas 56 per cent said the same of the BBC). The proportion stayed the same in 1993, and in that year 30 per cent felt that the Corporation 'does favour a particular party'.

Out of all the viewers, 23 per cent saw the BBC as biased towards the Conservative Party, only 5 per cent towards Labour. The explanation most often given by respondents for this bias was that the BBC is 'government-controlled' or 'government-funded'. However, few interviewees could offer a reason for the lack of impartiality they perceived. Channel 4 was seen as slightly more likely to be biased in favour of Labour than the Conservatives, and ITV as equally likely to be biased to either party.

## News and current affairs: an area under review

There has in recent years been some disquiet about the standard of news and current affairs coverage on television, and particularly on the BBC. We have seen that on 'Tory sleaze' the allegation has been made that television news has been reduced to the role of running other people's stories. The initiative came from the press, and on this and on other occasions major issues have often derived more from what is gathered from the newspapers than from original research undertaken by a television news operation. Investigation by TV journalists is increasingly a rarity.

The collapse of Baring's Bank in February 1995 is a good example of the limitations of television coverage. Much of the story as it originally broke lacked dramatic pictures, for many of the key contacts and relevant discussions took place behind closed doors. Whereas a story in a war zone or in an area beset by famine and pestilence can provide access and plenty of opportunities for human-interest interviews, the failure of a business operation is more difficult for the TV reporter to handle.

Complex detail of the type involved can be more extensively relayed in a quality newspaper, where the more specialist audience may sit down to read the information at its leisure. For prime-time television news, in which issues have to be compressed, made meaningful and interesting, the collapse was a demanding episode, and the broadsheet newspapers, especially the *Financial Times* or the *Wall Street Journal*, have better access, depth of reporting and quality of analysis.

There are some impressive programmes which provide City coverage in more depth, such as *The Money Programme* (BBC2) and Radio Four's the *Financial World Tonight*, but these do not occupy peak slots. The BBC knows that it has an obligation to cater for a specialised audience interested in the financial world, but such programming is inevitably of subordinate importance to the mainstream output. Television and business are an unlikely alliance, for ultimately business stories, even major ones, do not often allow for the 'must-watch' factor.

On most issues, however, people do get their news first-off from the television, next radio and then the newspapers. The two mid-evening bulletins, featuring ten or so stories a night, have a considerable impact. The indictment increasingly made is that stories are too much dictated by the ploys of spin-doctors and media experts who know how to manage the news, and that what results is an obsession with soundbites and picture opportunities. There may be more and more bulletins on different stations and at different times of the day, but much of it is simply the same information regurgitated with a slightly differing slant – depending on who is the news editor involved.

A similar point was made in the *Observer* by a journalist who noted that in one particular week John Major had been covered on a visit to Israel 'looking suitably sincere in a skull cap at the Holocaust memorial . . . yet there was no real story', and Prince Charles had received attention for his journey to Egyptian tombs where he 'paid homage to a host of other [dead] royal personages';[13] again, there was no significant story. In other words, the media advisers at Downing Street and in Buckingham Palace had scored more successes, courtesy of television news.

The article noted the 'knot between Millbank and Westminster, political journalists and politicians', and added:

> Where once the BBC's political editor did three interviews a day, he is now forced to do seven or eight, spending much more of his time stuck behind a microphone in that new citadel of political news management, 4 Millbank, the broadcasting headquarters of Parliament, where he is joined by queues of MPs desperate to get on air.

Broadcasters defend themselves against such charges, and usually dismiss the suggestion that their agenda is narrowing and that they are too liable to be the victims of skilful PR supremos in the party machines. They point to the differences between the *Nine O'Clock News* and *News at Ten*, and stress the range of different bulletins now available, with ITN producing news for the diverse listeners and viewers of Classic FM and Talk Radio UK, *Channel 4 News* and *The Big Breakfast* show, as well as for its main mid-evening slot. The danger is that although the stories may vary in their style of presentation, the same stories about the same issues and the same people tend to predominate.

At present, the area of News and Current Affairs is one under review. As Director-General, John Birt has for some time been uneasy about the quality of the Corporation's output. In the 1970s, he had co-authored a series of articles in which he elaborated his view that there was a 'bias against understanding' in television coverage, and he argued that there was a need for producers to identify issues which matter and present them in such a way that people could make up their own mind.

He was appointed in 1987 to the Deputy Director-Generalship with a brief to overhaul the style and approach of journalism and took close control of news and current affairs. In his Dublin lecture (see pp. 187–8), his belief in the merits of analytical discussion reasserted itself. He still believes in a serious treatment of serious issues. The gravamen of the Birtean indictment was that too much time is spent in discussing the 'tedious Westminster manoeuvring which was all we had to talk to them about'. He argued for more thoughtful coverage of matters which really did concern the public – crime, homelessness, social breakdown and the state of the environment, 'the events and forces that most shape our lives – and less of a preoccupation with disputation with those who rule or who aspire to do so'.

### Television as a source of political information: an assessment

Television has weaknesses as a source of political education, some of which relate to the need for balance and impartiality. In interviews with leading television personalities it is sometimes difficult for politicians to get their views across, for their replies can be cut off prematurely or they may not be given a chance to provide an adequate answer. Sometimes a sharp intervention by the chairman of a discussion is necessary to get a response from professional politicians who are skilled at being evasive, but on occasion the interview can be dominated by the personality of the interviewer more than by the answer being attempted (see pp. 173–89).

Furthermore, there is a need for speed and brevity on television, and great issues are sometimes not handled at length, arguments are left unexplored and to keep programmes alive and entertaining they can be superficial and trivial. In-depth analysis – how events came to be – is often lacking. Yet at best discussion can be profound, elucidating the arguments on key issues and exploring the backgrounds of incidents and decisions.

These criticisms have been taken up by a number of politicians who feel that TV trivialises important subjects. Several years ago, a leading Labour politician, Dick Crossman, hit upon this theme,[14] and it was taken up by the Labour left-winger, Tony Benn.

Benn suggested that: 'Listeners and viewers have come to expect from certain well-known broadcasters a particular line or thought which is peculiar to them, but which, through the power of the medium, inevitably shapes public thinking.' On the other hand, nobody 'is ever allowed to say all he wants to say in the way he himself would like to say it; all are subject to editorial control by the BBC'.[15]

There is a difficulty which both men recognised. Television does often trivialise and personalise politics, but to some extent this reflects the necessity of putting a message across within the limitations of the medium. There is bound to be a tension between what is desirable and what is possible. Many politicians might like to be able to make long speeches to expound their cause and to be given the chance to deliver their opinions without interruption. Many television people might also like the time to give more time to the serious discussion of politics in depth.

Both face the same problem. The politician is preoccupied with the marginal voter whom he wishes to impress with his grasp. The television producer is preoccupied with the marginal viewer, whose attention he wishes to hold. One is concerned with political survival, the other with economic survival. Both have to recognise that politics for most people is not the overwhelming interest of their lives. Their attention to the details of political debate and their knowledge about policies and personalities tends to be limited.

Politics is a minority interest, and the media have to cater for the majority. The difficulty is to reconcile the often conflicting demands of the half-attentive majority and of the intensely-interested minority. As the majority are now better informed and have more information than was ever once the case, this is less of a problem than it was. But it is the minority who feel that the quality of television coverage of news and current affairs is not always as good as it could or should be.

## Notes

1 Glasgow University Media Group (GUMG), as quoted in P. Trowler, *Investigating the Media* (Unwin Hyman: London, 1988).
2 J. Whale, *The Politics of the Media* (Fontana: London, 1977).
3 H. Gans, *Deciding What's News* (Vintage Books: New York, 1980), p. 119.
4 Alastair Hetherington, *News, Newspapers and Television* (Macmillan: London, 1985), p. 8.
5 P. Golding and P. Elliott, *Making the News* (Longman: London, 1979), p. 207.
6 GUMG, *Bad News* (Routledge and Kegan Paul: London, 1976), p. 1.
7 Moyra Grant, 'The Politics of the Media', *Talking Politics*, vol. 6, no. 2 (Winter, 1985).
8 M. Harrison, *TV News; Whose Bias?* (Policy Journals, Berkshire, 1985), p. 127.
9 N. Jones, *Strikes and the Media* (Blackwell: Oxford, 1986), p. 115.
10 *J'Accuse: The News*, as shown on Channel 4, 26 October 1994.
11 J. Wober, *Impartiality in Television: The Public's View*, ITC Monograph (John Libby & Co., 1993).
12 *Ibid.*, adapted from table 6.4.
13 R. Brooks, 'Who's Selling the News?', *Observer*, 19 March 1995.
14 R. Crossman, Granada Lecture, October 1968.
15 A. Benn MP, public speech, October 1968.

# 6

# The effects of the media

The effects of the mass media on popular attitudes are difficult to assess, and because of this there is a tendency to attribute much that happens in society to the power of those media. For example, it is easy to assume that, because a crime committed is similar to one shown in a cinema film or television programme, it is the viewing of it which provoked the incident. An obvious example here is the alleged link between the showing of a film in 1963 and the death of President Kennedy. *The Manchurian Candidate* included some scenes not unlike those which happened when Kennedy was assassinated in November 1963, and the film was quickly withdrawn after the shooting – yet there was no evidence that the assassin or assassins had ever seen it.

For many people, it seems to be evident that because television is so widely viewed, then it must be a very powerful force in shaping our attitudes and behaviour. But it is much more difficult to pinpoint what its effects might be, and of course they may be very different on different people.

Similarly with political influence. A viewer may spend hours watching the television or reading a newspaper, but this does not necessarily tell us that either or both are his or her main sources of information. People belong to a society in which there are many possible ways of obtaining knowledge, and it is impossible to separate that which has been derived from, for instance, conversations in the public house or at the workplace, from that which has been accumulated from elsewhere. Life is a continuing learning experience, in which knowledge and attitudes are liable to be influenced at many points in a person's career.

The task is the greater because there are so many different forms of media, and to distinguish between the effects caused by one medium rather than another is near-impossible. In developing their political attitudes, people might be influenced by television, radio, newspapers or quality journals, amongst other sources; it may more simply be an eye-catching poster which makes the greatest impression on them.

Yet many of the media have a narrow readership or a small audience, so that our main concern lies particularly with television and newspapers, which are the major sources of information for most people. Television is especially important, for many surveys have shown that is the means by which the majority of voters derive their political knowledge and understanding. It is the more important for those who are only irregular or non-readers of newspapers.

IBA and ITC surveys on attitudes to broadcasting provide an insight into the main sources of information which people recognise as having influenced them (see Table 6.1).[1]

Table 6.1  *Sources of British and world news (%)*

|  | 1980 | 1985 | 1993 |
|---|---|---|---|
| Television | 52 | 62 | 69 |
| Radio | 14 | 14 | 11 |
| Newspapers | 33 | 23 | 19 |
| Magazines | 0 | 0 | 0 |
| Talking to people | 1 | 1 | 1 |

In this and other similar research, the significance of television as the primary medium of communication would appear to be growing and that of newspapers declining. Regular readers, particularly those of the broadsheet press, still acknowledge their preferred paper as an important influence upon them. They become used to its style and approach, and are likely to pay attention to the line taken in editorial articles, general reports and features. Readers of tabloid newspapers are more likely to buy their paper for non-political reasons, and its coverage of news at home and abroad is probably of less relevance in forming their attitudes. For them, television is a more potent source of knowledge.

In *Media and Voters*, William Miller and his team of researchers carried out a more prolonged study than many others of media influence. They interviewed more than 3,000 people face-to-face in the mid-term of the parliamentary election cycle, and more than one-third of them again in the pre-campaign period. They then contacted between 1,500 and 1,800 of these respondents three times by telephone, once in the first fortnight and once in the second fortnight of the campaign, and then conducted another interview once the result of the election had been digested.

Their findings about the most useful sources of news are of interest, taken as they were after the election was over. They found that television, normally seen as the medium for getting to know personalities, was actually the one favoured by most people as the source of their 'issue-information' – whereas Miller and his team would have expected the quality press to be 'the medium for detailed understanding of the issues'.[2] But few of his respondents read the *Guardian* or *The Times*, and from the tabloids they often derived very little information: 'Our image of the typical newspaper reader in Britain has to be that of someone reading a tabloid, not a highbrow quality paper.'

Of course, some people found the media more useful than others, but their overall judgement, whether as a means of providing issue-information, leader-information or vote-guidance, came down clearly in favour of the television rather than newspapers or other sources, as Table 6.2 shows.[3]

Table 6.2  *The usefulness of the media (marks out of 10)*

| Source | Issue-information | Leader-information | Vote-guidance |
| --- | --- | --- | --- |
| TV generally | 7.1 | 6.3 | 4.5 |
| BBC TV news | 6.6 | 6.1 | 4.4 |
| ITV news | 6.3 | 6.0 | 4.3 |
| Newspapers | 6.1 | 5.6 | 4.2 |
| Party election broadcasts | 5.6 | 5.5 | 4.2 |
| BBC Radio news | 5.6 | 5.4 | 3.9 |
| Conversations | 5.2 | 5.2 | 4.0 |
| Commercial Radio news | 4.8 | 4.7 | 3.6 |
| Party leaflets | 4.4 | 4.2 | 3.5 |

Note: Not all of the interviewees were able to give a verdict on the most influential sources. The radio finding was based on a small audience only.

Many people found the media better at providing information than as an aid to helping them decide how to vote. Television was slightly preferred to the press as a means of voter-guidance, although 40 per cent claimed to find both media equally useful. Readers of the tabloids found television to be a far more useful source of information than their paper, but only a little more useful in helping them to make up their mind on the key voting issue. Surprisingly, readers of the broadsheets 'found their papers only scarcely any more useful than readers of the lowbrow press'.[4]

### The effects of television on elections/electors

The media, especially television, largely determine the form of the campaign and as such have replaced political meetings in importance; indeed, the large meetings addressed by leading figures in the party are now relayed on television. The campaign is staged for television, and each news bulletin accords coverage of the activities of the main politicians.

. The age of great open-air meetings has passed away. They survived at least into the 1960s when Harold Wilson was still addressing vast gatherings in the open air, and George Brown and [more surprisingly] Sir Alec Douglas-Home toured the country delivering short speeches 'on the stump.' Today, there may be local encounters when the candidate addresses a small group of voters in a town hall or from a raised makeshift platform, but the main meetings are 'made for television' occasions, in which stage-managed proceedings are timed for maximum television coverage and soundbites are delivered to grab the headlines.

Bowler and Farrell have illustrated the extent to which these trends mirror those which are happening in other democracies. They observe that 'it is now television which is everywhere the main tool in election campaigning', and quote the comment of Sundberg and Hognabba that 'free elections in a modern democracy would easily collapse if the mass media . . . were to ignore election campaigning'.[5] In a section on the French Presidential campaign of 1988, the writers draw attention to the fear of candidates that in addressing meetings they were neglecting the larger stage: 'All the candidates travelled a great deal . . . the preference for huge gatherings was apparent, and even then the candidates worried that they might be losing time,' given that 'the least important television show, even local, can give one tens of thousands [of viewers]'.[6]

At the local level, television has also had an effect. Local organisations and membership have gone into sharp decline; the roots of party activity are atrophying, and canvassing and pamphleteering are less in evidence. The real campaign is on television, and the local outcome is determined largely by the impression which voters form of the leaders and of party competence derived from their viewing habits. Studies of local electioneering are few in number, but the general conclusion is that quoted by Farrell: 'Local electioneering has been overtaken by the nationalisation of the campaign and the growth of the mass media.'[7] He does, however, go on to examine how the more shrewd local party activists sometimes seek to exploit the media for constituency electioneering purposes.

The media have another role in connection with the conduct of elections. Increasingly, they also help to set the agenda for the campaign. Journalists (or more particularly their editors) decide on what they consider to be the key issues which are worthy of investigation and follow-up reporting and commentary. Certain issues are kept in the forefront of discussion, as in the 1992 election when the claims and counter-claims over the 'Jennifer's ear' broadcast kept other matters off centre-stage in the first week, and the opposition stance on proportional representation and the possibilities of Lib-Lab cooperation dominated the last few days of the campaign.

## What can we say of the effects on the voter?

On electors, the effects of all this coverage are difficult to assess, for the reasons already given. Television has enhanced the degree of awareness and understanding of many people; nowadays, more people are more knowledgeable, better informed and in some cases more sophisticated in their understanding. The reasonably intelligent person can be a political pundit, making his/her own comments to colleagues based on what has been grasped from 'the box'.

Of course, a person's own background and environment will greatly affect his or her judgement. Parental attitudes, schoolfriends and associates all help mould a people's views as well as the media. Some voters are healthily sceptical of what they see and are very resistant to politicians who may be misleading them. They think all politicians simply attack one another and so believe none.

Three broad models of political influence have been advanced in the study of the impact of the media, and more recently television.

*The manipulative theory*

Back in the 1920s and 1930s, it was easy to think in terms of the importance of propaganda, for its usefulness had been highlighted in the war. In the 1930s, the experience of the dictatorships, particularly Nazi Germany, led people to assume that the media must have a considerable impact, for Dr Goebbels and others like him were making so much use of persuasive techniques. The survey evidence to substantiate such findings was lacking, and of course the effect of propaganda in a totalitarian regime is likely to be infinitely greater than in a liberal democracy in which people can think, act and react under less threatening conditions.

However, there are still those who take the view that the voter is an easy prey to manipulation. He or she absorbs what they see, and if the media is biased to the left or right then this will shape attitudes. This is the hypodermic-needle model which sees television as injecting the audience with a syringe, and it reacts to this injection just as a patient does when injected with an antibiotic.

A modern version of the manipulative theory is that which stresses the importance of agenda-setting. The GUMG argue that the media influence people by more subtle means. They influence the public by determining what is shown or read, and many of the viewers/readers come to accept what is offered as a representation of the main things which are really happening. If it is the case that dissenting ideas are generally shunned and that, because of the outlook of those who work in television, there is an anti-left bias in the way in which stories are handled and background detail explained, then this is likely over a period of time to generate attitudes which are both uncritical of the status quo in society and supportive of the conservative position. Hidden bias, in the form of references to the 'loony left', 'militants' or 'extremists', can only be damaging to a more radical party.

*The reinforcement theory*

In the light of interwar experience, postwar researchers such us Paul Lazarsfeld looked for evidence of the propagandist impact of the media in a liberal democracy. He was unable to find it. Using more modern and scientific techniques of investigation, his surveys found that there was no evidence to substantiate the idea of significant effects in the United States.[8] Taking the 1948 Presidential election as a case-study, his findings (*The People's Choice*) showed that few people changed their vote in the campaign, and that those who did so were as likely to cite discussions with relatives, friends and colleagues at work as the major reason rather than television or newspapers.

This led Lazarsfeld to expound the 'minimum effects' model of media influence, which recognised that attitudes may crystallise in a campaign, but that voting behaviour itself was little influenced by television. The explanation for this was to be found in what was later known as the 'selective exposure theory'. As Miller puts it, listeners and viewers 'can filter out and suppress unwelcome messages while paying particular attention to those they like'.[9]

In contrast to those who discerned the hypodermic needle at work. Lazarsfeld stressed that there was no uniform response. In the face of so many possible influences, it was difficult to isolate any one of them. People already have their own ideas and attitudes before they view the programmes of their choice. When they see or hear information which does not accord with their preconceived judgement, they have to find a way of handling it, According to this view, they do so by a psychological process referred to as 'cognitive dissonance', an idea researched and expounded by an American, Leon Festinger, in 1957.[10]

The central idea of this theory is that when an individual becomes aware of two cognitions or perceptions which are not consistent with each other, this induces a state of psychological unease or tension. His or her own beliefs are at odds with the facts which have become available, and this 'dissonance' has to be handled.

A classic example would be the issue of smoking. An intelligent person who smokes would understand the strong connection between smoking and cancer. If we assume that the person would prefer not to have the disease, then he or she has to find a way of dealing with this discomforting situation. The way in which this may be done provides an insight into our study of how a voter deals with information which does not fit his or her beliefs. The smoker may cast doubt on the evidence or convince themselves that for some reason they are unlikely to be a victim. So the voter may seek to reconcile the contradiction or dissonance between what they believe and the facts with which they are being presented, which appear to run counter to their accepted notions.

According to the theory, he does this by three psychological processes:

1 *Selective exposure*; people are selective in their choice of programme or newspaper, and avoid those that give rise to conflict. Strong Conservatives are unlikely to choose the *Guardian*, and neither do many Labour voters read the *Telegraph*. On television, committed Conservatives are more likely to watch a Conservative broadcast, and when they decide to view a Labour one it is mainly to deride it and use it as further ammunition to illustrate Labour incompetence or untrustworthiness.

2 *Selective perception*; people tend to perceive information which fits existing expectations. They see different things from each other, for they individually choose those aspects which coincide with their preconceived notions.

3 *Selective retention*; people tend to retain information which supports existing attitudes and to ignore that which presents conflicting views. The inconvenient material is conveniently ignored.

Via these three devices, the viewer or listener filters out what he or she does not wish to see or hear, the result being that any dissonant facts which get in the way of the interpretation are either ignored or made to fit in with existing attitudes.

This view of the various media as essentially reinforcing agencies has a long pedigree. Milne and Mackenzie studied voting behaviour in North-East Bristol in 1955 and found that only 45 per cent of people acknowledged any type of propaganda source as an explanation for their voting.[11] Trenaman and McQuail came to this conclusion in 1961, for their study of the 1959 election came up with largely negative findings.[12] People knew more as a result of their listening and viewing, but their attitudes to the parties and their policies were largely unchanged.

Back in 1964, Birch concluded that these and other studies:

> showed that people exposed themselves mainly to communications with which they were predisposed to agree and that they tend to remember the content only of those items with which they had agreed. These studies suggested that, while the mass media may have the effect of reinforcing some people's opinions, they rarely have the effect of changing them. There was some evidence that people who exposed themselves to many communications on political matters were better informed than others, but since better-informed people were more interested in politics and more likely to read or listen or watch political items, it was impossible to determine the nature of cause and effect.[13]

The idea of reinforcement rather than fundamental change was later refined in the work of Blumler and McQuail who developed the consumer model of media influence. Under this theory some viewers and readers may seek reinforcement of their views, others may consciously seek guidance in helping them to make up their minds as to for whom they should vote. A significant number have no interest at all, and may watch merely because the set is on; they are not looking for guidance or reinforcement, and may react either by being uninterested in the message put forward, or may passively accept it in an uncritical manner. Here, in what is sometimes seen as the 'uses and gratifications' model, as Miller puts it: 'The essential idea of the consumer model is simply that there is a variety of motivations for media exposure, and that motivations condition the message.'[14]

For years, this type of approach was the standard orthodoxy, but today it is much more open to question. In some relevant respects things have changed since the 1960s. We now have much greater experience of the media, and in particular television has become a significantly more pervasive medium since Birch wrote that passage. With almost every home now having a television and people viewing so extensively, it is hard to believe that the effects are so minimal as he implied.

Another change in the last generation has been the traditional party allegiance of sections of the electorate. It is now a commonplace to speak of declining voter-partisanship, and the erosion of the class basis of voting has left electors more open to the possibility of media influence. If class is no longer a determining influence on voting behaviour and people are more receptive to a change of mind, it seems reasonable to suggest that the media, especially television, may have a greater effect than ever before. After all, the research of psephologists suggests that around a quarter of the electorate changes its vote during the election campaign. Denver observes that: 'As . . . enduring ties have loosened . . . it seems likely that voters have become more open to influence during campaigns. Fewer will have their minds already made up when the campaign begins.' He goes on to note that: 'There has been no full-scale study of the effects of television upon voting behaviour in the period of dealignment'.[15]

Hence, the problem with the reinforcement approach is that it does not square with what might seem a common-sense view of likely media influence. Those who seek to market our politicians do not have such a low view of media influence, for otherwise they would spend much less time, effort and money on seeking to put their message across in the most effective way. Today, as we have seen, much of an election campaign is concerned with 'made for television' events, ranging from photo opportunities to staged rallies at which set-piece speeches are delivered at a time designed to make the evening headlines. Are professionals doing this purely because the other side is doing so, and they cannot take the risk of losing out in the struggle just in case there is a significant impact on key voters in marginal constituencies?

## The independent effect theory

In the light of this greater awareness, a third model is in vogue today. The independent effect theory is now sometimes advocated by sociologists, and this suggests that the media do have an effect on public attitudes, even if those effects are difficult to monitor and variable in its impact. It may be a negative one – e.g. by ignoring certain parties, the media make people believe that they are not important or do not exist. It may be small-scale and short-term influence, but it is naive to write off the power of the media. Whilst Blumler could write that 'the magnitude of measured communication effect has typically proved modest and unlikely to be able to override strong countervailing forces',[16] he proceeded to highlight certain features which suggested a degree of influence beyond straightforward reinforcement.

Some evidence to substantiate the effect of television is provided by a study of the 1976 Presidential election in the United States. Patterson's survey invited participants to assess the performance of the two candidates, Jimmy Carter and Gerald Ford.[17] Those who gave their verdict within twelve hours generally inclined to the view that Ford had won, whereas those who gave it after that period inclined to the view that Carter had come out ahead. The people interviewed later had been able to take on board the judgements of the media correspondents about who had won, and many of these were harsh on Ford believing that a gaffe he committed was a costly error. Their exposure of the mistake and comment on it may have swung opinion against him.

The truth is that no one really knows what the effects of television are and different research points to different conclusions. People react in several ways. Some are partisans who seek to back up their beliefs with examples derived from the programmes they view; others are monitors genuinely seeking information with which to make up their minds. There are also those who are merely passive spectators watching out of apathy or without great commitment. In other words, it is misleading to speak of the impact of the media as though this was the same impact on all groups in the population. The effects of television exposure may be entirely different on such categories as the young and the old, the employed and the unemployed, those in the private sector and those in the public sector – and in none of these cases can we assume that those involved act in a homogeneous way. There are many effects on many different people.

One of the many difficulties in studying the effects of television is the difficulty in distinguishing between the short term and the long term. It is inevitably difficult and costly for researchers to mount a detailed study of attitudes over a really long period. It would be impractical to monitor the same people over many years, but it may well be that the effects of the media are considerably more long-term than has ever been allowed for. As Denver puts it, they may be 'slow and subtle – but none the less real'.[18]

The general election campaign, which is normally the basis for study, or even a longer piece of research over several months, cannot provide a whole picture of the development of people's political attitudes, and the contributory factors to any changes which occur. Negrine has made the valid point that elections are sometimes 'preceded by events which have a significant impact on the outcome of those elections themselves – so much so that the result is never in doubt. This happened in 1979 and also in 1983.'[19]

In determining people's attitude to the Labour Party, the events of 1978–79 (the 'Winter of Discontent') have had a profound and long-lasting effect in making people perceive Labour as 'soft on the unions' and unable effectively to handle their 'too-close' relationship with them. Negrine uses the illustration of the Falklands conflict in 1982 to show that, having achieved an opinion poll lead of 15.8 per cent by the start of the campaign, the Conservatives never looked back; they proceeded to win with a 15.2 per cent margin of victory.

There is no easy conclusion concerning the impact of the media (especially television) on the electorate. Television provides the major learning experience of democratic politics, and David Butler has argued that television exposes the electorate 'to a larger body of rational evidence than ever before'.[20] At election time the elector faces a barrage of material from the mass media including news bulletins, discussion programmes and party broadcasts. Given the saturation coverage, the careful marketing of the product and the fact that almost every home has a television which is constantly watched by some members of the family, one would expect there to be some influence on popular opinion and consequently on voting behaviour. If the effects are not readily apparent in the short term, then over a longer period exposure is more likely to make a deeper impression.

### The effects of television on politicians

Some politicians are telegenic and perform well on television; it can help to destroy or create a reputation. Ronald Reagan, significantly an ex-actor, was good at the 'soft-sell' whereas Richard Nixon often inspired mistrust for he could often look 'crooked', hence his nickname 'Tricky Dicky'.

A good performer (Macmillan, who did not like appearing, or the young Wilson) can do well, and benefit from having the opportunity to speak directly in your living-room. By contrast Douglas-Home was unconvincing and seemed out of touch. Mrs Thatcher was able to use the medium to convey her strength and resolution, and with careful coaching from professionals was successful in adopting a 'softer' style of voice and appearance to accompany her message.

In the case of John Major, much has been made of his affability and ordinariness, playing to his alleged strengths. He appears to me more successful in talking to a group of people than in addressing a large rally, and broadcasts have often surrounded him with such a set of supporters. That Labour chose Tony Blair as leader was an indication of the importance attached to people who have a telegenic appeal, which is media-friendly. Abrasive and argumentative politicians can seem very unattractive to the public.

The arrival of television in the House of Commons meant that politicians had to show a new awareness of the demands of television, and many of them sought expert advice as to how they should present themselves when the camera might be recording their appearance and mannerisms. Of this, much more is written in Chapter 10.

### The press

Like television, newspapers have also been generally assumed to reinforce the views held by their readers rather than to convert them. Many readers are unconscious of the papers' bias or indifferent to it. It has often been assumed that the obvious partisanship of the press may be counter-productive, and Glyn Parry has been an exponent of this viewpoint: 'Far from resulting in a massive conversion of waverers and doubters, it creates a feeling of repugnance amongst normal supporters.' [21]

He notes that Labour developed as a mass party despite the overt hostility of much of the press, and that anyway there is much more to newspapers than political coverage. In the nineteenth century, when papers were geared to the needs of an educated minority, politics loomed largely in their content; in the twentieth century, the emphasis has been upon mass circulation, and its significance has diminished. Papers are purchased more for news of sport, social gossip, fashion and crime, and in some cases, for the pin-ups they display, than for anything else; they are sources of entertainment which opt for sensationalism and titillation, more than sources of political information.

The quality broadsheets do provide more detailed information and analysis, though Jack Straw (a Labour frontbencher) has noted that the amount of space devoted to Parliamentary reporting has declined over the past few years. His findings point to a significant drop in typical daily coverage in the period since 1988.[22] The *Guardian* and *The Times* were especially criticised, but so was the *Daily Telegraph* to a lesser extent. Straw sees the reduction as a danger to public knowledge and understanding, seeing political argument as a 'vital ingredient in democracy'.

The traditional view of the impact of the broadsheets has been that whilst it may widen knowledge and affect readers' attitudes on specific issues, it has much less impact on general ones on which people may already have their own views; they tend to choose a paper they admire, and probably would find within it more backing for their existing opinions.

It is difficult to say with any certainty whether newspapers of any kind do more to mould the views of their readers, or whether (as we have speculated) that the readers choose the papers anyway because they agree with their views. MORI's survey in 1975 suggested the latter, for it showed that 70 per cent of *Telegraph* readers were Conservative voters, and 57 per cent of *Mirror* ones voted Labour.

Of course, the 1992 election reopened discussion of the influence of the press in the light of the tabloids' behaviour in so belittling the Labour leadership and condemning the party's policies (see also pp. 40–1). The effects of the *Sun*'s coverage are open to dispute, and those who deny or downplay the role of newspapers in affecting the outcome note that more of that paper's readers voted against the Conservatives than for them (50 per cent for Labour/Liberal Democrats, as against 45 per cent for the Tories). They point out that the press has always been overwhelmingly against the Labour Party, but that has not stopped Labour from reaching leading-party status in the twentieth century and winning elections under Harold Wilson.

The ferocity of the tabloid onslaught is now greater than it was then, however, and many of the conclusions often put forward about press influence on voting behaviour are based on old research. More recently, William Miller's enquiries into the 1987 election (*Media And Voters*) suggested that the tabloid press was influential over the voting preferences of voters, particularly those who were uncommitted. He found that the more tabloid the newspaper the greater its influence on the result, and that in general papers had more significance than broadcasting:

British television is still very much an information medium rather than a propaganda medium . . . The tabloids in particular carried relatively little in-depth information but a lot of propaganda. So we should expect readers of different papers to be influenced in different directions depending upon the content of their own particular papers. We should expect the mass-selling tabloid press to have a stronger influence on public attitudes and choices than on public information and perceptions. Highbrow papers might be more like television, primarily affecting their reader 'information and perceptions'.[23]

Kenneth Newton is another academic who has discerned the possibility of a growing press influence. He argues that:

even those who identify with a given party and believe in its policies are more likely to vote for another party if, over a period of time, they regularly read a paper which supports the other party. Evidence is accumulating to suggest that the political impact of the national press may not be insignificant after all.[24]

Other academics remain less convinced, and have tended to stress that inasmuch as there is much press influence, it is likely to be of the reinforcing rather than the changing variety. Harrop's study[25] echoes the older view of Butler and Stokes[26] that there is little evidence of electors their switching their allegiances because of what they have read. Where there was no established preference, then the findings showed that there could be a modest press impact on voting behaviour.

Denver retains an open mind on the issue of press influence. He notes that there is certainly:

a correlation between the papers people read and the party they vote for . . . [though] the relationship is far from perfect – only a minority of the readers of the extravagantly pro-Conservative *Sun* actually voted Conservative . . . and the surprising preference of the *Financial Times* apparently left its readers unmoved.[27]

Like other analysts, he is unsure as to whether people deliberately choose a paper which is politically attractive to them, or whether the readers of particular papers are influenced by their choice of reading material: 'People may read the *Guardian* and vote Labour, but that does not mean that they vote Labour because they read the *Guardian*. Rather, they may read the *Guardian* because they vote Labour. In other words, the data may reflect selective exposure.'

If the effects of papers are the subject of contentious discussion, the press may have a different importance which is not to convert readers, but to determine the issues of the campaign. Campaigns may be increasingly fought on television, but the stories in the morning newspapers and the way in which they are handled by the editor may help determine what radio and television take up in their news bulletins and discussion programmes. In other words, they help to determine the national news agenda, and as well as throwing up issues for debate they can help in creating images of leading personalities which then feed through into the questions of television interviewers. Neil Kinnock suffered from many such stories which began in the press and may have helped determine people's opinion of him when he was interviewed in television studios.

## Notes

1   *Attitudes to Broadcasting*, IBA survey, 1985, and *Sources of News, in Television; the Public's View*, ITC survey (John Libby & Co.).
2   W. Miller, *Media and Voters* (Clarendon Press: Oxford, 1991), p. 119.
3   *Ibid.*, p. 118.
4   *Ibid.*, p. 131.
5   S. Bowler and D. Farrell (eds), *Electoral Strategies and Political Marketing* (Macmillan: London, 1992), p. 229.
6   *Ibid.*, ch. 6.
7   *Ibid.*, p. 229.
8   P. Lazarsfeld, *The People's Choice* (Columbia University Press: New York, 1968).·
9   W. Miller, *Media and Voters*, p. 2.
10  L. Festinger, *A Theory of Cognitive Dissonance* (Peter Row: Evanston, IL, 1957).
11  R. Milne and H. McKenzie, *Marginal Seat* (Hansard Society: London, 1958), p. 161.
12  J. Trenaman and D. McQuail, *Television and the Political Image* (Methuen: London, 1961), esp. p. 192.
13  A. Birch, *Representative and Responsible Government* (Allen and Unwin: London, 1964), p. 181
14  W. Miller, *Media and Voters*, pp. 2–3
15  D. Denver, *Elections and Voting Behaviour in Britain* (Harvester Wheatsheaf: London, 1994), p. 113.
16  J. Blumler, *The Political Effects of Mass Communication* (Open UniversityPress: Milton Keynes, 1977), p. 42.
17  T. Patterson, *The Mass Media Election* (Praeger: New York, 1980).
18  D. Denver, *Elections and Voting Behaviour in Britain*, p. 122.
19  R. Negrine, *Politics and the Mass Media in Britain* (Routledge: London, 1994), p. 156.
20  D. Butler, *Political Communication; The General Election of 1987* (Cambridge University Press: Cambridge, 1989).
21  G. Parry, *British Government* (Arnold: London, 1978), p. 24.
22  J. Straw, 'Ask no questions, hear more lies', *Independent*, 24 October 1993.
23  W. Miller, *Media and Voters*, p. 132.
24  K. Newton, 'Political communications', in I. Budge and D. McKay (eds), *The Developing British Political System: the 1990s* (Longman: London, 1993), p. 122.
25  M. Harrop, *Press Coverage of Postwar British Elections, Political Communications: The British General Election Campaign of 1983* (Cambridge University Press: Cambridge, 1986).
26  D. Butler and D. Stokes, *Political Change in Britain* (Macmillan: London, 1969).
27  D. Denver, *Elections and Voting Behaviour in Britain*, p. 125.

Part II

# Parties, politicians and the media

# 7

# The role of the media in the political process: pressure groups, local government and privatisation

Much of our coverage concerns the way in which political parties and politicians have responded to the developments in the media which they try to use for their own advantage. Yet they are not the only organisations and individuals which seek to propagate their views and thereby influence public opinion. Members of any body which wishes to have an impact on the government or the governed will quickly appreciate the importance of using the tools of the age, particularly newspapers and television, and ensure that they adopt techniques which are media-friendly.

For any persons charged with conducting a public campaign, whether they belong to an industry or utility undergoing privatisation, a local authority or a pressure group, a knowledge of the outlook and working methods of journalists and broadcasters is essential.

## Pressure groups and the media

In Britain and America, pressure groups use the media to help create a more favourable climate of opinion. In the USA, this might be especially important in states which employ constitutional devices such as the referendum and the initiative, for in those areas there is a real possibility that an impact on the public may affect the outcome of voting on polling day.

In either case, Britain or the USA, the scale of publicity employed must depend upon the financial and other resources of the group. Television advertising is permitted in America (see pp. 133–7), but because of its expense it is little used by most lobbyists other than in the build-up to an election campaign, when the Political Action Committees spend lavishly on short thirty-second spots. But such an outlet is considerably more costly than a full-page ad in a newspaper, so that the print media are more useful than the electronic form for most of the time. As a campaign reaches its climax, an American group might be more willing to invest in air or viewing time.

Newspapers and journals are more frequently used. In the way that the American Medical Association has resorted to such means to explain the outlook and anxieties of its members, so too has the British Medical Association made extensive use of poster and press advertising – not least in its campaign against Kenneth Clarke during his period as Health Secretary.

Business enjoys a special advantage, for those involved have the money to use propaganda on an extensive scale. They know how to deliver their message effectively, or at least can afford to find an agency to do it for them. Some industrialists are active in the campaigning by free-enterprise groups such as the Economic League and Aims for Freedom and Enterprise.

New technologies have increased the reach of interest groups, particularly the development of computerised and targeted mass mailing. For years some organisations have sent out large mailings to people whose names are in telephone directories, but this is an indiscriminate approach. With today's technology, personalised mailing is possible and increasingly widely used. It creates the illusion of personal interest, and can be a useful means of fund-raising and mobilising an already committed group into taking action – such as writing letters, taking part in protests or turning out to vote.

Targeting has often been used to contact people likely to have a common concern, such as members of environmental groups. The ideas of the environmentalists have also received a regular airing on television. Sometimes, specific programmes have drawn attention to national and international problems, whilst there are regular 'nature' and 'health' series which cover some of their territory. The groups involved will often be represented in particular programmes, so that the adoption of a media-friendly image is important for their spokespersons. Key figures in Friends of the Earth have had a close association with the media, some having at one time worked in television or the newspaper industry.

The Campaign for the Preservation of Rural England once operated mainly through personal contact in Whitehall, but the arrival of a new Director in 1980 brought about a change. He had been involved in advertising, and done freelance work for radio and television. A new awareness of the importance of propaganda was evident, and there was a conscious attempt to influence public opinion.

Within the food industry, the media have played an important role in the emergence of a series of related issues concerning food additives and the quality of products for consumption. This is one of the new issues which Wyn Grant[1] has identified in the realms of pressure-group activity, and one in which numerous organisations operate under the umbrella of the National Food Alliance.

The media have been active in publicising food scares, and whereas food safety 'trundled along without too much publicity'[2] until the late 1980s this is no longer the case. As Grant has indicated: 'The campaigning groups, operating through the media, have changed the politics of food from a technical subject dealt with in a closed community into a politicised arena operating in a more open policy setting.'[3]

Alf Dubs, a former Labour MP with an interest in lobbying techniques, has described some of the means by which a group can popularise its case. He mentions the value of press conferences which can be used to publicise new findings or launch a policy statement. If they are held in London, they are more likely to attract the attention of an MP. The press can be useful to a group, the more so if summaries and pictures are made available:

> The aim is to interest the press and give them a chance to ask questions . . . if your group has something urgent to say you can always ask an MP to inform the Press Association at the Commons . . . if [the chief reporter of the PA) thinks it is an interesting story, he will put it out on the PA tapes, and this should be good coverage.[4]

Groups can approach local radio stations or even seek to get their story on the BBC Radio Four *Today* programme. Again, it is easier if they can involve an MP who is willing to ask a Parliamentary Question or put down an Early Day Motion, for then the radio editor is more likely to follow the matter up.

Some campaigns have been particularly skilful in advancing their cause. Baggott quotes the example of the English Collective of Prostitutes which managed to persuade an advertising agency to produce posters free of charge. These were placed on seventy sites around the country, and drew attention in a humorous way to the case for abolishing the laws which regulate the activities of 'the oldest profession'.[5] A very different – but also locally popular – concern was that taken up by the supporters of a football team.

## The Valley campaign

An interesting example of a group campaign was that concerned to save the Valley as the football ground of Charlton Athletic FC. After serious financial problems, the Club no longer owned its ground which needed substantial renovation. It decided to share facilities with Crystal Palace at Selhurst Park, but this move never won much backing with the supporters who disliked the idea of driving ten miles across London to see a home game. For two seasons, in 1985–97, supporters chanted at every match that 'we should have stayed at The Valley'. Even a return to the First Division, as it was then called, did not arouse their complete enthusiasm, and in 1987 the directors decided on a return to their home area. They repurchased the Valley, and intended to build a new ground which would be a modern, all-seater stadium.

The Labour-controlled Council claimed to support the Club's return, but was unwilling to grant permission for the commercial development of the site which would make the plan viable. Some of the aggrieved backers of the scheme decided to fight the Council. They decided to form themselves into a political party, the Valley Party, the specific aim being to return the Club to its traditional home. The formation of the group did not encourage a more emollient attitude from the Council as was anticipated, and so the Party decided to fight a full-scale election campaign through the ballot box.

It was necessary to generate media attention from the broadcast media and national newspapers, and in addition canvassers used door-stepping and leaflets to publicise the cause. They contested each of the wards and put up a total of sixty candidates. With only £3,500 at their disposal, television was patently beyond financial practicality, radio uneconomic, and the local press superflous, for it was already sympathetic to the campaign. Posters were an obvious choice, and thirty-five sites were booked for most of the month before the April 1990 election.

The outcome of the elections was that the Valley Party won an impressive 10.8 per cent share of the vote. All of the main parties lost support compared with the last elections in 1986. In 13/36 wards the Party came second or third, ahead of at least one major party, and Labour suffered serious losses, including the defeat of the key figures in its resistance to the Valley cause.

Media coverage was an important part of the success, and although funds were limited the Party was able to attract national coverage of what was a local issue, both at the press conference to launch the campaign, and in items on *Thames News, Newsnight* and LBC and Capital Radio. Articles in the *Guardian* were seen as helpful. Above all, however, advertising was 'at the heart of an effective campaign. It was the advertising which generated the powerful media coverage and helped to recruit sixty citizens who in the space of a couple of months became a potent political force in the Borough (Greenwich).'[6]

The Club did eventually return to the Valley early in the 1990s, following a change of attitude on the part of the Council.

*Direct action*

By direct action, we refer to any attempt to coerce the government or those in authority into a change of viewpoint. The form may be violent or passive, but in either case an attempt is made to use pressure or force, rather than persuasion through the usual democratic channels. The most common method involves marches, sit-ins and other such demonstrations. If they are well-organised and attract media coverage, they can be effective in achieving the aim of those who participate.

Animal rights activists have been willing to disrupt events and stage several forms of demonstration, in the knowledge that they are likely to command media attention and thereby draw attention to their cause. It is the prospect of gaining widespread publicity which has made direct action a more useful and popular means of protest over the last generation. This was seen very clearly in 1994–95, when the media were almost ever-present as protesters tried to prevent the export of live animals abroad for slaughter.

Greenpeace has also been able to draw attention to its high-profile campaigning through the media, whether it be against French nuclear tests or the dismantling and dumping of an obsolete oil rig. Grant observes that this has led to criticism: 'engaging in media stunts . . . may . . . mislead supporters into thinking that policy has been changed'. He quotes one writer who has suggested that 'a handful of heroic Greenpeace "rainbow warriors"' may be less effective than 'a steadier engagement at the international level . . . [Predominantly] symbolic acts . . . may simply soothe the public.'[7]

## Communication by other organisations

Effective communication was important in the privatisation campaigns (see also p. 131) of the early to mid-1980s, and was used skilfully in promoting the sale of British Gas and British Telecom. An extensive programme of qualitative research was carried out to monitor and assess attitudes to British Gas in the pre-flotation period, and it showed that, partly as a result of the corporate advertising campaign, the image of the company improved significantly among potential investors.

The programme was conducted in three stages, the Announcement phase, the Information phase and the Countdown phase. The strategy was to encourage participation in 'The People's Share Offer', and this was done by illustrating that people from all walks of life could be involved – builders, divers, riders and singers among them. The creative device common to each episode in the campaign was a character called Sid, who never actually appeared, but was seen as a metaphor for the general public. Sid was seen on television, but also heard on radio, and featured in the press and in ads on poster hoardings.

Local authorities have sometimes used advertising to promote their interests. Particularly effective was the campaign to counter the Conservative Government's 'Paving Bill' which prepared the way for the abolition of the Greater London Council (GLC). Advertising was used by the Labour-controlled GLC to stimulate widespread opposition to the proposed legislation, and was effective in gaining wider media coverage so that the issue became one of popular interest and concern. This success may well have been a factor in helping Labour to overcome some of its traditional opposition to the use of advertising in national party politics. It showed that a left-wing party could deploy advertising techniques without compromising the radical tone of the message.

It is to the use and abuse of the media by parties and national politicians – as well as by broadcasters and journalists – that we must now turn our attention.

## Notes

1  W. Grant, *Pressure Groups, Politics and Democracy in Britain* (Harvester Wheatsheaf: London, 1995), p. 53.
2  *Ibid.*, p. 54.
3  *Ibid.*, p. 55.
4  A. Dubs, *Lobbying: An Insider's Guide to the Parliamentary Process* (Pluto Press: London, 1989), p.188.
5  R. Baggott, *Pressure Groups Today* (Manchester University Press: Manchester, 1995), pp. 186–7.
6  '"Vote Valley": Changing the Agenda in a Local Government Election', in *A Winning Case History, from the Institute of Practitioners in Advertising* (NTC Publications: Henley-on-Thames, 1990).
7  W. Grant, *Pressure Groups, Politics and Democracy in Britain*, p. 89.

# 8

# Governmental manipulation

In the process of political communication, there is inevitable conflict between the interests of the three elements involved, government, the media and the public. The government has a viewpoint which it wishes to put across to the the electorate, but the media may have a different set of priorities and wish to question the viewpoint of those in authority.

It is the same in all countries. Governments of various shades of opinion tend to be suspicious of the media because they wish to determine what information should be in the public domain and suspect that the media have their own agenda which they wish to convey. They resent the influence which broadcasters wield, and envy their ability to control the supply of information. There is a natural tension between the newspaper or journalist on the one hand, and government (be it local or national) on the other. One side wishes to expose wrongdoing and spotlight the failures of government policy. The other side wishes to highlight its achievements rather than dwell upon the things left undone or done badly.

Any government long in power – such as the Conservatives since 1979 – becomes particularly suspicious. It cannot easily blame its predecessors for what has gone wrong, and when problems in society are pointed out it feels vulnerable to criticism. It is always easier to expose failure rather than defend the status quo, for some individuals and groups inevitably suffer injustice or are the ones left out in the bid for material prosperity.

Ministers tend to feel sensitive to the media and fear that their policies will be misinterpreted, their achievements ignored and their deficiencies emphasised. Any reasonable and inevitable differences of outlook between them will be magnified out of all proportion and used to create an impression of serious disunity.

Labour and Conservative governments seek to manage the media in the hope that a favourable impression of their work can be created. In their endeavours, they are helped by the fact that although Britain is a reasonably liberal and tolerant democracy and has been so for many years, it has a highly secretive system of government which the media find difficult to penetrate. Whitehall has traditionally adopted a highly restrictive attitude to the unauthorised disclosure of official information. It is hard to seek out the truth for much information is protected. Special legislation exists which curbs the availability of knowledge and among the controls is the legislation on official secrecy, on the security services, and that relating to privacy and confidentiality.

## Government control over information

The Home Secretary has direct powers concerning the British media, for under the terms of the BBC's Licence and the legislation concerning the ITA the Minister has the right to lay down the hours of operation, though normally this would only be done in an emergency. He has the power to veto the broadcasting of any particular topic or type of topic, though again this is very much a reserve power. In normal circumstances, it is inconceivable that he or she would actually stop the expression of opinion through direct censorship, though in times of war such as in the Falklands dispute or the Gulf conflict then different rules prevail.

As the Report of the Committee on the Future of Broadcasting noted back in 1977: 'It is inevitable that Ministers will be tempted to intervene. In the last resort, the Government, not the broadcasters, must make the decisions about national security.' It distinguishes between the legitimate practice of Ministers and Departments 'making representations . . . about programmes dealing with matters for which they are responsible', 'representations about specific programme matters made through political channels, or by Departments with responsibilities for the subject matter of the programme', and 'attempts to influence programmes or programme control generally, by Ministers brandishing the threat of using the Home Secretary's powers of direction or, to the BBC, the threat of withholding an increase in the licence fee'. Representations of the first kind are inevitable, but few allegations or instances of the second have come to use from any source'.[1]

It prefers the present system of giving Ministers the power to veto transmission when there is an alleged question of national security or the imperilment of civil order to one where responsibility was transferred to the broadcasting authorities, for they would find it difficult to resist if devastating consequences of transmission were shown.

> In the present system, a Minister can state his grave objections; the Broadcasting Authorities can then reject these objections and can inform the Minister that under his power he is at liberty to ban the programme; but if he does, they will tell the public that he had done so. We believe that this is the best way of reconciling the freedom of the broadcasters with the legitimate concerns of the government.[2]

D-notices act as a means of offering informal advice on matters of security and are operated by an official Press and Broadcasting Committee. They are issued to prevent the publication of sensitive information, and they amount to a form of self-censorship. Many journalists dislike a system in which some of their fellows are willing to be compliant, and feel that it smacks of the 'old boy' network. D-notices were not referred to in the 1989 legislation, but they are still in use.

These limitations add up to a series of important controls on the supply of information, and on what items can be reported. Beyond the statutory restrictions, there is a tradition of secrecy in British government which can be understood in questions of national security (though the term can be used to conceal information on a vast array of subjects) but which extends into many areas of policy-making. Governments are very protective of their interests, and cling to any information which it is inconvenient to release. This cult of secrecy is not matched or balanced by any Freedom of Information Act, unlike the situation in countries ranging from Australia and New Zealand to the United States and Sweden. There is no constitutional requirement to place information in the public domain.

Issues of free expression, what might be printed or spoken, are ultimately resolved by the courts. There is no Bill of Rights, and traditionally the British judiciary has erred on the side of security considerations. In the Spycatcher case, the Government was keen to muzzle the press, and a judge explicitly stated that the interests of the state were not distinctive from the interests of the government of the day.

The result is that important information on matters ranging from events in Northern Ireland to the nuclear accident at Windscale in 1958, or to defence procurement, are concealed from the public.

## The television authorities and postwar governments: a history

As we have indicated, the media are committed to the notion of free expression and are not disposed to afford the government a quiet life. Clashes have a long history, and back in 1940 Churchill hoped to establish more effective control.[3] A document uncovered in the Public Record Office reveals that the Prime Minister was intent on making the Corporation more of a propaganda arm of the Government. During the Battle of Britain, a few months later, he was again attacking it as 'one of the neutrals' and 'the enemy at the gate'.

In many issues since the war conflict has arisen between the two sides, Ministers and media personnel. One of the early areas of disagreement in postwar Britain was at the time of the Suez Crisis, in 1956. The background to the British intervention remains shrouded in some mystery and confusion, as the key documents were not revealed after the statutory thirty years had elapsed. Press reporting varied according to the political line of the paper, with pro-Conservative papers being in favour of the invasion and anti-ones against. Inevitably, the agenda set by critics in Fleet Street was taken up by the broadcasters.

Eden was angry at the widespread criticism of Government policy, and wanted to stifle such free discussion. He took the view that dissenting voices should not be heard at such times, for they provide 'comfort to the enemy by reporting domestic divisions, thus weakening the credibility of our threats'[4] So exasperated was he at the coverage given by the broadcasting authorities that he contemplated taking control of the BBC. He shrank from such an intervention, and indeed assured the Chairman of the Board of Governors that 'the Government have no intention of interfering with the freedom of the BBC'. He was appealing to the Corporation to show restraint, and it resisted considerable pressure, much of which was of the informal kind.

The Wilson and Callaghan Governments were similarly keen to ensure that the media were kept in their place and were as keen to manage the output of the media as were their Conservative predecessors. Wilson was anxious to ensure that Ian Smith, the Prime Minister of what was then Rhodesia, was kept off the screen after the African country had illegally declared its independence from Britain, in 1965, and made representations to that effect. The Labour Governments of the 1970s also concealed the fact that they were modernising the Polaris missile-heads from the gaze of the media and the public, because this was a costly and controversial act of policy.

However, it is in the period since 1979 that the relationship between the media and the politicians in power has come under the greatest strain. On several issues Ministers felt that they were getting unsatisfactory coverage from journalists. Particularly on matters of national security, but also on matters of day-to-day politics, the Government attempted to suppress information and/or conveyed a distorted version of events. In the 1980s they were willing to resort to the courts to defend that concern with security, and judges on occasion showed a willingness to go along with their wish to prevent disclosure. Such an obsession with secrecy and the careful management of news has made it difficult for the media to seek and find the truth.

## Governments and the media: some problems in the 1980s

### Argentina

In the Falklands War, Mrs Thatcher was dissatisfied with the way in which television handled the confrontation with Argentina. She did not expect the media to be neutral, but rather to wave the flag on behalf of 'our boys innnn the South Atlantic'. She felt that the official (i.e. the Government's) case was not being adequately presented, and that there was too much examination of the viewpoint of those who disagreed with the war. A *Panorama* programme cast doubts upon the wisdom of Government policy, and this was much resented in Downing Street. So was the way in which *Newsnight* referred to 'British troops' rather than 'our troops'. The Prime Minister conveyed her views to the House of Commons on 6 May 1982:

Many people are very concerned indeed that the case for our British forces is not being put over fully and effectively. I understand that there are times when it seems that we and the Argentinians are being treated almost as equals and almost on a neutral basis.

The media authorities wanted to explore the background of the dispute, and felt that it was their role to be objective and detailed in their reporting of hostilities. They were conscious that there was some division in the country over the rights and wrongs of Government policy (though not comparable to that over Suez), and saw this as a legitimate area for investigation and discussion. Opponents of the war felt that, if anything, the Corporation was being too uncritical in its acceptance of the ministerial viewpoint, and took note of the observation of the Chairman of the Governors who had assured the Prime Minister that the BBC was not neutral on the merits of the dispute.

During the war, the media was hampered in its activities by the tardiness of the Ministry of Defence in releasing film of the action until it had been carefully vetted. As film was immediately released by the Argentinian side, the broadcasters used this and this meant that the British version lost some of its impact.

### The bombing of Libya, April 1986

The Americans suspected that the Libyan Government of Colonel Gadhafi was involved in acts of international terrorism, and they used their air base in Britain to fly bombers to that country to bomb its military installations; Gadhafi was also a target. The British Government gave permission for the flights and seemed thereby to be endorsing the operation. This led to much controversy for the Opposition and many journalists were unhappy with the British decision.

The Conservatives were very critical about the coverage of the bombing raids by the BBC, for whereas the ITN accounts gave high priority to Libyan involvement in terrorism, the Corporation's reports placed more emphasis on the effects of the bombing, the casualties involved, and discussion of the rights and wrongs of the raid. According to a complaint from Central Office, terrorism was mentioned 'only in the last breath'. The Conservative dossier, prepared by Norman Tebbit (who had a high profile in the clash between the BBC and the Government) stated that coverage of the events was 'riddled with inaccuracy, innuendo and unbalance', charges which were vigorously refuted. It seemed as though the Party Chairman was 'softening up' the BBC in the run-up to the election.

A further difficulty in the relationship of the media and the Government arose in 1986 over a series of programmes made by the BBC on security matters; one episode related to the spy-satellite communications system, Zircon. The programme was banned and searches were made of the homes of researchers of the journalists involved, and of the offices of *The New Statesman* and BBC Scotland. Tapes and files were seized. Members of the House of Commons were able to view the programme which eventually (two years later) was shown on television.

### Events concerning Northern Ireland

There is an obvious security implication to discussion of events in Northern

Ireland, and coverage of events in the province has caused problems for broadcasters on several occasions.

The army has been for many years seeking to hold the ring between republicans and loyalists in a situation of dangerous sectarian strife. The two groups have entirely different allegiances, the nationalists denying the legitimacy of the Northern Irish state, the unionists being committed to the maintenance of the six counties as a distinct and separate entity. As violence or the threat of violence has occurred, the military have been expected to deal with the situation using only a minimum of force, although sometimes soldiers have found themselves in life-threatening situations. It is an uneasy balance in which there were always likely to be occasions in which excessive fire-power was used, and in which innocent bystanders might suffer.

When things went wrong, tragedies occurred, and the media were keen to probe events and find out what really happened. Ministers were keen to suppress open reporting, sometimes out of a desire to display their backing for the security forces, and on other occasions to avoid giving publicity to the IRA or any other terrorist group. In 1976, the Secretary of State for Northern Ireland, Roy Mason, had accused the Corporation of disloyalty in the battle against terrorism. He had taken the opportunity to remind the Governors and staff of their dependence on the licence fee, and this was a threat which was to be heard again in the following decade. Tory Ministers frequently found themselves at odds with broadcasters and the BBC was at the mercy of pressure, direct and indirect.

Soon after she took office, Mrs Thatcher was affronted by the BBC for showing a programme which contained an interview with a spokesman for a terrorist group, INLA. This followed closely on the assassination of her friend and colleague, Airey Neave, at the hands of terrorists. The complaint was to be the precursor of many similar ones, for there was no obvious agreement between Ministers and the media over what constituted legitimate areas for transmission. Broadcasters claimed the freedom to report events which they considered newsworthy and important.

*Real Lives* (1985) was a programme in which two people from either side of the religious divide were portrayed and interviewed in their various settings. It enabled a picture of life in the Catholic and Protestant communities to emerge. The episode was postponed after an appeal by the Home Secretary, Leon Brittan, and shown a month later with thirty seconds added.

Brittan recognised in a letter to the Chairman of the Governors that it was 'no part of [his] task as the Minister responsible for broadcasting policy generally to attempt to impose an act of censorship on what should be broadcast in particular programmes', for this would be to deny the constitutional independence of the BBC. But he claimed the right to express his anxiety about the impact of showing Real Lives on the fight 'against the ever-present threat of terrorism', and felt that the Corporation would be handing to the IRA 'an immensely valuable platform' for its ideas.

Faced with a request that the Corporation should not 'give succour to terrorist organisations', the Board of Governors discussed the programme and decided to go ahead with it. At this point, and almost without precedent, the Governors asked to see it prior to its transmission. The Chairman later responded to the Home Secretary's letter, and confirmed that *Real Lives* would not be shown 'in its present form'. He elaborated on the decision a few days afterwards, and suggested that it 'was not balanced [and] showed terrorist organisations in a favourable light'.[5] Another Governor was more explicit about the danger inherent in broadcasting the programme: 'The opponents' argument was that TV is a great image-maker. Once you show a terrorist as a nice guy with a baby on his knee, it becomes difficult to shake that image.'[6]

In 1988, it was the commercial channel which caused grave offence by showing *Death on the Rock*. The ITV programme concerning the shooting of three IRA activists in Gibraltar by the SAS argued that the shooting was probably unlawful as they were not acting illegally at the time or posing a threat to the representatives of the security forces. Thames and the IBA went ahead with the programme despite pressure from the Foreign Office, and the Government was bitterly critical. They argued that the timing prejudiced the inquest yet to be held. An independent enquiry by a Conservative Peer, Lord Windlesham, cleared the programme-makers of the charges against them and noted that it 'reflected the virtues and limits of television journalism in the late 1980s'.[7]

In the same year, under the terms of the 1981 Broadcasting Act, the Home Secretary, Douglas Hurd, imposed a ban on the broadcasting of direct speech by representatives of certain organisations, notably Sinn Fein, the UDA and the paramilitaries. Programmes could include the 'reported speech' of such supporters, or an actor's voice could read a quotation, but they could not speak for themselves. Ministers wished to deny terrorists what they called 'the oxygen of publicity'.

The National Union of Journalists challenged the ban in the courts, for they saw it as a limitation which prevented the media from fulfilling their obligation to be impartial and to provide balance in their political programmes. The case was lost in the European Court, but the restriction continued to cause much dismay among broadcasters, who believed that it barred them from informing viewers and listeners fully and fairly. Hugo Young suggested that Ministers seemed incapable of seeing that 'the freedom of the press [and broadcasters] is not about the freedom of journalists but the liberty of the subject'.[8] In practice, the ban was undermined by the way in which the dubbed voices were sometimes made to synchronise very effectively with the lip movements of the interviewee. In 1994, Southern Ireland lifted a similar prohibition, and a year later the British Government brought it to an end as part of its 'peace process'.

### The clash of the BBC and the Government in 1995

Relations between the BBC and the Conservative Government nosedived early in 1995, and in the process much damage was done to morale within the organisation. It was felt by many within the Corporation that John Birt's nerve failed when programmes were critical of the Administration and due to go out at a politically sensitive time. This had been evident in a series of episodes in the previous four years.

In 1991, a *Panorama* programme suggested that the Government had turned a blind eye to Saddam Hussein's efforts to develop an Iraqi supergun. It was dropped, for it was felt that it might offend public opinion on the eve of the Gulf War. In the spring of 1994, the hierarchy of the BBC withdrew a programme involving revelations concerning alleged malpractices in the Tory-controlled Westminster Council until after the local elections – though the original story first appeared on *Panorama* (1988), when some of the evidence was unearthed which had inspired the District Auditor to carry out an investigation.

Taken together, these and other incidents suggested that there was reason to think that the Birt regime was especially susceptible to political pressure from the Government. He appeared to be doing it a favour by his attack on over-powerful interviewers in his Dublin Speech (see pp. 187–8), for any 'toning down' of their methods would give members of the Cabinet an easier ride.

In March 1995, there began an assault on the BBC by certain individual Ministers. Jonathan Aitken accused the Corporation on 'open partisanship', noting that on the *Today* programme the Chancellor had been interrupted thirty-two times by John Humphreys. Aitken reiterated the comment of a colleague, John Redwood, that the BBC was in danger of becoming the Blair Broadcasting Corporation, run by an Islington Blair Band.

Others joined in the Government broadside and it was a Deputy Chairman of the Conservative Party, John Maples, who noted that: 'It does always seem to be the good news which does not get the prominence and the bad news that gets it.'[9] It transpired that key figures in the Cabinet are sometimes unwilling to debate with Opposition shadow-spokespersons, and if they do so they insist on being given the last word. On other occasions, Central Office seeks to close down an issue for discussion, by refusing to field a Minister until the last possible moment.

The attempt to lean on the BBC seemed suspiciously like an attempt to 'rough it up' well before the election, in the expectation that this would ensure that Ministers would be given an easy ride when the campaign gets under way. However, much of the pressure imposed by governments of any colour is of a less overt nature.

## Governmental attempts to manage the news

Government control of propaganda is not a new phenomenon and individual politicians of the last 100 years have appreciated the benefits to be derived from a cosy relationship with journalists. It is in their interest to seek to control, or attempt to control, what appears in print. More than 100 years ago, Joseph

Chamberlain was most effective in exploiting his contacts with newspaper editors, and was well known for publishing unsigned articles critical of his colleagues as well as of the other party.

However, the coming of television which, whilst independent of government is nonetheless in many ways beholden to it, has changed the situation. Governments understand the power of television and its reach to almost every household, and so they have developed the management of the supply of information into an art form. Much of the information is rather humdrum, but particular attention is given to ensure a sympathetic coverage of the main stories.

Managing the media involves keeping a careful eye on what information is made available, when it is released and how it is presented. Ministers legitimately seek to persuade people of the validity of their viewpoint, but in the process they are often 'economical with the truth', only conveying facts which are beneficial or at worst neutral to their reputation, and concealing those which are detrimental. The evidence of Sir Robert Armstrong (the Cabinet Secretary) in the Spycatcher episode revealed that there is a (modest) difference between failing to tell the truth and actually lying. Sir Bernard Ingham has written of his responsibility, on occasion, 'to preserve credibility without lying'.[10]

In the late twentieth century, much attention is paid by all governments to the careful management of the news; they wish to shape it for their own purposes. Several players are involved in the process, for the developing tendency is for those involved to specialise in one particular area.

Foremost among them are the people who set out to brief the media, the various spokespersons for government departments of whom the main ones are the Press Secretaries. These people seek to 'put a spin' on events and ensure that they put a gloss on them, particularly those on which some damage limitation is necessary. There are also those whose task it is to see that occasions run smoothly, without the hiccups which could create an adverse impression of the competence of those in power. These 'minders' arrange news conferences, interviews and other such occasions, and check on the administrative arrangements and the settings involved in order that the pictures 'look good'.

Speechwriters, or 'wordsmiths' as they are commonly known, provide much of the script for the big speech, and are charged with the task of enlivening its contents with the soundbites and humour which may make the headlines. In addition, there are the various assorted advisers who know the topic under discussion and have ideas on how to present it in a way which the media might be willing to use.

The United States and Britain provide many examples of politicians in power who have sought to use the media for their own advantage. Sometimes, powerful magnates of the newspaper world (such as Lord Beaverbrook in World War Two) were given office. Others have been allowed such privileged access to those in power that they responded by applying self-censorship to what was written. Geoffrey Dawson of *The Times* was known to modify or suppress despatches from the paper's Berlin correspondent, in order not to undermine the policy of appeasement being then pursued by the British Government. The editor of the *New York Times* did a similar thing in the period leading up to and following the Bay of Pigs episode in 1961.

In the age of television, opportunities abound for governments to control the supply of information. They understand that it is often the brief soundbite which makes the main news, and speeches are often littered with *bons mots*, the catchy words or phrases which get the headlines. Televised press conferences in the United States and carefully rehearsed interviews and speeches in Britain and across the Atlantic are opportunities to convey a memorable message which can be widely publicised.

Brendan Bruce has given a vivid account of the way in which the modern Prime Minister prepares for a public occasion at which he or she is to make a televised speech. He points out that in the days of Attlee, things were much more straightforward. The Prime Minister's wife would have driven him to a hall where he would have taken out a scribbled note and then delivered remarks which would have been reported without comment the following morning in the press. Today, things are very different, and he indicates that for a speech at a party conference Mrs Thatcher (whom he served) would have used a team of over fifty assistants: 'All of these people are striving (just as a theatrical production team does) to flood the viewer with data and reduce audience participation.' [11]

As politicians have arrived at a better understanding of the media and its potency as a means of communication, so they have sought to control it and use it to serve their purposes. The advisers or 'briefers' to whom we have alluded have a key role in assisting them in managing the media. On the one hand, they can be used to restrict access to themselves, but they can also be used to develop a fruitful relationship with the media which they have 'neither the time, expertise nor inclination to build'. Bruce describes the chief tasks of the briefers as to be

the public voice of the principal; to fill in the background facts; to provide a context for the events and issues of the day; to correct misconceptions and factual errors; and to act as a liaison for media 'bids' (e.g. requests for interviews, etc.).[12]

### The means by which governments manage the news

In seeking to communicate information, the Ministers have at their disposal the Government Information Service of about 1,200 staff, part of whose task it is to manage the news. On the one hand, it conducts government advertising as described on p. 131. It also puts out information expressing the Government's view of its work. Public relations officials are adept at 'putting a spin' on the story they have to tell, and easy slogans are used to sum up, often misleadingly, the labours of a Government Minister or Prime Minister, so that they seem to have been entirely beneficial. The verdict on the Maastricht Treaty, after the Prime Minister had waged a delaying battle to fend off the Social Chapter and economic and Monetary Union, was that John Major had secured a negotiating triumph; he had won 'game, set and match', a phrase which was much reflected in media coverage. The Franks Report on the Falklands which contained some serious criticisms was nevertheless presented in a more favourable light.

Among the sources of communication from government to journalists, there are official, on-the-record briefings, unofficial ones where the reporter can say that 'It is my belief that' or 'sources tell me', planned leaks designed to test the waters and press conferences. Little use has been made of the latter in Britain, and when Edward Heath used the Lancaster House conference to announce his policy on incomes there was much opposition to his choice of method.

The general view is that initiatives of this type should first be announced in Parliament. In many other democratic countries, the use of press conferences is more extensive, and they are viewed as a perfectly proper and normal means of communicating newsworthy information. Needless to say, the press favour them, for they give journalists an opportunity to question those in power. Ministers are enabled to make announcements and comment on the background to their decisions, though this does not, of course, prevent them from delivering a sanitised version of the topic on which they wish to expound.

However it is particularly via the Lobby System that governments in Britain convey their message. In the Thatcher years, it was the Lobby and the role of her Press Secretary, Bernard Ingham, which became a source of interest, not to say contention, on occasion.

### The role of the press secretary

In his autobiography, *Kill the Messenger*, Sir Bernard Ingham has described the task as he saw it on taking office;[13] according to his account, he was acting only as his predecessors had done, and was doing his job in the same way at the end as at the beginning. He recognised three major tasks, to:

1   Serve as spokesman for the Prime Minister and, as the occasion requires it, the Government as a whole.

2   Act as adviser to the Prime Minister on his or her presentational programme and to the Government as a whole on the overall presentation of its policies and its measures.

3   Co-ordinate, at official as distinct from Ministerial level, the Government's presentational programme – to conduct the Government's communications orchestra.

As Press Secretary, it was necessary to be well informed about the news, and to be able to provide a service attuned to the needs of different journalists, some writing for a British audience, others wanting an angle to present in Europe or America. He was concerned both with the national and regional press, and recognised the need to ensure that both received a good service. He was particularly aware of the importance of the provincial press, which he viewed as an important feature of the communications industry: 'It reaches deep down into the community and is read more extensively than the national press'.[14]

The background of Press Secretaries is either an official one, deriving from their work in the Civil Service – as Ingham's was – or, less commonly, it is a party political one. Either way, on appointment they become temporary Civil Servants for the duration of their term of office. Whereas previous incumbents had often served for only a few years and been much less visible, Ingham's eleven-year stint inevitably made him a more high-profile figure and the target of much publicity. As he was so often seen with the Prime Minister, he was closely identified with her approach and outlook, and enemies of the one tended also to be enemies of the other.

In Mrs Thatcher's premiership, Bernard Ingham became much more powerful than this predecessors, for they had not been as closely identified with the Prime Minister of the day as he was with Mrs Thatcher. It was a relationship of mutual trust and understanding. He understood her likely reactions and often could express himself in language which she herself might have used. In talking to him, journalists were in effect talking to the voice of the Prime Minister. He was an adroit manipulator, and under a good-natured, blunt and blustering Yorkshire exterior, he was effective at concealing the true intentions of Ministers. He gave out a picture which often concealed the true state of affairs or rubbished the work of Ministers who had fallen foul of the Premier.

Ingham was much more suspicious of television journalists than those of the press. He found the Corporation 'the most awkward organisation I was ever likely to deal with'.[15] He felt that its executives were arrogant, and disliked the attitude of television producers and reporters who were 'not so much left or right wing as anti-government'. It was a medium in which many key figures felt that they were there 'to challenge authority of whatever political colour'. This was his explanation for the differences between the Government and the media during the Thatcher term.

Journalists were more likely to complain about 'news-management', a charge to which Ingham was happy to plead guilty:

Journalists see us all as consummate Machiavellis . . . Of course, I tried to manage the news . . . to ensure that Ministers spoke with one voice . . . that Ministers were aware of what each other was doing and whenever they were likely to cut across each other . . . But news management, in the sense of ensuring that nothing is allowed to get in the way of the story the

Government wants to get over, is impossible in the modern world . . . A
chief information officer can plan and plot and generally bust a gut in trying
to clear the way for an important announcement. But he is not in charge
of events, or journalists.[16]

He argues that it is impossible for governments to manipulate the media in
the way that is claimed. They are the mercy of events which happen at times
inconvenient to the government, so that rather than being the master of the
information they convey they have to react to outside forces. Even if careful
steps have been taken to manage the news to get an appropriate headline,
anything from an earthquake to an air crash can suddenly assume pre-
eminence as a lead story. He makes the point that television and newspaper
editors select what goes into news bulletins, and claims that: 'It is television
which predominantly dictates news values for the masses; either there are
pictures or there are not, and if there are not pictures there is no news.'[17]

Yet this understates the extent to which press officers do control information. They are the focus of many stories in the British press and on television,
and the slant given to news can seriously distort the picture which emerges.
Ingham appreciated the importance of 'maintaining relations with the media'
and saw this as one of his key achievements. By this, he meant not merely
the press briefings which he held as Press Secretary, but also the informal
relationships between briefers and the media. Because his Prime Minister was
largely unsympathetic to the media and its mode of operation, 'being secretive
both by nature and by training',[18] he saw the importance of redressing the
balance and taking the initiative with key people in the media, sometimes
representing their wishes to those in authority. He did this effectively in 1982
when he persuaded the Ministry of Defence to allow journalists to sail with
the Task Force *en route* for the South Atlantic.

Much of the Press Secretary's work is less concerned with policy announcements than with 'bringing the work of the Government together in
one presentational whole and serving as an interpreter for the media on the
import for the conduct of the Government of the Prime Minister's approach'.
Hence, he would say, the desirability of his contribution being not in the form
of press conferences, which are used more extensively in the United States,
but more by way of unattributable background briefings.

Ingham has estimated that he gave some 5,000 of these briefings to jour-
nalists and probably six times that number in answer to individual inquiries.
Of his fourteen weekly briefings, ten were for the Lobby, though the Thursday
afternoon session was normally conducted by his deputy. It is to the Lobby
System which we now turn, the Lobby being an organisation with which
Ingham had a sometimes tempestuous relationship.

### The Parliamentary Lobby

The Parliamentary Lobby is a term employed to cover the activities of some

200 or so accredited journalists who by virtue of their privileged position have access to MPs and Ministers. Its origins are unclear, for a fire which broke out in the blitz destroyed many early records; however, Gladstone was known to meet a select handful of journalists to brief them on affairs of the day. Since the late nineteenth century it has developed considerably, and it is now much larger and less exclusive than in its early days.

Those who belong to the Lobby can roam the corridors of Westminster and enter restricted areas to which normally only elected representatives have access, the only exclusion being the Chamber itself. They can attend the daily briefings of the Downing Street Press Office, and also attend the special ones given by the Press Secretary. Conversations are assumed to be off the record, unless specified to the contrary. In other words, the journalist must resort to such introductory remarks as 'The Prime Minister is understood to be intending' or 'Sources close to the Prime Minister say', rather than stating the precise source of any observation as being the occupant of Number Ten or the Press Secretary. In Mrs Thatcher's time, it was not difficult to guess who was behind the quote, if only for the choice of vocabulary which Ingham was wont to employ. His expressions were often distinctive, with words like 'balderdash' and phrases such as 'she's not best pleased' littering his briefings.

Ingham has described a typical occasion:

My deputy and I sat in extremely comfortable arm-chairs on either side of the grand fireplace . . . I would tell them what the Prime Minister was doing that day and what Government news events, announcements or publications to expect, and then I would place myself at their disposal. They could ask anything they liked and I would answer as I wished. We would each form our own conclusions. The questions could range from what the Prime Minister had for breakfast – which would have been relevant, had she made a habit of having breakfast, during a salmonella, listeria or BSE scare – to the intricacies of Anglo–Soviet relations. Sometimes it became lively; on others, the briefing died of boredom.[19]

Opinions vary about the system. Many experienced political journalists on several papers have been happy to acquiesce in the system as a way of extracting a great deal of information which would otherwise be time-consuming or difficult to obtain. They are able to acquire the basis of a good story, for the Lobby is a means whereby they can be made aware not only of news, but also a steady stream of opinions and gossip on which to base their account. Armed with such information, they are able to gauge the mood of those in government and take the political temperature.

In the last few years there has been much controversy over the Lobby system which some newspaper people found too cosy, as generous hospitality was dispensed along with selective and sometimes incomplete information. From the time it first appeared, the staff of the *Independent* refused to participate in the Lobby game, and the *Guardian* and the *Scotsman* followed their lead shortly afterwards. The objections raised by those working for these papers reflect a belief that it is a means of communication which is too beneficial to the government of the day.

Ministers and officials can leak such things as bad economic indicators at a convenient time, so that when the news becomes official no one will be too surprised and the markets will not react in panic. Ministers are free to try out their ideas by floating them in such briefing ('flying a kite'). They can then assess the public and media reaction, and if it is hostile then the story can subsequently be denied.

Some journalists feel that they are being used, and dislike the way in which sycophantic colleagues are manipulated by the Press Secretary and his team. The Prime Minister may wish to undermine the reputation of individuals in the government whom he or she fears as rivals. Harold Wilson and Mrs Thatcher both used this method to discredit those around them. An attempt may be made to encourage sympathetic journalists to take a harsh view of a particular member of the government, or indeed to let it be known that his or her services are unlikely to be retained for much longer. When John Biffen was said to be only a 'semi-detached member of the government', it was time for him to consider his future and make alternative plans! He was said to be insufficiently committed to the on going nature of the Thatcher revolution.

Journalists are liable to be fed incomplete or misleading information which, because of its source (Number Ten), has the impression of truth about it. Those who abhor the system dislike being manipulated, and their editors do not wish to have 'managed' facts and figures. In the view of Martin Linton, a *Guardian* gallery reporter, the essence of comment and criticism is that it should be attributable; you need to know who said it, before the information can be assessed.[20]

They would prefer a much more open system in which stories are attributable and those who make them are accountable for the accuracy of what they say. They would favour more open arrangements and look with envy to other countries where accurate information is less difficult to obtain, because of their Freedom of Information legislation.

As sources of accurate information, most systems have their disadvantage, for the truth is that governments around the world all have an instinct to conceal full information, including not only key facts but the underlying motives involved in pursuing particular policies. Even in a more transparent form of government, there is a need for journalists to ferret out information, especially when an administration such as the Nixon one in the early 1970s was perverting the course of justice in its handling of the Watergate case. Then it was the determination of persistent journalists to dig deeply and regard any information deriving from the Oval Office with scepticism that unearthed the extent of the scandal and the President's role within it.

Britain is a liberal democracy and has eschewed direct control of the media, except in time of war. A privately-owned press is less amenable to pressure but as we have seen is very vulnerable (especially via the Lobby) to news management. The broadcasting authorities, especially television, are more vulnerable to pressure from left and right. Harold Wilson was obsessed with the BBC after the row over *Yesterday's Men* in 1970 and Labour became deeply suspicious of the Corporation.

The experience of the Thatcher years shows that whilst Ministers may parade the virtues of the democratic system they are not immune from a desire to influence what is said in the press and on television, and this can involve the deliberate manipulation of the truth and a resort to bullying tactics. Relations between those in the media and those in government are at times inevitably strained. In the 1980s, they deteriorated sharply, and in the early Thatcher years journalists found themselves in the position of providing the only effective opposition to Ministers. Programmes which dared to query the motives and integrity of Government policy were seen as hostile rather than as legitimate inquiry, and interviews by well-known television journalists were seen as needlessly offensive.

The particular circumstances of that decade made it seem that this was an unusual state of hostility, but all governments which are experiencing an electoral trough tend to blame the media, which are alleged to be preventing them from getting the Ministerial message across effectively.

For their part, broadcasters resent any attempt to stifle the free flow of debate and are understandably defensive when they feel that they are being leaned on or manipulated. To avoid critical and investigative programming seems to them to be an abdication of their responsibility, and pressure on them to tread warily seems to be a denial of their professional judgement. They are in the business of portraying important stories, and see themselves as the people best qualified to judge what is newsworthy and appropriate for transmission.

However, they may also become fearful, particularly if they belong to an organisation which is dependent on the government of the day for the level of the licence fee. The BBC has shown signs of much greater timidity in recent years, and allegations have been made of programmes being withdrawn at the last minute because of, or in anticipation of, political pressure. The appointments made to senior positions, especially those to the Board of Governors, have sometimes been political ones, and in the Birt–Hussey era there have been more signs that the Corporation is conscious of its vulnerability under a government which is regarded by many of its members with deep suspicion and unease. Those in authority in the broadcasting media cannot ignore the voice of the political masters.

The grounds for tension are readily apparent. The two sides have different priorities and expectations, and when issues arise in which the material under discussion is itself politically contentious (and possibly a matter with security implications) the likelihood of combustion is much increased.

## Notes

1 Report of the Committee on the Future of Broadcasting, 1977, Cmnd 6753.
2 *Ibid.*
3 A. Rawnsley, 'Box of Political Tricks', *Guardian*, 9 September 1988.
4 Ibid.
5 L. Brittan, letter to Chairman of Governors, Stuart Young, as quoted in R. Negrine, *Politics and the Mass Media in Britain* (Routledge: London, 1989), p. 114.
6 Chairman of Governors, *Guardian*, 7 August 1985.
7 Another Governor, as quoted in the *Observer*, 4 August 1985.
8 Hugo Young, *Guardian*, 17 November 1988.
9 J. Maples MP, quoted in the *Guardian*, 29 March 1995.
10 Sir B. Ingham, *Kill the Messenger* (Harper Collins: London, 1991), p. 321.
11 B. Bruce, *Images of Power* (Kogan Page: London, 1992), p. 132.
12 *Ibid.*, p. 133.
13 Sir B. Ingham, *Kill the Messenger*, p. 177.
14 *Ibid.*, pp. 342–3.
15 *Ibid.*, p. 354.
16 *Ibid.*, p. 187–8.
17 *Ibid.*, p. 188.
18 B. Bruce, *Images of Power*, p. 303.
19 Sir B. Ingham, *Kill the Messenger*, p. 193.
20 M. Linton, addressing a conference of the Politics Association, 1989.

1 Election scenes at West Islington. Photo shows a novel scheme adopted by the West Islington Conservatives to arouse electors to the poll by means of loudspeakers.

2 'Make Great Britain Great Again', Conservative Party poster.

3 'Labour Isn't Working', Conservative Party poster.

**NEW** *LABOUR*
**NEW**BRITAIN

**NEW LIFE FOR BRITAIN**
Labour's plans for
government

**IT COULD BE WHO?**
Richard Branson on the
lottery

**THE YOUNG ONES**
New deal for a lost
generation

FREE! pledge card with
Labour's five early pledges.
Order more for your
friends turn to page p21

COME
ON YOU
REDS!
Alex Ferguson's
radical roots

Labour

THE MAGAZINE FOR LABOUR PARTY MEMBERS

4 'New Labour New Britain', magazine cover.

5 Paddy Ashdown surrounded by the media.

6  Tony Blair addressing delegates and journalists.

# 9

# Selling politicians

In the years after the 1867 Reform Act, when the franchise was extended for the first time to artisans in the urban centres, the nature of politics underwent a profound change. The wider electorate called for new techniques of election-eering, and new methods of persuasion were required. This involved a greater emphasis upon explaining policy, via manifestos and speechmaking tours. Leaflets were handed out and voters were carefully canvassed so that on election day the maximum party vote could be mobilised.

The period up to 1945 was the golden age of the political meeting. Politi-cians spoke directly to sometimes surprisingly large gatherings, or small groups in draughty town and village halls. The arrival of the mass media changed all this. It was one of the Beatles, John Lennon, who remarked that he could communicate with more people in one concert than Jesus Christ ever did in his whole lifetime, and politicians too have seen the potential of using the media opportunities available today. The process of communication is less often as direct as it once was. Now the media are intermediaries between people and the politicians. In a single news item on television, they can address more people than they ever could in bygone days.

## The parties and publicity: a history to 1922

The Conservatives have always recognised the need to get their message across by the available means of the day if they were to capture the allegiance of the mass electorate of the twentieth century. They have been in the forefront of using new techniques and campaign strategies. In the 1920s, they ran courses on public speaking to assist their candidates, and Central Office acquired nearly 100 public-address systems and a fleet of loudspeakers. Pointing to their understanding of the potential of film, Richard Cockett writes: 'By 1929 the party had a fleet of cinemas touring the country and screening custom-made propaganda in towns and villages, reaching a larger audience more effectively than the traditional string of public meeting.'[1]

The first advertising agency which the Conservatives employed was the Holford-Bottomley Advertising Service, but Benson's was perhaps the one which became best known. This was the company which had the contract to publicise the merits of Guinness. But in the late 1920s, they did much to publicise the Conservative case. The party Conservatives spent £300,000 on their campaign in 1929, more than half of it on publicity. Central Office distributed half a million posters and printed more than 8 million manifestos, a British record.

It was Benson who first put Stanley Baldwin on cigarette cards and thereby reached a large populace. He was also the one who first gave the medium of film his serious attention, and with the introduction of sound in 1930 he quickly realised the scope offered by the new media development. At a time when cinema audiences reached some 20 million a week, here was an excellent means of communicating with a vast, and in many cases working-class, audience.

## The postwar years

Since the last war, in the use of television and in exploiting the services of media professionals, the Conservatives have again been in the vanguard of using market research, managing the message, developing the party political broadcast and giving a key role to advertisers such as Saatchi and Saatchi. Labour has paid the Conservatives the highest compliment of seeking to emulate such professionalism.

In the 1950s, Mrs Crum-Ewing was the Central Office figure responsible for ensuring that the party used television to advantage, and she analysed the qualities needed for success on television:

> Generally, it is the interesting rather than the handsome face that charms the viewer. American research places the four winning qualities in this order – friendliness, conviction, sincerity and intelligence. Nothing in our experience contradicts this finding.[2]

She was responsible for writing the scripts for party broadcasts and for staging courses in mock studios at Central Office. At the same time an attempt was made to make broadcasts more interesting and realistic. The Conservatives had used interviews of a 'question and answer' variety for some time, and developed the technique by bringing in independent broadcasters to ask the questions on themes provided by Central Office.

The 1950s was a decade of development in political advertising, and from the 1950 election the Conservatives made use of Colman, Prentis and Varley to run their poster campaign. Posters became more appealing and eye-catching. The company was keen to use ordinary people for news and posters, and it adopted uncomplicated language which made the message easily memorable. It continued to run campaigns up to and including the 1964 election, but their techniques reached their peak in 1959 when a series of posters was produced which assured voters that 'Life's Better with the Conservatives', and gave the warning 'Don't Let Labour Ruin It'.

If the Conservative poster campaign was effective, nonetheless Labour's broadcasts were thought to be more so, partly because more professional television communicators were available to them. But in Harold Macmillan the Conservatives had a more adroit performer than their opponents, one whose theatrical gifts were made for television.

For much of the 1960s, the media initiative lay with Labour, for Harold Wilson was a far more able performer then Sir Alec Douglas-Home or Edward Heath. Heath was not a 'natural' for television, but in spite of the difficulty of 'selling' his particular qualities there were further moves towards increased professionalism on the Conservative side.

Geoffrey Tucker (a copy-writer for Colman), whose work in 1959 had been particularly impressive, was involved in the mid-1960s in the launch of Ariel, the biological washing powder. He employed the skills developed in that advertising and marketing campaign to Conservative propaganda. Tucker was instrumental in developing a new range of party political broadcasts, and made them independently of the resources of the BBC at Garret's studios, in Shepherd's Bush. A young producer there was Gordon Reece, who was influential in the new style of broadcasts; he was to become a key advertising figure.

## The Thatcher years

It was the arrival of Mrs Thatcher as party leader which saw the development of a more consistently professional approach, and Gordon Reece was made the new Director of Publicity, a post he held to 1981. It was he who employed the advertising agency Saatchi and Saatchi in 1978, and its fortunes soared in concert with those of the party.

Saatchi was not the first agency to handle publicity, but it was to be the most famous. Unlike others, its services were retained between elections, though inevitably its work peaked in the run-up to polling day. In 1978, it was already a large and well-known agency and it had done some political advertising for the Manpower Services Commission. Its brief for the Conservatives was to handle all aspects of publicity, from press and poster advertising, to research and television.

Saatchi worked well with Central Office and its sympathetic Party Chairmen, at first Lord Thorneycroft and then Cecil Parkinson, 1981–83. Its Managing Director, Tim Bell, Gordon Reece and Mrs Thatcher achieved a rapport. She was keen to receive their authoritative advice on the use of the media, as well as taking their counsel on the way in which she projected her own image.

Reece proffered sound advice on her handling of the media and even arranged a voice session with the actor, Lord Olivier, for her. He stressed the benefits to be derived from appearing on popular shows such as Jimmy Young's, as well as making more serious appearances in the *Panorama*-type interview. She thus obtained coverage in an array of programmes, and was able to cultivate a popular image.

Of all the publicity ploys of the backroom team of media advisers, it was probably the Saatchi campaign prior to the 1979 election which was most famous and most successful. The poster 'Labour Isn't Working', consisting of a long dole-queue snaking out of sight (actually they were Young Conservatives, but that did not matter) was particularly effective in making its point, and other advertising and party broadcasts made the campaign in 1979 supremely successful. The same personnel were, in varying degrees, involved in the 1983 and 1987 campaigns as well. In all cases the result of the election was so favourable to the Conservatives that the effect was probably to reinforce the scale of victory rather than to change the outcome of the election.

During the Thatcher years and subsequently, Central Office was actively involved in the new professionalism of publicity, for in the same year as Saatchi were appointed so also was a Public Relations Consultant employed. In 1979, Harvey Thomas began to use American-style electioneering rallies, mingling show-business stars with politicians, and the technique was developed in the following two elections. Attention was also paid to the staging of such events to make the greatest impact on television.

Experience of television production is a necessary precondition of appointment as either party's Director of Communications. Shaun Woodward, who assumed the role for the Conservatives in 1991, had been a television producer, and that background made him an ideal candidate, in some ways the more so because of his work with *That's Life*, once a popular consumer programme. It was he who hired John Schlesinger, the British-born Hollywood director, to make a series of party broadcasts in 1991–92.

## Labour in the 1970s and 1980s

The Labour Party was much slower to appreciate the need for a new approach to its publicity, and its failings in the use of the media were only too evident in 1983. Labour then provided a model example of how not to conduct a propaganda campaign, with Foot scorning American-born techniques. His campaign made few allowances to television, and he made little attempt to provide the visual images which media men craved.

Following its heavy defeat, more thoughtful members of the party realised that Labour must improve its own publicity; in a television age it was futile to hold out against the tide. It was not so much that the use of the media might turn defeat into victory, more that without the skilful use of the media Labour might never be able to gain the sympathy of the electorate.

Over the next nine years, publicity was to develop in a remarkable manner, and there was a new awareness of the importance of image. Neil Kinnock saw the potential of television and realised that Labour suffered from its outdated image. He was determined to revolutionise the way in which the party presented its case, and make Labour appear as a modern party. He understood the relevance of the entertainment aspect of television, hence his appearance in a Tracey Ullman video and his enthusiasm to be seen in the company of rock stars.

Supported by a new General Secretary, Larry Whitty, who was sympathetic to the Kinnock programme and shared his belief in the importance of 'projection' as well as organisation and policy, was able to get the National Executive Committee to appoint Peter Mandelson, a former TV producer, as the man charged with improving Labour's presentation. His main creation was to be the Shadow Communications Agency (SCA), which proceeded to revolutionise Labour's campaigning methods and approach.

The Agency, set up in 1986, comprised Labour-supporting advertising and marketing experts. Mandelson did not scorn the visual, and he was instrumental in creating a new identity for the Labour Party. Out went the dated 'red flag' image. The red rose symbol was designed by a corporate identity consultant, Wolff Olins, and this was to reflect the style of a gentler, more sophisticated, more distinctly English image, as opposed to the increasingly discredited forms of hard-line socialism dying out in Eastern Europe.

In particular, the SCA projected Kinnock as the most important figure in the modern Labour Party, for in 1987 he was viewed as an asset. The 1987 campaign was built around this, and the broadcasts were presidential in tone, notably the enthusiastically-greeted 'Kinnock: the movie' broadcast. The whole Labour campaign in 1987 was skilfully orchestrated, and arguably made the best use possible of Labour's possibilities – given that it was unable to offer a convincing and distinctive vision to the Government. Yet for all of the improvements in style and presentation, Labour still lost. However impressive the packaging, the message failed to convince the electorate.

## The 1992 election

Both parties sought advice from American television consultants in the run-up to the 1992 election. Again, Labour produced an impressive visual campaign. It had also done a great deal to make its policy more acceptable, yet it was still unsuccessful. The message was still not one which had a clear appeal to many voters who doubted whether, despite the trappings, the substance had really changed.

Nonetheless, the slick pre-election policy launches which Labour has adopted in recent years, and the glossy presentation of its case in the last two general elections show how far the party has come in embracing the requirements of the modern age. On both occasions, the news media received an abundance of visual images and senior party figures organised their schedules around television rather than mass rallies.

The one major rally in Sheffield, which in many ways was reminiscent of the sort of occasion staged by Conservatives in previous elections, seriously backfired. It was visually striking, full of glitz and glamour, stage-managed to a T, treating its characters more as movie stars than as politicians striving for office. Some people did not like such a display of fervour, which had overtones of the Nuremberg rallies of the 1930s.

The Tory campaign, like that of 1987, was again in many ways unimpressive, and there were many suggestions from within the party fold that there was a lack of vitality in the organisation. No one seemed to be able to galvanise and coordinate the campaign. Yet it had its successes, including its skilful poster campaign.

John Major is not a natural for the public platform, and certainly not a speaker in the same class as Neil Kinnock. But he possesses a personality which lacks jarring features. Whereas in 1992 some voters might have been repelled by Kinnock's displays of Welsh emotion, the Prime Minister's was a modest, easy-going style, one more attuned to small conversational gatherings than to the mass meeting.

It was the idea of the soapbox – which apparently came from Major himself – that caught the imagination. Though used on only a few occasions, the image it portrayed was of a leader prepared to take to the streets and risk running into opposition. He appeared to be battling for power, whereas Neil Kinnock in the Sheffield Rally appeared to be assuming that it had already been granted to him.

### Further Americanisation?

In 1992, there were plenty of signs of the extent to which the Americanisation of British electioneering has gained a foothold. The photo opportunities, the soundbites, the made-for-television all-ticket rallies, the use of film directors and other ideas all showed how much British parties had derived from American techniques in their efforts to create television events. However, the necessity for good visual images is considerably greater in the United States where there is much less of a role for national newspapers and far fewer lengthy national news programmes and political interviews.

It may be that there will be a reaction to the style of recent campaigning, and Labour would be foolish to again adopt a rally of the type organised in Sheffield. But there is unlikely to be a significant turning away from modern forms of electioneering, for in either case party managers have to use the tools of the modern day. Whether or not the propaganda, in broadcasts, television 'events' or poster campaigns, makes any measurable difference to the result, no party would run the risk of cutting itself off from the main means of communication available. This would enable their opponents to monopolise the campaign, for these are the things which get reported.

## Market research and opinion polls

The application of modern marketing techniques to the selling of politicians began in the United States. It was to be some time before British parties saw the benefits to be derived from doing their own market research, though research into voting intentions has a longer history.

Opinion polling has been conducted in Britain since 1938, the first poll being an offshoot of the US Gallup organisation. The American practice became more popular after the war, and other organisations as well as Gallup were involved in early surveys, such as the National Opinion Poll (NOP). In the 1950s and 1960s, the polls had a good record and several were remarkably accurate in pinpointing the outcome of elections. Since 1970, the performance has been a mixed one, for in four out of seven elections (including that one) several have not succeeded in forecasting the winning party, and if they have done so they have often been inaccurate about the scale of the advantage enjoyed by the winning party.

More polls were published in the run-up to the 1992 election than in any previous campaign, fifty-seven by eight different organisations. Most of these were concerned with the level of party support rather than the issues involved, though some combined both features. They asked questions on voting intention, with further ones on perceived competence on economic policy and other topical concerns.

## Purposes of polls

Most political polls which are published in newspapers are concerned with the voting intention of the individual approached. However, others are concerned to find out about the attitudes of voters to specific questions, the idea being to provide a profile of what the public wants and believes.

Answering questions on voting intention may seem straightforward, though there are difficulties in measuring even this. Surveys of attitude pose additional problems. Much depends on the question asked, and a different form of basically the same question can evoke a different response; unless carefully drafted, the question might imply a particular answer. Again, another difficulty in asking for an opinion is to assess the strength of the person's conviction. For instance, should a weighting be made for strongly-held opinions, or for those which are based on greater knowledge? The person interviewed may know virtually nothing on the topic, and such a view might not be helpful to those interested in formulating policy to meet popular demands. This is a serious difficulty, and some who answer 'don't know' in response may be genuine in being unable to make up their mind. Some may not understand the topic or the question; others may be simply apathetic or uninterested.

The lack of information on many issues which impedes the ability of many voters to offer a worthwhile judgement has been tackled by a different form of poll, the much more recent Deliberative Poll, which may be difficult to employ on a regular basis, but which does give a worthwhile guide to public feeling when knowledge is provided.

## The influence of the polls

The early success of polls on voting intention meant that much significance was attached to the findings which they highlighted. Newspapers have been pleased to print their results, and political commentators regularly refer to them in providing their analysis. For all of the possible flaws, they nonetheless still seem to be the most effective method of gauging public opinion.

For party leaders the polls are a useful guide to the state of public opinion and give a broad indication of their relative standing among the electorate. They have become important to the parties in making their policies and in planning their strategies. For the Prime Minister they are an additional weapon in his or her armoury which makes it difficult for opponents to remove him or her. In calling the election he or she will wish to see an established lead in the polls over a prolonged period, and some Prime Ministers have been extremely successful in 'playing the polls'. They can use polls to assess the reaction their policies are having on the voters and wait to see the results of any pre-election stimulus to the economy feed through into poll results.

But the Opposition also benefits from information about the regard with which the voters view the party. Labour used polls when conducting its Policy Review after the 1987 defeat, to such an extent that critics on the left of the party claimed that Walworth Road was more interested in asking what the public wanted and devising policies to match these requirements than it was in sticking to Labour's eternal principles. It was argued that policies should not be trimmed to the passing whims of the voters, and that it was more important to 'sell' the ideas and policies which members believed in.

Polls also assisted the party by pointing to the public feeling in and after 1992 that Labour still suffered from its close association with the unions, and that the public still had doubts about its economic competence. They indicated the areas of popular concern, and Tony Blair's seizure of the 'law and order' issue was a response to public demand. His slogan 'tough on crime and tough on the causes of crime' seemed to respond to the mood for strong action based on intelligent diagnosis and understanding.

### The growing sophistication of market research

Whereas early research was into voting behaviour and public attitudes on policy areas, the key development of the 1980s was that parties began to see how the use of surveys could assist them in their bid for power. Rather than merely finding out what people felt about education, health or defence, the attempt was made to understand voters and their concerns more thoroughly, and to sell the core beliefs of the parties in such a way that it seemed as though they were able to cater for popular aspirations. This required the identification of particular target groups within the electorate, and an attempt to direct campaigning to their hopes for the future well-being of their families. The attempt was made to go beyond a preoccupation with issues alone, and to ascertain why the voters felt as they did.

Writing of the campaign to get Ronald Reagan elected to the White House, Bruce records how in the United States:

> voters were encouraged in interviews to express their feelings about what was important to them in their daily lives and the reasons for this importance . . . From this data it was possible to draw a line directly from the values that the voters held, to the issues that were important to them.[3]

Reagan was then encouraged to 'tap into' these enduring values and issues, such as family, neighbourhood, workplace, peace and freedom, and his advisers ensured that he was sold to the American public as a person who was in tune with those basic ideas.

The 'This is a Man' film, the one which later inspired 'Kinnock: the movie' (see pp. 126–7) in Britain, was deployed to portray the candidate as a man who was in sympathy with those concerns because he was brought up by people who shared them, and in an atmosphere where they were part of his daily life. As the commentary said, he was 'raised in America's heartland, small-town Illinois. He gained from his close-knit family, a sense for the values of the family, even though luxuries were few and hard to come by.' With his service record (to emphasise his patriotism), his presidency of the Screen Actor's Guild (to show his leadership quality) and his Governorship of California thrown in, the effect was to ensure that Reagan seemed to be the man for the times. So appealing was the image, that it was successful in wooing many Southern Democrats away from their traditional allegiance.

This example was not lost on the British parties, especially the Conservatives. It took opinion surveys into a different realm, for 'values research' showed how you could move beyond discussion of the virtues of the National Health Service, to show that the reason people liked it was because it gave them a 'sense of security' and catered for their 'peace of mind'. It was a way of presenting familiar issues in such a way that they gelled with the values that really mattered to many voters. Once the careful research had been completed, then the skilful advertising and direct marketing campaign could play to these themes.

The value of skilful marketing had been indicated as far back as 1959 when, as Bruce has written, 'favourable associations were conjured up by the mention of the party's name, rather than expounding policies'.[4] 'Life's Better with the Conservatives. Don't Let Labour Ruin it' was effective in 1959 just as 'Britain is Great Again. Don't Let Labour Wreck it' was eighteen years later. But in the 1980s and 1990s, there has been a far more sophisticated understanding of what makes the voter tick.

The Conservatives used special 'focus groups' in 1979 to enable them to prepare their campaign, 'Labour isn't Working'. In so doing, they were drawing on American experience, just as was the Labour Party when it began to employ them four years later. An advertising agency gathers together a small group of citizens who are persuaded to express their inner feelings in answer to some projective questions, such as: 'If Bill Clinton was a colour, which one would he be?', or, more directly, 'How do you rate Bill Clinton?' The responses enable the person in charge of the enterprise to understand the target market better, and to adapt the message to the beliefs and values of those whose influence matters.

Labour discovered such groups four years later, and in 1983 Robert Worcester of MORI made use of them to assess the state of popular feeling about the party. He found out just how wide was the gulf between 'the language of Labour's campaign, and the concerns of floating voters'. Subsequently, Philip

Gould was brought into Labour's advisory team with a special brief to measure the state of public opinion over a range of issues. In 1992, on the basis of his research, he was able to warn Neil Kinnock not to believe the good news in the polls, for this was at variance with his own findings.

In the 1980s the propagandist and the pollster began to operate hand-in-hand. Polling was seen as something which was helpful to politicians, for now that television had become the means of mass communication it gave them a way of finding out public reactions. When addressing them on the public platform, candidates could assess those reactions for themselves, but now that direct contact with the voter was emphasised less, so a reliance on surveys mattered more.

The danger with such polling is of course that whereas it was once an adjunct which can be a useful guide, it becomes the be-all and end-all of political operation. The party begins to address only those concerns which the public communicate, and instead of providing leadership on a range of subjects it slavishly follows the voice of the public whose views have been transmitted to those who conduct the market research.

Rees quotes Dottie Lynch, a Political Editor with CBS who was herself once a pollster. She observed that whereas an incumbent would once run on their record this was less the case in the mid-1980s: 'more and more candidates who either didn't have records or didn't have positions fully formed on issues [began to ask] "What do the polls tell me I ought to believe?".'[5]

This question is a step further than candidates asking what the voters think of their beliefs. They don't need to have any, and the opportunistic politician of flexible or no principle can succeed if the presentation is appropriate, as the parties are well aware. Rees has illustrated what he calls 'the tyranny of the polls' with an American example. He describes how those in charge of propaganda in a particular region pored over maps showing the detailed social composition of a target area, and produced advertisements and other material especially geared to the particular set of voters in each district:

> In the ghetto, it was a commercial calling for more employment oppor-
> tunities for the inner cities; in the affluent middle-class suburbs, it was a
> commercial calling for more resources for the police to help fight crime . . .
> It isn't a question of having just one policy decided by the pollsters – the
> candidate might have several policies specially targeted to specific voters'
> needs.[6]

Not all politicians like the reliance on the market researchers and pollsters. In August 1996 Clare Short (a Labour front-bench spokesperson) attacked 'the obsession with the media and focus groups' by 'people who live in the dark'. Others have also been uneasy about the use and abuse of the market-research approach, and see the people involved as too powerful, and a threat to the health of the democractic process. They may dislike the increasing reliance on pollsters, but at least their findings are open to interpretation by the person receiving them. They are often even more suspicious of those who conduct focus groups, and who – having sifted through their accumulated evidence – come to their own conclusions and report them to the leadership. For they are in a position to convey the message to which they are personally committed.

More than this, 'focus group-campaigning seems to take politics further away from principles and policies, and more towards the most cynical kind of market manipulation'. Yet the picture can be overdrawn, and there are still politicians of principle on both sides of the Atlantic. British parties do have more identifiable beliefs than American ones, and the task of the propagandist is to present those beliefs in such a way that they are relevant to the values and concerns of the individual voter. In this, they have become markedly more adept in the last decade.

## Presenting the candidates and the message

In recent years, a new industry has developed to help present candidates for public office in a more favourable light. Media advisers are concerned to train their candidate in the ways of the media to ensure that he or she safely navigates the possible pitfalls and enhances their prospects by looking and sounding convincing.

All parties are aware of the need to give advice on image and interview technique, and on how to handle enquiries from the press and television reporters. Smaller ones lack the resources of Labour and the Conservatives, but they too attach importance to providing candidates with assistance on the timing of press releases and on matters of appearance. The Scottish National Party uses the experience of its Parliamentarians to train new candidates.[7] Apart from calling upon such expertise, Plaid Cymru has compiled a brief handbook available to those likely to be in the public eye.[8]

The 1983 election campaign was the classic example of what can happen if a party or its candidate ignores the media. Michael Foot's campaign was seriously disorganised, so that even in Walworth Road there was sometimes doubt as to where the candidate was. He seemed to actively shun the media as they attempted to seek him out and interview him, and preferred to concentrate on meeting a few people in the streets and to address large rallies which made little allowance for television. Since then, the Labour Party has learnt a lot, and in the Mandelson era there was an abundance of visual material and the main party figures were keen to ensure that their appearances coincided with the presence of the cameras.

Amongst the gurus who now surround the party leaders and work in the backroom, there are specialists in news management to ensure that any statements get maximum impact. They realise the importance of seizing any opportunity to gain publicity, and are aware that the striking visual image or the memorable phrase or headline can be significant in forming people's perception of the candidate and party, and their suitability for office.

In recent elections, candidates have been concerned to take advantage of photo opportunities, carefully stage-managed episodes in which the leading figure is set against a particular background – perhaps to demonstrate concern for the area or its industry. For instance, Mrs Thatcher was pictured against a setting of dereliction in the North-east. On another occasion, she was shown nursing a new-born calf in East Anglia to demonstrate that she was a caring personality and thereby tone down any public perception of stridency and excessive toughness in her image. In 1986, whilst on holiday in Cornwall, she borrowed a King Charles spaniel so that she could then be pictured on the beach with the animal pulling her along – another humanising shot for popular consumption.

Visits to factories or disaster areas might fulfil the function, and in 1992 Labour ensured that Neil Kinnock was pictured in schools and hospitals. Politicians have been keen to do walkabouts so that they can be can be filmed out on the street meeting people, although this can go wrong, as Sir Geoffrey Howe found in 1987, when on one occasion few seemed to recognise him and even if they did they exhibited little sign of interest. Usually, walkabouts are staged with sufficient care to ensure a good result, and the emphasis is upon exploiting occasions which show the candidate to advantage, or the opponent to disadvantage. In the United States, George Bush was often filmed in front of naval destroyers which served to remind voters of his war record, whereas Ronald Reagan preferred the image of the all-American cowboy, riding on horseback into the sunset – conjuring in the elector's mind an image of the great outdoors as part of the wholesome American dream.

On both sides of the Atlantic, politicians have become aware of the value of the soundbite, a short saying, full of concentrated meaning, which consists of a few easily-remembered words, and yet conveys a particular message. Tony Blair, before he assumed the leadership, was already demonstrating an awareness of the value of the pithy catchphrase. 'Tough on crime, tough on the causes of crime' was a useful summary of his policy towards law and order, as part of a bid to wrest this issue from the Conservatives. It suggested a politician who understood people's anxieties on the topic, but was realistic enough to appreciate that a strong policy needed to be balanced by one which tackled root causes.

The Americans have produced some effective soundbites, such as Mondale enquiring of Reagan 'Where's the beef?', or the same President when he suggested that 'You ain't seen nothin' yet.' Most famously, or infamously, was George Bush's 'Read my lips. No new taxes', a slogan which backfired when as President, he found himself supporting higher taxation.

Spin-doctors are part of the media team, their task being to change the way the public perceive some event, or to alter their expectations of what might occur. They are a recent phenomenon, and are charged with the careful management of news with a view to extracting the best possible outcome from any situation. They want to massage the message.

Those in power have always wanted to put a gloss on events to present them in the best possible light, but in the last decade or so spin-doctoring has been perfected as one of the most important political arts, its development coinciding with a growing anxiety on the part of politicians about the image they present in the media age. The term 'spin' derives from the spin given to a ball in various sports to make it go in a direction which confuses the opponent. Applied to politics, a spin-doctor is someone who provides a favourable slant to an item of news or potentially unpopular policy on behalf of a particular personality or party. Five types of spin have been distinguished:

1   ante-spin – a preparation before the event;

2   apres-spin – a gloss after the event;

3   tornado-spin – the attempt to whip up interest into something which is not of inherent fascination;

4   crisis control – management of things getting out of control;

5   damage limitation – management of things which are already out of control, to prevent further deterioration.[9]

Spin-doctoring is often loosely used to suggest the role and work of any image-creator, but Brendan Bruce reminds us that it has a more specialised meaning which derives from the Carter–Ford Presidential debates in which each side sought to claim victory.

Worried that Robert Dole, the Republican nominee for the Vice-Presidency, would show up badly against Walter Mondale, Republican advisers wanted to 'get in first' with a series of favourable verdicts on their candidate's performance. It was arranged that three prominent figures would each address the voters on three different television stations immediately after the debate was over. They left their seats to give the live interviews which announced Dole's victory before anyone had commented on the Mondale performance. Careful management also ensured that, again 'live', Dole was soon able to receive a congratulatory call from President Ford. On this occasion, the effort backfired, for remarks made by the candidate were soon pursued by the media in a way discreditable to him.

Since then, there have been several notable examples on both sides of the Atlantic, a classic one concerning the Tory Party Chairman, Kenneth Baker, who handled the 1991 local election results most adroitly. They were disastrous, for Labour won nearly 500 seats and the Conservatives lost nearly 900. However, the effect of his more favourable interpretation was that the outcome seemed less bad than anticipated, for in the run-up to polling-day the spin-doctors had made it seem as though the two results to watch were Wandsworth and Westminster, which the Conservatives managed to retain. The headlines the following day were more favourable than might have been expected; for example, 'Conservatives hold on to Wandsworth', rather than 'Labour makes massive gains'.

Liberal Democrats, afraid that in a by-election they might do less well than expected (because everyone assumes they will win), might seek to dampen expectations by suggesting that they will do well to win at all. In the 1994 European elections, at a time when the media were talking of a strong Liberal Democrat challenge, with the prospect of their gaining several seats, they were concerned to say that it would be very pleasing if they achieved a first Euro-victory; one or two would be good for them. When they got two eventually, it looked less of a disappointment.

Spin has become an accepted feature of campaigns in the US since the Dole–Mondale contest, changing people's perceptions about how well or badly they expect a candidate to do. In the New Hampshire primary in 1992, former President Nixon suggested that the right-wing evangelical Pat Buchanan would probably get 40 per cent, knowing that if he obtained 30 per cent he would be doing well. By talking up his chances, the effect was to make people think that he had done disappointingly when he eventually obtained what was in reality a creditable 30-plus per cent against an incumbent Presidential candidate. Nixon therefore gave a boost to the campaign of George Bush, and helped to damage the momentum of the Buchanan campaign.

The exact techniques vary from occasion to occasion, but in essence the purpose and often the procedure are broadly the same. Bruce, as Director of Communications for the Thatcher-led Conservative Party after 1989 and now a private consultant, is in a good position to comment on it. He describes it thus:

> Spin patrols haunt the press room at party conferences, helpfully pointing out key passages and significant phrases to journalists hard-pressed to deliver their copy. To help the television reporters, copies of the speeches are supplied with suggestions as to which passages should be selected for airing.[10]

Experts in the field are aware of just how important it is to protect the candidate from potentially damaging situations. When Neil Kinnock fell over on a Blackpool beach or Gerald Ford fell down the steps to Air Force One in front of the world's press, the front-page shots helped to create an impression of incompetence and at best ineptitude.

Media advisers need to get the timing of their initiatives right, and they tour with the candidate looking for opportunities for him to meet the media. They stage-manage meetings to ensure that the cameras can record in time for the message to be transmitted on peak-time evening news bulletins, and this means that even large meetings are organised carefully so that the effect is made for television. This can go wrong, as the Sheffield rally did for Labour. Meant to be a demonstration of Labour's confidence and preparedness for government, it proved to be a serious error which backfired badly on campaign organisers.

Candidates tend to hold few meetings, and they are held in accessible places at convenient times. Sometimes it is a case of making the best of a poor situation. John Major was clearly ineffectual when addressing a mass rally, and was always likely to be outperformed by Neil Kinnock as an electioneer. But his advisers found that he responded well in small groups. In the more intimate atmosphere, his friendly, conversational style was shown to advantage. He also liked his soapbox, a device more often alluded to than actually used.

If the candidate has obvious disadvantages, it is a question of seeking to minimise their impact. In seeking to sell President Ford in 1976, his managers adopted the 'rose garden strategy'. He would meet the journalists only once a day, in the White House gardens, the timing being sufficiently late-on for him to have been thoroughly briefed beforehand, so that his inadequacy and lack of knowledge could be concealed.

*The American experience*

America has led the way in selling its public figures. Three of them in the twentieth century have been 'naturals' for the broadcasting age. Franklin Roosevelt, though he was confined to a wheelchair in his later years, was photographed from the waist up so that his physical disabilities were concealed. He was a master of the fireside chat, and his technique was supremely professional. Having rehearsed with the utmost care, and learnt his speech by heart, he was nonetheless able to make it seem as though he was addressing the individual voter in the intimacy of his or her home. 'My friends', he began, and in a slow and relaxed voice, he was calmly reassuring to Americans at a time of depression when they needed to be comforted and given hope for the future. He assured them that 'the only thing we have to fear is fear itself – nameless, unreasoning, unjustified terror which paralyses needed efforts to convert retreat into advance'.

Roosevelt was to be the first President to address an (albeit very small) audience on television in 1939, but his communication skills were those of the pre-television age. He did make use of the cinema, which he recognised as another powerful medium. (Goebbels and Baldwin were others who would have recognised the force of Lenin's dictum: 'Of all the arts, the cinema is the most important for us.')

John F. Kennedy had an image of youth and glamour, the more so as he could be portrayed as a war hero. His appeal to 'get America moving again', his call for his country to pursue 'new frontiers', his suggestion that Americans should ask what they could do for their country rather than what their country could do for them, were all memorable phrases which showed him to be a true and loyal patriot who was in the driving-seat himself, but who wanted to get the best out of his fellow countrymen. His appeal was especially meaningful to younger people, for as America's youngest elected President he represented a new generation which wanted to boost US power and influence in the world. In the 1960 Presidential debates (see p. 149), he recognised that 'It was TV more than anything else that turned the tide.'

Ronald Reagan was a trained actor. He looked good, and his soft-soap style and easy charm enabled him to say very little but appear and sound sincere. Much attention was paid to his appearance to conceal his advancing years, and by the use of a teleprompter, he was able to speak directly to his audience in tones to which they could warm.

If these were the masters of the soundbite and photo opportunity, television can be damaging to a politician's prospects. In Britain, it failed to advance the cause of Sir Alec Douglas-Home in 1964 or Michael Foot, who appeared to be elderly and out of touch. His donkey jacket was an unfortunate choice of clothing when on display at the cenotaph. Moreover, his hair often seemed to be undisciplined and untidy.

Similarly, Mondale suffered by comparison to the assured and composed Reagan, and complained in 1984 that television lighting was set in such a way as to make him look like a racoon. Sometimes a potential disadvantage can be concealed, as with Dukakis, the Democratic challenger four years later, who had a 'height problem'. The use of a box in the television debates made him seem taller and more impressive than he was, a need all the more important as he was the shrimp in the 'wimp versus the shrimp' Presidential battle against Bush.

President Carter collapsed whilst jogging, President Bush vomited at a reception for him in Japan, and these and other images of feebleness and exhaustion tend to suggest that a person is not up to the job. Voters like young candidates who look in control, and after the Kennedy era, Lecanuet in France, Mayor Lindsay in New York and Wilson in England were keen to capitalise on their comparative youth and dynamism. If not youthful they need to be able to give the impression that their faculties are intact, and to compensate by other qualities as Reagan was so skilfully able to do.

Some politicians rather resent the new techniques by which their performances are so carefully packaged and sold. For Labour, Roy Hattersley spoke of his sadness that the party had concentrated too much on presentation at the expense of ideas in the 1987 election. Five years later, there were similar misgivings expressed on the Tory side. Professor Kavanagh quotes his findings from private interviews with John Major and Chris Patten, both of whom resented the preoccupation with photo opportunities and soundbites. Hence the leader's reported question to his advisers: 'Do I have to do this?' [11]

Party media specialists clearly see a need for such exposure. They know that journalists and TV producers provide a saturation coverage of political events, particularly at election time. Programme and press editors cannot show everything, and they attempt to select those areas which look to be of potential interest. The 'minders' know that it is up to them to ensure that plenty of good copy and favourable images of their candidate are available at the right time and in the right place.

There is a natural tension between paid communicators and party politicians. They share a mutual interest in 'getting the message across', but whereas the professionals might prefer to condense the message into a few well-chosen words, the politicians would prefer to elaborate (often at some length) about their vision of the country's future in their hands. Politicians may recognise that presentational skills are now important, but many wish it were not so. In an ideal world, they would probably prefer to do their own persuading.

Another Kavanagh interviewee who has advised the Labour Party on communication has highlighted the difference of approach:

> Politicians do not think in marketing terms. They like to think that it is their personal charisma or their speeches on a one-to-one basis or before an audience that decides elections. In contrast, advertising people objectivise the whole process, they ask what the objective is and then how we can achieve it. This means that the skills of the politicians are not so unique or special as the politicians believe.[12]

## Party political broadcasts

Party political broadcasts appeared on British television for the first time in 1951. Inevitably, the early efforts were very amateurish, as politicians inexperienced in the medium tried to cope with the heat of studio lighting and the need to memorise large chunks of script. They varied from the straight talk to the studio interview with an allegedly unbiased (but very genteel) interrogator, from the homely, cosy fireside chat of Lord Attlee to the complacent discussion of Harold Macmillan and his colleagues at Chequers as they contemplated the next five years. In the opening one the Liberal, Lord Samuel, was terminated abruptly for running over his allotted span of time.

Despite the poor stage-management of the Chequers performance ('very inappropriate for the mass media', according to David Butler[13]), Macmillan soon revealed himself to be a skilful operator, and from 1959 there was a growing professionalism in PPBs, as they quickly became known in the media. Labour's expert was the young Anthony Wedgwood Benn, and his broadcast was set against the background of a contemporary television theme-tune. The parties began to use speakers who were versed in the media, and the Liberals – lacking the money of of their rivals – began to employ well-known television stars to add a touch of glamour and/or humour to the occasion, at first a James Bond actress, later a disc jockey and in the 1980s (as part of the Alliance), John Cleese.

By the late 1960s, the allegation was emerging that politicians were being sold like soap powder; in the words of one newspaper headline, it was a choice between 'OMO Wilson or DAZ Heath'.[14] The age of the ad-man had arrived, and was to remain an important feature of the election scene. However, it is since 1979 that the idea that politicians could be packaged and marketed has really gained a strong foothold.

Sir Tim Bell saw the potential of the Party Broadcast, and under his guidance the Conservatives began to adopt a new style more reminiscent of television advertising. He wanted to get away from the long-established constraint of the ten-minute film, or 'talking heads' approach, and introduced two innovations:

1   Broadcasts were to be made more like television commercials, catchy, with memorable slogans.

2   They were to be shorter, and he reduced their length by half from ten minutes to five, on the assumption that long programmes were dull and made too many demands on the viewers' patience (they certainly had been much derided by a public, who claimed to see them as an opportunity to make the tea).

Bell was keen to see more effective broadcasts, and believed that by shortening them they would convey their message more clearly. This was an unusual view at the time, and the prevailing outlook was that if you had free air time then it was wise to exploit the opportunity to the full. In 1979, he had outlined[15] his preference: 'We put in a strong plea for two-minute PPBs . . . Ten minutes is . . . a nightmare for a professional, to have to produce to this length.' In the 1987 campaign, only two Conservative broadcasts ran for the full ten minutes.

In that year, however, it was the Labour Party which produced the most memorable PPB, the one subsequently dubbed 'Kinnock: the movie'. It was the high spot of the campaign, and is the example that is always referred to as an illustration of what can be done by a professional director. Hugh Hudson, of *Chariots of Fire* fame, portrayed Neil Kinnock and his wife strolling hand-in-hand over the Welsh hills towards a headland, to the accompaniment of Brahms's First Symphony and soaring seagulls overhead. Here was a particularly fine set of visual images which exploited the medium in a new way, and reflected the partnership which had been developing between Peter Mandelson and Hudson over a period of time. The broadcast also had a strong script by Colin Welland, and besides its romantic pastoral scenes it showed Kinnock in a series of favourable settings; taking on Militant Tendency in 1985 at the Labour Conference, and thus depicting his strength, but yet also showing his love of country and commitment to 'decent' community values.

Reaction was favourable, and the *Sunday Times* described it as 'masterly . . . breaking new ground in TV political history'.[16] The television industry uses its own measure of programme popularity, the Television Rating (TR), and this pointed to widespread approval for the recording. The effect was to boost his personal ratings by 16 percentage points (Mass Observation Research) and to raise the morale of the Labour campaign. However, the figure so often quoted needs to be put into some perspective, for as Brendan Bruce points out, the increase was among those already intending to vote Labour; support for Kinnock among the electorate actually increased much more modestly, from 21–27 per cent over the course of the campaign, and one strong PPB was unable to convince the floating voters of his leadership quality.[17]

Butler and Kavanagh describe the broadcast as a 'stunning invocation of the Labourism of the 1940s by the media techniques of the 1980s'.[18] It was also a testimony to the 1984 American influence in selling politicians, for it owed much to the American weepie, 'This is a Man', dubbed the 'Nancy and Ron show'.

Conservatives might well complain of glossy packaging, but the approach was an obvious development of trends which had been around for some while and which they had done so much to pioneer. What it showed was that television is a good medium for telling a story, and professionals who surround our party leaders have realised that by relaying their candidate's life they can provide the sort of television coverage that might remain in the voters' mind – strong Mrs Thatcher, caring Mr Kinnock or, more recently, nice Mr Major. Biography, according to Laurence Rees, is 'one of the few areas of TV political propaganda that can sustain a theme for as long as ten minutes'.[19]

In the 1992 election, two broadcasts were the cause of much discussion, one on John Major and one on the Health Service. The opening Conservative PEB was the first to have its own title, *The Journey*. It relayed John Major's early life and career in Brixton, hence its nickname, 'John Major returns to his roots'. It said little about his policies or his achievements as Prime Minister, but that was not its purpose. What it set out to do was to display a picture of an approachable and affable character with whom voters could identify, one who had made it to the top himself and who wanted the same opportunity for others as well. It was reassuring, for here was a man with whom voters could feel at ease. It bore the imprint of people who understood the medium, and Shaun Woodward's experience of consumer programming and John Schlesinger's direction ensured that it was a clever piece of propaganda. It showed a sure touch in portraying a person to advantage, which television can do effectively.

The final Conservative broadcast returned to John Major's personal appeal, as he talked to camera and expressed his wish to see 'a country that is at ease with itself'. The final Labour broadcast also attempted to capitalise on the personal qualities of the leader, for having dwelt on the loss of a sense of identity and community which many people felt, it then used famous people from all walks of life to pay tribute to the values of Neil Kinnock.

An earlier Hudson production was a visually impressive depiction of England, and it took an upbeat line about its future possibilities. Whereas American advertising is normally negative in style, this was a strangely positive image to promote. Butler and Kavanagh quote the remark of a Labour official: 'It makes the country look so bloody marvellous, you'd think; why change the government?'.[20]

However, the main cause of controversy was the second Labour broadcast, the one which told the story of Jennifer's ear – or rather the story of two girls and their similar problems of 'glue ear'. The parents of one girl were able to use private health care to remedy their daughter's affliction, whereas in Jennifer's case they were reliant on the NHS. The trouble was that Jennifer's case had been inadequately researched, for although it was supposed to be representative of any such example it was sufficiently specific to set the media hounds off in search of the poor victim and her family. It was a heaven-sent opportunity for newsmen and their investigations, and the revelations and subsequent denials and explanations brought little credit to anyone concerned. They also meant that the real issue which Labour was seeking to highlight, funding of the Health Service, was lost, and a week or so of the campaign was wasted in the rather fruitless process of claim and counter-claim. The technique was a very American one. It was a professionally accomplished broadcast, strong on emotion and with the added-extra ingredient of a sickly child. It failed in its purpose.

## The purpose and impact of party broadcasts

Via these broadcasts, the political managers convey the message which they wish to put across, explaining policies, introducing or familiarising the leader to the voters and seeking support. As to their impact, several studies have been conducted, many as research papers for the IBA/ITC by J. M. Wober. One, in 1974, attempted to relate the number who turned out to the size of the viewing audience for political programmes, including PEBs, and found that among those who indulged in heavier viewing there was a diminished disposition to vote; in areas where Labour broadcasts were widely viewed, there was a smaller percentage who voted Conservative, whereas in areas where Conservative and Liberal broadcasts were watched in greater numbers, there was no similar improvement in their vote. The study was an exploratory one, at a time when such measurement of viewing habits was in its infancy.[21]

A further study in 1979, conducted by the same analyst, showed that the public preferred a straight broadcast to one which used a dramatic or comic approach. Labour's programmes were better received, in that they dealt more with issues, whereas Conservative PEBs were seen as stressing individual personalities. In both cases, those interviewed felt that such programmes had helped them to appreciate the party viewpoints, although this was not the case for the Liberals who had fewer broadcasts anyway.[22]

In 1983, the Labour concentration on transmitting a Keynesian economic policy and avoiding 'slickness' did the party little good, and four years later we have seen that the switch was made to paying more attention to the leader than before. By then, Labour broadcasts were well made and portrayed it in a more favourable light, whereas the Conservatives appeared to have lost their effectiveness. It may be that this improvement in communication skills helped Labour to fend off the challenge of the Alliance and strengthened support for the party and its leader; but ultimately the Labour campaign, of which the PEBs were seen as a key aspect in improving Labour's image, failed in its attempt to provide the party with a significant boost on polling day.

The findings of all of the IBA surveys suggest that there may have been some benefit in influencing the knowledge of voters and their voting habits. In particular, the one conducted after the 1987 election noted that a number of viewers found the broadcasts 'interesting and thought-provoking', even if they were less persuaded that the issues covered were especially important; around half of the viewers claimed to have found them 'helpful'. It pointed again to the lack of knowledge and understanding of the Alliance position, and made the point that if one function of PPBs and PEBs is to demonstrate parity or equality of status between the parties, this had not been achieved; people did not have a 'similar and thorough knowledge of all the main parties' policies'.[23]

Evidence of a higher or lower turnout amongst those who watched several broadcasts was not found to be significant, but PPBs seemed to have been more successful at informing and persuading viewers than those put out in the election campaign. Wober made the point, however, that broadcasts can have other indirect effects:

A PEB which gains critical acclaim may enhance the morale of party workers and even politicians, leading to better performance in news and current affairs interviews and on the streets facing the voters. It would be extremely difficult to demonstrate such effects let alone to quantify them.[24]

For Butler and Kavanagh, PPBs and PEBs are a medium in decline: 'Once they *were* the election. Now, on radio, most of the party broadcasts were slightly reworked soundtracks of the television broadcasts.'[25] They used to be transmitted simultaneously; now they are put on at different times, ITV in 1992 getting in before the evening coverage of the election produced a state of bored indifference among many voters (6.55 p.m.), whereas the BBC placed them in a slot after the mid-evening news.

The main parties devote much time and manipulative skill to the production of their broadcasts, and there has been a steady growth in their professionalism over many years. All are in a sense television commercials, though for the reasons we explore in the next section they are different in kind from American political advertising. In the same way that we react to advertisements, we remember them when they are well done, and some have been very successful in conveying a sympathetic image of the parties and their leaders.

## Political advertising

The Institute of Practitioners in Advertising defines its purpose as being to present 'the most persuasive possible selling message to the right prospects for the product or service at the lowest possible cost'.[26] To Bolland, advertising is concerned with 'the paid placement of organisational messages in the media'.[27] In the world of politics, then, those who place adverts are interested in passing information to the general public, via the purchase and use of advertising space, in the hope that they can influence popular perceptions of what they (and perhaps their opponents) stand for.

For several years now American political parties have attached great importance to selling the message via television commercials, and although party political advertising is not allowed on British television the technique has been widely used on hoardings, in newspapers and, in a different way, in Party Political Broadcasts.

Party managers have realised the significance of marketing their product, and have used professional agencies to help them do so. Using private opinion polling to assist them, they have carried out market research, to enable them to better identify, anticipate and satisfy customer requirements. They then seek to produce and market an image and a policy stance which the public wants to buy.

Advertising is costly, but the cost is justified if its works effectively, and a good campaign achieves the desired results within an acceptable budget. The questions a campaign manager must ask are:

1   What is to be achieved?

2   Over what period is it to be achieved?

3   What is the strategy by which new converts to the party will be won over and existing voters 'firmed up' in their intentions?

4   What tactics, what creative ideas will help achieve this strategy?

Since the 1950s television has been a major advertising outlet in Britain, although the cinema is another obvious means of expressing a case. Cinemas cater for a predominantly young audience, and this makes them a specialised medium for advertisers wishing to influence that age group. Governments wishing to impart information and promote public awareness on a topic such as Aids may find either medium useful, but depending on what they wish to convey, they also use large hoardings and place adverts in newspapers or magazines.

Advertisements have to conform to certain standards of public taste and decency, all of them supposedly being 'legal, decent, honest, honest and truthful'. They are monitored by the Advertising Standards Authority (ASA), which in cases of blatant misuse has the power to order them to be withdrawn and/or can impose penalties. In April 1993, the ASA produced new guidelines on political advertising. The new rules mean that the 'honest and truthful' requirement has been extended to cover 'public policy' and issue advertisements placed by charities, unions and other pressure groups.[28] Until this amendment, the British Code of Advertising Practice precluded the ASA from investigating misleading factual claims in items placed by such bodies. The same principles now apply to the overwhelming majority of public policy and issue posters as to any others within the orbit of the Code.

Advertisements placed by central or local government, and those concerning government policy are also covered, and must be capable of being substantiated. Party political advertising is an exception to the need for adverts to be based on verifiable claims, and there is no comeback when they fail to do so.

Government advertising may cover such things as Aids, as we have mentioned, but more controversially, from a party political point of view, it also includes that done as part of the privatisation campaigns of the 1980s and 1990s. There was a feeling that the distinction between the use of advertising for purposes of information and for the promotion of party propaganda had become blurred. 'Tell Sid' and other such adverts had a legitimate purpose, in seeking to give the public information about a forthcoming sale of a nationalised concern, but the cause they put across is one which coincides with the attitudes and actions of the Conservative Party.

Privatisation has been a highly contentious area of party dispute, and the masses of money spent on promoting the sale of gas, telephone, electricity, water and other industries and utilities is seen by some critics as a propaganda boost for the Conservatives, one which costs them nothing. It cost some £40 million to promote the sale of British Gas, and critics see such spending of public money as part of an attempt to encourage people to approve the Government's policies, rather than a genuine attempt to impart information.

The Conservatives used government advertising much more extensively than their predecessors had done, and annual spending rose from £35 million in 1979 to nearer £200 million in 1989. In September 1989, a *Panorama* programme claimed that public money had been used to put across the idea of water privatisation even before the measure had been passed into law – so that in effect the Government was using funds for political purposes.

Ministers also used advertising extensively to sell their policies for reform of the National Health Service. On this occasion, the British Medical Association used hoardings to respond to Ministerial claims with its own highly successful poster campaign. It emphasised the damage which the 'reforms' would impose, and the posters were the more effective because they made people think that if the doctors who had to work the new system were so uneasy, then something must be wrong.

Another example of government advertising later in the decade was that concerned with selling personal pensions. Adverts stressed the liberating quality of taking out a private pension plan as a means of security, 'saving for the future'. They showed people being bound and gagged to the occupational scheme then in existence. The new plans would be portable, easily transferred from one area of employment to another, and transfer to them would be facilitated by the generous national insurance benefits which would be offered to those who quit the state scheme. People would be empowered, in the true spirit of the Thatcherite ethos. The claims were to be inflated ones, and on the basis of what the public was told by advertising (as well as by insurance companies) some 1½ million people are said to have been sold inappropriate policies.

*The use and extent of party political advertising*

What is not covered by the Code (even in its amended form), is party political advertising. Any advert whose function is to influence public opinion for or against a party or candidate contesting an election or referendum is exempt. In 1978–79, the Conservatives in Opposition attacked the Government's employment record, claiming that 'Labour isn't Working'. When they won in 1979, and within two years presided over a tripling of the unemployment figures, there was no comeback. Neither was the Code able to meet complaints made in 1992 about Conservative Party advertisements. Nor is there any effective control over the use or abuse of party time on television, but political statements by the parties are confined to the fixed allocation of Party Political Broadcasts which they can use as they wish.

Press and poster advertising is a standard feature of campaigns. Both parties have followed the American practice of adopting negative knocking copy in framing their advertisements. Such was the case with the 'Labour's Policy on Arms' poster, in 1987. Neil Kinnock had indicated in an interview with David Frost that a nuclear deterrent-less Britain would defend itself from invasion in the way that the Afghanistan guerillas had done against the Soviet Union, employing 'all the resources you have, to make any occupation totally untenable'. Saatchi saw an opportunity to exploit, and produced an effective and memorable piece of propaganda for the Conservatives; their poster made a telling point about Labour's defence policy, depicting a soldier with his hands up. They also effectively highlighted 'Labour extremism'.

The Labour Party was slower off the mark in getting its material into the press, and the tone of its theme 'The Country's Crying out for Labour' was a depressing one. Using visual images more than comment, they showed a country of gloom and despond, with suffering all around, the danger being that such depressing scenes become more associated with the party placing the advertisement than with the object of the attack. The Alliance made a virtue of its smaller resources and, using the back of an own-label packet, offered a reminder and a warning that 'The best products rarely come in the flashiest packs.'

In 1992, the most stunning impact was made by the Conservative poster 'Labour's Tax Bombshell'. It was a strikingly eye-catching piece of propaganda, and showed a silhouette of a huge bomb against a red background. It addressed the concern (which Conservative propaganda had done much to implant) of some people who worried that even if they really favoured a change of government, they could not afford to pay the price of a Labour victory.

As Rees points out, the 'tax bombshell' attack coincided with other propaganda, which questioned the personal competence of Neil Kinnock who was portrayed in the Tory press as an untrustworthy 'windbag'. However much Labour might protest that it did not intend to increase taxes, the impression depicted of Mr Kinnock made the voter question whether or not a party led by him could be believed on the tax issue.[29]

Advertising is also placed by organisations sympathetic to the main parties. In 1983, this was extensive, less so in the following two elections. Aims for Freedom and Enterprise and the Economic League convey the free-enterprise message in newspaper advertisements, and in 1987 the Committee for a Free Britain, an Aims for Industry derivative sharing the same address, placed anti-Labour material in the *Sun*. Pro-Labour bodies were more active five years later, and Butler and Kavanagh[30] found that NALGO's seventy-three pages of newspaper inserts (mostly on health and education) made it the 'largest single political advertiser in the press during the campaign, exceeding even the major parties'. In fact, Labour itself spent more overall on press advertising than the Conservatives in this election, a reversal of the usual trend (Conservatives £1.1 million, Labour £1.9 million). Much of the advertising by either party in this election was actually done in poster campaigns, rather than in newspapers.

Britain lacks the brief television advertising employed in America, and via party broadcasts it is less easy to convey such a strong and dramatic effect. The cinema film made by the Saatchis, in 1979, was only ninety seconds long. On this and other occasions the Conservatives have implicitly recognised the difficulty of sustaining interest by using less time than that to which they were entitled.

Research in Britain and America has shown that it is negative advertising which plants the most remembered images in the voters' minds. 'Feelgood' images are helpful in producing an aura of contentment and satisfaction, but for a party unable to find much to make people feel good about, attacks on the alleged deficiencies of the rival parties make an impact, as American experience illustrates.

## Political advertising in the United States

In the absence of clear-cut ideologies to distinguish the parties, the advertisements of American candidates place greater emphasis on themselves as individuals, and on the personal demerits of their opponents. In doing so, they can be blatantly unfair, and not subject to restraint.

Election broadcasts in Britain are carefully controlled, whereas in the United States there are no such restrictions. A candidate may spend as much as he or she wishes to, and it is this which enabled the billionaire Ross Perot to mount his independent campaign again Clinton and Bush in 1992. Much of this money was spent on paid television time.

The scale of such advertising has significantly increased in recent years, and in 1988 the Bush and Dukakis campaigns were each reckoned to have spent some $30m on television alone. In the November 1994 Congressional elections, there were countless examples of candidates using money extensively to seek support. Some of the more familiar ones were to be found in:

1   The Senate race in California, for which the Republican Michael Huffington and the Democrat Dianne Feinstein between them spent $27 million (more than £17 million) on their campaign.

2   The Senate race in Massachusetts, where Mitt Romney was taking on the incumbent Democrat Ed Moore, and where Edward Kennedy was seeking to defend his family seat.

American advertising recognises few limitations. It is overwhelmingly negative, for research in Britain and the United States has shown that this is the most effective variety. It goes for the jugular, and is severely damaging in personal terms, often being concerned to expose deficiencies in the moral character of an opponent. There is little point in protesting at its unfairness, or in resorting to litigatory action, for not only is this costly and slow; more importantly, by the time of any legal suit, the harm to prospects of election has already been done.

Adverts which attack the opponent's financial wheeling and dealing are common, as are those which remind the voters of personal weaknesses. Those used against Edward Kennedy suggested memories of Chappaquiddick, an incident in which a lady friend was killed when Kennedy's car left the road and plunged into a lake; they also reminded electors that he had a drink problem, and the unflattering physical images implied that too many whiskies and good dinners had taken their toll of his physique and personality.

Kennedy's opponents and his supporters have all resorted to vicious personal abuse of a similar kind. In Oliver North's campaign for a Senate seat in Virginia, the incumbent's marital fidelity came under fire, in an advertisement which opened with a picture of a *Playboy* magazine cover, depicting a former Miss Virginia rumoured to have had an affair. A voice intoned: 'Chuck Robb won't tell the truth about the beauty queen in the hotel room in New York. He says it was only a massage.' In Tennessee, a candidate was congratulated for 'kicking [his] chemical dependency'.

American advertisers are only too aware of the amount of information which the public can assimilate at any one time. Advertisers have decided over the years that this is much less than was once the case. During the Vice-Presidential race in 1952, Richard Nixon took thirty minutes of paid television time to answer charges of corruption in front of 58 million viewers. He defended himself in his famous or infamous 'Chequers' broadcast, in which he and his wholesome-looking family appeared together to create the image of a loving family in support of a worthy candidate. It worked effectively.

Since then, paid time has been markedly reduced, and now advertisers specialise in the sixty- or (more often) the thirty- or even fifteen-second commercial which makes a point briefly, yet dramatically. They try to implant a view in the public mind and change their perception of particular politicians. In 1960, the Nixon campaign for the Presidency suffered from the posters which made him look like a crook and which asked 'Would you buy a second-hand car from this man?'

One of the most devastatingly effective attacks was that on the Republican Vice-Presidential nominee, Spiro T. Agnew, in 1968. A close-up of him was shown on the right-hand side of the screen, from which gradually spread out a caption accompanied by uncontrollable laughter at the other end. The caption read: 'This would be funny if it wasn't serious.' No reason was given, no message was offered, but the caption gelled with some people's concern about his fitness for office.

In 1988, there were more negative advertisements from the Dukakis side than from the Bush camp, but they did not impinge on the memory to the same extent. Research carried out for the Republicans had shown that many voters, including many floaters who leaned to the Democrats, were alarmed by two issues, that Dukakis did not make a recital of the pledge of allegiance compulsory in schools, and that he supported the furlough release programme which allowed convicted prisoners to receive weekend passes towards the end of their sentences. The first one could be used to show Dukakis as a foreigner (he was of Greek origin) and therefore not the man to safeguard American traditions, the second that the Democrats were insufficiently tough on crime.

In that second context, one of the most damaging pieces of propaganda was the Willie Horton ad placed by the Bush campaign. Horton, an Afro-American, had been released from gaol on weekend leave, and whilst out of prison he had raped a white woman. The implication of Republican advertising was that the Democratic Governor of the state, who was also the party's presidential candidate, was personally responsible.

Like many other negative advertisements, it was a blatantly misleading and unfair comment. It was a Republican Governor who had conceived the system, and forty-five other states had similar schemes in operation. But the combination of a black offender and a liberal Governor meant that the episode could be used to demonstrate the folly of liberalism.

In 1992, advertising encouraged voters to ring a special line on which they could hear alleged recordings of Bill Clinton's affair with his alleged mistress, Gennifer Flowers. In 1994, the Huffington backers accused Feinstein of being a jukebox for special interests: 'You put your money in and get what you want.' Poll evidence suggested that this left large numbers of Californians regarding her as untrustworthy.

Bill Schneider, an American political scientist, believes negative advertising to be a very efficient tool:

> For one thing, it's easier in 30 seconds to turn people off your opponent than to build a positive case for yourself – especially since television is a medium particularly suited for carrying negative, warning-style messages . . . you get more bang for the buck by running negative ads.[31]

As yet, Britain has been reluctant to follow the American example, and propaganda attacks have tended to have more substance than those in the United States. The campaign is not conducted through advertisements, but in the PEBs, the extracts shown on television news, in interviews for the current affairs programmes and in the coverage of the national newspapers. Even when the tone is negative, as with 'Labour isn't Working', the focus has been on a general theme rather than on one isolated event such as the Willie Horton ad.

Negativism has been cleverly used in recent years. The Labour Party ran its 'Yesterday's Men' campaign in 1970 to warn the voters against letting their opponents back into power. However, the Conservatives have come up with some of the most striking negative ads, as in the 1978–79 'Labour isn't Working' campaign, the 1987 poster on Labour's arms policy and the 1992 one on 'Labour's Tax Bombshell'. These were highly effective items of propaganda. Advertisers are agreed that it works well. Bruce quotes a Labour consultant, Barry Delaney, as saying:

> In recent years in this country, all the most memorable ads are Tory party knocking ads, and the value of them is that they encourage your own supporters, discourage waverers and infuriate and demoralise the opposition . . . knocking copy, when it's well done, is probably going to be more effective than any other kind of advertisement.[32]

However, it can provoke a reaction. The Conservatives' use of the 'New Labour, New Danger' campaign in the summer of 1996, portraying Tony Blair as a 'demon' with burning red eyes, was denounced not only by the opposition parties and individual Conservative MPs, but also by some church leaders. Critics found it an offensive image, and lamented what they perceived as a further step in the adoption of American political practices. The ASA agreed, and warned Central Office against further use of the posters.

One of the effects often attributed to such negative advertising is that it produces disillusion with the Washington politicians and the political system in general. This cynicism is said to have been a factor in the falling turnouts of the last generation. In the 1994 elections, it was again suggested that one of the most toxic campaigns in living memory had left many people turned off politicians. American voters have become more disengaged from political strategy, as the style of advertising increasingly antagonises them.

However, advertising men are attracted to the negative style when seeking to sell politics and politicians. They cannot use television to tell a brief story, so they need a concise slogan to get the message across. As Professor Kavanagh remarks: 'It is easier to promote a negative message about the opposition than a positive one about their own side.' [33] He quotes an advertising consultant who worked for the SDP in the 1980s: 'Positive advertising does not work, because all parties favour the same goals – peace, prosperity, better welfare services, safe streets and so on. The challenge is to say how they will achieve, and that is too complex for an advert.' [34]

Not all US advertising is of the type described. Americans have often been shown adverts which are autobiographical in style. Television is good at handling personalities and stories, and some of the most effective advertisements judiciously combine the two elements. Rees provides an example:

> One of most skilful of such 'endorsement' ads was in Oregon when Joe Slade-White made it for the incumbent governor. An old man was sitting on a bench, and said: 'Some people say Neil Goldschmidt is a big spender, but I happen to know that he was taught about money by one of the toughest economists in this state'. The picture widens to show a grey-haired, smiling lady, 'his Mom'. [35]

In 1980, when Jimmy Carter was standing for the Democratic primary, propagandists portrayed him as 'Husband, Father, President', before adding 'He's done these three jobs with distinction.' No mention was made of his rival, Edward Kennedy, but the contrast with his troubled life was implicit. Dissonance is important, for the campaign cannot conflict with the candidate's known character, as those who tried to sell Kennedy as a family man soon realised. It was a dissonant image, not compatible with people's impressions; it seemed to be an inversion of the truth.

### The impact of advertising

The impact of posters and newspaper inserts is thought to be negligible. American research by Horner, Collis and Kirvan [36] suggests the effect on voting behaviour is small, but that it helps to sharpen people's perception of what the parties stand for (in the case of the knocking copy so common in the United States, it increases the cynicism of the electorate about politics and politicians). If the effect is small, why do parties go in for it?

When there is money available to spend parties naturally tend to use it. In 1983, the Conservative Party Chairman did cancel expenditure of £3 million out of his £10 million advertising budget, when things were so clearly going in its favour. This is untypical, and campaign organisers are reluctant to provide their rivals with any possible advantage by not using any means at their disposal. They normally deploy all their possible ammunition, for it is never easy to say exactly what is going to make the difference between success and failure. The point was well made by Brendan Bruce, when he suggested that parties go on investing in advertising for the reason given by an American businessman when talking of the same question:

> On a trans-Atlantic flight, someone once asked the chewing gum tycoon, Philip K. Wrigley, why he continued to spend so much money on advertising when his business was already such a success. 'For the same reason', replied Wrigley, 'that the pilot of this plane keeps the engine running when we're already 30000 ft up in the air.' [37]

Advertising may boost the morale of supporters and help to implant a theme in people's minds; it is part of the accepted setting of an election campaign, and if it makes the onlooker remember the product and its alleged advantages over its rivals, it is worth doing. Barry Delaney has summed up their usefulness to the parties effectively: 'They are the authentic voice of the party. In all the claims and counter-claims, advertising is distinguished as the message that the party wants to convey, in a tone of voice and style that it determines – unperturbed by Jeremy Paxman, unsullied by the comments of *The Sun*.' [38]

If a party has an unpopular policy, then no amount of presentational glitz can save the party or the candidate. The 1987 election shows that in Britain good propaganda is not enough to woo the voters round, and it was Roy Hattersley who speculated after his party's defeat on whether or not smart packaging actually drew attention to the lack of real content in the area of policy.

In a close contest, of course, it may be that skilful use of party political broadcasts and advertising will make a difference, by implanting a message in the public mind. The American academic, Samuel L. Popkin, has observed that 'people make up their minds on voting according to past experience, daily life, the media and past campaigns', [39] all of which are susceptible to influence from the propagandists.

### Recent trends: a reflection

It may be that there will be a reaction to the style of recent campaigning, and Labour would be foolish to again adopt a rally of the type organised in Sheffield. But there is unlikely to be a significant turning away from modern forms of electioneering, for in either case party managers have to use the tools of the modern day. Whether or not the propaganda, in broadcasts, television 'events' or poster campaigns, makes any measurable difference to the result, no party would run the risk of cutting itself off from the main means of communication available. This would enable their opponents to monopolise the campaign, for these are the things which get reported.

### The American experience

What the American experience teaches is that those who succeed in politics are those who clearly preach a message which the voters will favour. The optimistic broad themes of President Reagan, conveyed via an intelligent use of the available means of communication, were attuned to the aspirations of many Americans.

As television has become such an important medium of political propaganda and manipulation, consultants have assimilated certain beliefs which they exploit ruthlessly. Much of their work is concerned with producing material which is unfair, but also unanswerable. The influence of these communications experts is all-pervasive, and their numbers have grown dramatically. According to Rees,[40] there are now 10,000 of them, compared with only 100 two decades ago. He quotes the consultant to the Democratic Party, Raymond Strother, as saying that: 'In America today, without good professional help, if you're running against a person who has professional help, you have virtually no chance of being elected.' [41]

Such is the impact of the America – consultant in field of propaganda, that several of them have gone to work elsewhere, some of them in Britain. As we have seen, Britain has anyway developed its own media gurus, who have latched on to their methods. The medium of television has allowed the political consultant to flourish, but there are differing estimations of their significance.

In *Packaging the Presidency*,[42] Professor Kathleen Jamieson argues that television is just one more way by which our politicians seek to put across their ideas. She quotes examples from the nineteenth century, and amongst other things makes the point that handbills were circulated which falsely accused rivals of all sorts of dubious practices. There were also 'pseudo-events', such as when Daniel Ebster in 1840 'camped with Green Mountain boys in a pine wood before an open fire, ate meals from shingles, paid tribute to log cabins and challenged at fisticuffs anyone who dared call him an aristocrat'.

There have always been forms of political communication, for they are a necessary component of a mass democracy. But what is so different is the number of people who can be contacted at any one time, and, more importantly, the fact that television, the medium, has itself changed the nature of the message. Marshall McLuhan has been the prime exponent of this point, and in *Understanding Media* he has demonstrated that television is not just another channel of communication.[43] It has changed what is said, as well as how it is said.

For any politician in the 1990s, considerations of appearance and manner are highly important. People who gained office earlier in the century might now be unable to do so for their lack of telegenic appeal could be a barrier to their election. In the United States, where advertising can be bought, a combination of money and charisma can enhance the chances of success, though the packaging of Nixon could ensure that – if the means of salesmanship were appropriate – a less-than-charming person could gain the highest office.

*Britain and America compared: British reservations*

Britain has gone some way down the American road, though there are significant differences. It tends to lag a few years behind in media developments, and parties have as yet made more use of advertising agencies than consultants, though the latter are a growing breed. Colmans and Saatchis are companies whose main work was in the field of product advertising, and some of their techniques could be adapted to selling politicians.

Britain has no party political advertising on television, though there have been thirty- or sixty-second political adverts for cinema, such as the Saatchi one in 1979, 'Labour isn't Working', which, like the poster, featured a long queue supposedly overspilling from a job centre. Denied the opportunity to show an American-style commercial on television, Britain has to adapt other forms so that they provide entertainment as well as information – whether it be the celebrity 'showbiz' rally, the professional party political broadcast made by a film producer or the light interview on the Jimmy Young show.

The emphasis is upon producing material and circumstances which elevate the spirits, make people feel optimistic about their situation and inspire their trust and confidence in those who aspire to rule. But although television has increased the importance of the way in which parties portray themselves and has concentrated the attention of the electorate on personality more than ever before, it remains true that there is a significant difference between political coverage across the Atlantic. Party ideologies and policies have traditionally been more distinctive in Britain, and as Mandelson reminds us there are limits to the extent to which you can succeed without getting the programme right. American parties have never had such an ideological basis, and though there are differences of degree and emphasis between Republicans and Democrats, the narrowness of that divide means that there is a greater emphasis upon the individuals running for office.

Film and television propaganda has flourished in the United States for thirty years and is basic to parties and candidates in elections. In Britain, contemporary political professionals have followed the example, as always a few years behind. In an age of television, viewers make their assessment based on the visual image more than the spoken word, and propaganda works most effectively if it engages the emotions rather than the intellect, if it emphasises themes rather than policies. In 1992, the Conservative campaign was redolent of any American one, driven by personality and not issues.

Not everyone in Britain is happy with the new forms of electioneering, and selling politics in the American way. In 1987, Conservatives attacked the 'glossy packaging' of the Hugh Hudson broadcast, though they had made extensive use of similar techniques of persuasion themselves. According to Tyler,[44] the programme was 'shrugged off as rubbish' by most of the occupants of CCO, and Mrs Thatcher never saw it. Many members of the Labour Party were similarly dismissive of the approach, which seemed to smack too much of the marketing man and the image consultant; they felt that increasingly it was the wrapping rather than the content which mattered. They detected 'designer socialism' as the new ideology, and disliked the triumph of style over substance. They also lamented the tendency to follow rather than lead public opinion, and felt that Labour is too concerned to put forward an agreeable image than to sell its traditional ideas and policies.

There remains a feeling among some people that political advertising is wrong in principle, and that the methods of the persuasion industry are unsuited to a topic of such *gravitas* as politics. There is a danger that the public can be manipulated, that their doubts and anxieties can be unfairly used by those in power. Politics may increasingly be all about marketing men and advertisers giving the public what they want.

Such reactions are probably not typical of those of the voters, many of whose opinions of Neil Kinnock were at least temporarily improved by the Hudson broadcast. The makers of that programme were aware of the needs of the day. They understood that no party can afford to ignore the means of communication now available. This has long been the case, and parties have made continuous adjustments to cope with the demands of a mass franchise in the period since 1867.

John Smith, though not averse to the new forms of communication (and himself a supreme example of how to deal with the television interviewer), toned down the glitzy presentation, and in his short spell as leader concentrated more on the message than on the way it was communicated. His successor, Tony Blair, was chosen among other reasons because his youthful charm made him a naturally telegenic figure, and he is likely to ensure that the media relays the changing message of the party in ways which maximise its impact.

In the past, there has been some dissonance between what the message says and the way it is being said. Labour has perhaps now achieved a better understanding of the fact that it is difficult to sell an unwanted message. Tony Blair has been concerned about the content, not just the packaging.

## Unjustified alarm?

There may be some reasons for optimism among those who are perturbed about recent trends, and the most recent general election provides them. The examples of Jennifer's ear and the Sheffield Rally may be indications of some consumer resistance to excessive slickness. The ordinary voter could confound the professional politician more than the paid interviewer. On *Election Call*, very unlike any American experience, Tony Blair and Michael Heseltine ran into awkward questioners, in a way that would never happen to an American politician.

The charge is often made that image dominates everything, and there is ample evidence that politicians and their minders have become image-conscious. But they cannot sell a product which the public shows no interest in accepting, and Labour's defeats in 1987 and in 1992 proved that the message has to be one which strikes a chord with the mass of voters. Bruce believes that the public have an unerring ability to 'spot a wrong-'un', and that: 'Image-makers may be able to alter physical appearance and modify body language, but they can't create what really matters – strength of character and inner conviction.' [45]

It may be that the smoothness, slickness and all-too-evident professionalism of recent campaigning will evoke sales resistance. Sincerity and candour cannot be entirely simulated in a society which still respects these qualities. Heavily-researched products advertised on television can still be a flop if they fail to suit their purpose, and so too a political campaign, however skilful, cannot conceal the lack of appeal of a party with an unwanted message.

## Notes

1   R. Cockett, 'The Party, Publicity and the Media' in A. Seldon and S. Balls (eds), *Conservative Century* (Oxford University Press: Oxford, 1995), p. 561.

2   Mrs W. Crum-Ewing, quoted in *ibid.*, p. 566.

3   B. Bruce, *Images of Power* (Kogan Page: London, 1992), pp. 84–5.

4   *Ibid.*, p. 97.

5   D. Lynch, quoted in L. Rees, *Selling Politics* (BBC Books: London, 1992), p. 84.

6   L. Rees, *Selling Politics*, p. 86.

7   Letter to author, 1 December 1994.

8   Plaid Cymru, *Encountering the Media* (Plaid Cymru: Cardiff, 1995).

9   *Panorama*, 30 September 1976.

10  B. Bruce, *Images of Power*, p. 137.

11  D. Kavanagh, *Election Campaigning: The New Marketing of Politics* (Blackwell: Oxford, 1995), p. 171.

12  *Ibid.*, p. 169.

13  D. Butler, as quoted in *There Now Follows* (BBC Television), 8 October 1993.

14  As shown in *There Now Follows*.

15  Sir T. Bell, as quoted in *There Now Follows*.

16  *Sunday Times*, as quoted in D. Butler and D. Kavanagh *The British General Election of 1987* (Macmillan: London, 1988), p. 154.

17  B. Bruce, *Images of Power*, pp. 112–13.

18  D. Butler and D. Kavanagh, *The British General Election of 1987*, p. 154.

19  L. Rees, *Selling Politics*, p. 44.

20  D. Butler and D. Kavanagh, *The British General Election of 1992* (Macmillan: London, 1992), p. 177.

21  J. Wober, *Television Coverage and the First 1974 British General Election*, IBA Research Paper, 1974.

22  J. Wober, *The May 1979 General Election: Viewers' Attitudes Towards Television Coverage*, IBA Research Paper, 1979.

23  J. Wober, *Party Political and Election Broadcasts: Their Perceived Attributes and Impact Upon Viewers*, IBA Research paper, 1987.

24 *Ibid.*

25 D. Butler and D. Kavanagh, *The British General Election of 1992*, p. 174.

26 The Institute of Practitioners in Advertising, free leaflet.

27 E. Bolland, 'Advertising v. Public Relations', *Public Relations Quarterly*, vol. 34, no. 3 (1989).

28 Committee on Advertising Standards, Advertising Standards Association, pamphlet on political advertising.

29 L. Rees, *Selling Politics*, p. 120.

30 D. Butler and D. Kavanagh, *The British General Election of 1987* and *The British General Election of 1992*, p. 206.

31 B. Schneider, quoted in J. Friedland, 'The Great Democratic Turn-off', *Guardian*, 29 October 1994.

32 B. Bruce, *Images of Power*, p. 105.

33 D. Kavanagh, *Election Campaigning: The New Marketing of Politics*, p. 159.

34 *Ibid.*, p. 160.

35 L. Rees, *Selling Politics*, p. 58.

36 As quoted in D. Butler and D. Kavanagh, *The British General Election of 1987*, p. 178.

37 B. Bruce, *Images of Power*, p. 108.

38 D. Kavanagh, *Election Campaigning: The New Marketing of Politics*, p. 195.

39 S. L. Popkin, *The Reasoning Voter*, quoted in L. Rees, *Selling Politics*, p. 120.

40 L. Rees, *Selling Politics*, p. 12.

41 R. Strother, as quoted in *ibid.*, p. 12.

42 K. Jamieson, *Packaging the Presidency*, as quoted in *ibid.*, p. 13.

43 M. McLuhan, *Understanding Media*, as quoted in *ibid.*, p. 13.

44 P. Tyler, *Campaign! The Selling of the Prime Minister* (Grafton: London, 1987), p. 153.

45 B. Bruce, *Images of Power*, p. 179.

# 10

# Politicians selling themselves

### Political speeches

The nature of public speaking has undergone a considerable change in the past seventy years. Before then, oral communication was limited to addresses at a public meeting or rally, and speeches in Parliament. In the House of Commons, politicians on the government side were concerned to argue the ministerial case for things done and left undone, and there were some classic expositions. One of the most famous was the Don Pacifico incident in 1850 when Palmerston insisted on the rights of English citizens abroad, in a five-hour review of British foreign policy over the previous generation. Gladstone responded more briefly in a masterly three-hour performance in which he gave a considered rebuke to the Foreign Secretary.

What Gladstone could do was to blend moral judgement with logical exposition, and his gifts were employed in many great parliamentary occasions of the century – most famously in the debates over Irish Home Rule. They were equally if not more effective on the public platform. He blended reason and emotion, and was able to lambaste the Disraeli Government over the alleged impiety of its Imperial policy in vigorous yet eloquent tones.

Today, speeches range from humdrum pronouncements on routine occasions to largely inattentive audiences – a Minister defending the policy of his Department in a near-empty chamber – to the set-piece performances of the leading speakers on either side. On the public platform, there is much less need for oratory than was once the case, for most of the election speeches by the party leaders are made-for-television events. Otherwise, there are the relatively small number of speeches in which local candidates address a tiny gathering in a school hall. Most speeches are now made with the viewer in mind, and even those given at Party Conferences are continuously televised.

Conference performances vary in quality, and the party spokespersons on these occasions often markedly contrast in style. They all face the difficulty of addressing two audiences, one present and one at home. On occasion, the problem is compounded, when there are three sets of people to target. In 1995, Paddy Ashdown was speaking to the viewers, many of whom would only see and hear the highlights (the soundbites), his audience (whose enthusiasm needed to be aroused), and also the leaders of the Labour Party (whose overtures for a more cooperative approach by the opposition parties required a response).

Party leaders at conference time are aware of the value to them of their personal slot, for they appreciate – as Kavanagh reminds us – that the hour-long slot 'amounts to a party's total allocation of broadcasts at a general election'.[1] In other words, it is free and prolonged coverage. He goes on to observe that 'eloquence is a trait often sought but rarely found in a party leader'. Skill in debate or the possession of a fine voice do not guarantee that a person can write or deliver a good set-piece speech.

Several prominent politicians have been able to turn in a good Conference performance, Macmillan, Wilson and Callaghan all being able at their best to carry the hall with them. Gaitskell was not a leader to whom the party could easily warm, but his 1960 'fight, fight and fight again' performance was a highlight in the history of political speeches, as much for the importance of its content as for the manner of delivery. Labour Conferences in those days preferred the burning passion and socialist conviction of Nye Bevan.

Party leaders such as Sir Alec Douglas-Home and Ted Heath have lacked speaking skills. In the case of the latter he could frustrate the efforts of his speech-writers by throwing away a good opportunity to put his listeners into good heart. Often, he would erase the punch-lines so carefully prepared for him. There was little humour in what was left and the delivery was dull, and often lacked timing.

Neither was Mrs Thatcher a natural orator, and her speeches had to be carefully prepared and carefully rehearsed throughout the night before she was ready for the big occasion. Humour needed to be handled with caution for it was sometimes delivered with the wrong intonation. But she worked at getting the timing of her jokes right, and could be effective in addressing the faithful.

Of other recent leaders, Neil Kinnock was at his most effective before a party audience, at Conference or in any other gathering. He was not a good performer in the television interview or in the House where – thrown by interruptions from barracking backbenchers – he was unable to relax and deploy the wit at his command. Before he delivered his Conference speech, the efforts of his advisers would be carefully read and rewritten in his own words, and then the speech would be 'internalised'[2] and rehearsed. When on top form, the result could be triumphant, as in his attack on Militant in 1985 in which he poured scorn and derision upon those who ran local government in Liverpool.

## The techniques of public speaking

Public speakers adopt a variety of devices to enable them to make an impact upon their audiences. Many of their speeches are written by advisers who understand their subject's thinking and approach, and the strengths and limitations of their manner of delivery. Theodore Sorenson wrote many of President Kennedy's most remembered phrases, though JFK was no mean performer in scripting his own lines. In common with other American orators, he was fond of using linked phrases in which the word order in the second of two parallel phrases is reversed (chiasmus); for instance, 'Ask not what our country can do for you, but what you can do for your country.' Less inspirational was the example coined by Bob Dole in his 1996 presidential campaign: 'For the government cannot direct the people; the people must direct the government.' Other American and British politicians, most recently John Major, have employed anadiplosis, repetition with a subtle variation – as in Abraham Lincoln's Gettysburg address; in the definition of democracy as 'government of the people, by the people, for the people'.

Alliteration, litotes (deliberate understatement, as in 'no mean performer') and paronomasia (punning) are common, the latter deployed effectively in Margaret Thatcher's 'you turn if you want to; the lady's not for turning'. Styles vary from Paddy Ashdown's matter-of-fact plain-speaking, laced with sudden rhetorical (almost Churchillian) flourishes and references to topical songs or sporting occasions, to the more thoughtful and serious Tony Blair, whose impassioned and moralising appeal to his listeners is enlivened by an occasional (and often self-deprecating) joke to lighten the intense atmosphere. Often the Labour leader's speeches are reminiscent of those of the preacher in the pulpit, an indication that the American tradition of evangelical political preachers (Martin Luther King and Jesse Jackson) has been tapped by speakers here. The Blair style is highly personalised, as he summons up the spirits of the Old Testament prophets rather than more well-known heroes of his party's history, and vows to deliver his array of pledges (as at Blackpool, 1996) to be honoured.

In that conference speech, the well-crafted test, rich in sporting allusions to 'Labour's coming home', the Blairite performance skills were particularly in evidence. He could hardly be faulted in the way in which he delivered his message, an aspect highlighted by a *Guardian* columnist:

> From the taut, presidential status on podium-arrival, to the perfectly coor-dinated head-swivelling, to the active darting right hand – now an imploring little claw, now a sweeping new broom, now a stabbing finger, now a fist clenched in victory . . . The trio of facial expressions and matching tones of voice – fierce intent, broad good humour, throat-constricted contempla-tion – were no less well deployed . . . [as were] the ruthlessly sentimental references.[3]

By contrast, John Major, vividly described by Mark Lawson as 'the anti-ora-tor of modern politics',[4] has a simple, low-key approach, though he too can incorporate the sentimentality of several American politicians, especially in references to his family. Bill Clinton told a Chicago audience in 1996 of his gratitude to the city for producing 'the love and light of my life, Chicago's daughter; Hillary [turning to her], I love you'. Similarly, at the party con-ference of the previous year, John Major invoked the memory of his father in a testimony of his personal beliefs: 'He made garden ornaments forty years ago; some fashionable people still find that very funny. I don't. I see the proud, stubborn, independent old man.'

Having analysed three speeches, Peter Bull was able to write of his findings on the use of hand gestures in public speaking.[5] He observed how they were related to intonation, and how they could be used by the speaker to elicit and control applause. In particular, he commented on the way in which Arthur Scargill was able to enthuse his audience by the adroit use of rhetorical devices matched by synchronised gestures, to the extent that he seemed to be able to conduct his audience.

Bull sees the hand gesture as being 'especially significant because of its greater visibility than, say, facial expression or gaze', whereas in the television studio there is more emphasis on facial attributes. Some have commented more on the rhetoric itself, and have pointed to the limited range of devices employed. In a number of publications, Atkinson has noted the effect of contrast and three-part lists, both ploys which are particularly popular with speakers, and are often picked up by the media.[6] Others have mentioned the changes in pitch, rhythm or volume which are often associated with body movements such as the use of the outstretched index finger, or the raising of the forearm. Much of the research is based on a relatively small number of speeches, which limits the general applicability of the findings, but reading of political biographies and personal observation confirm much of the highly detailed analysis which such studies employ.

With the finest orators, their effect is one which is carefully calculated and the techniques are perfected after long practice – sometimes in front of the mirror. In the case of Adolf Hitler, listeners would at first be lulled into thinking that the speech was almost disappointing, for its content and delivery seemed unremarkable, but then, perhaps after twenty minutes or so, without being conscious of how or why it happened, members of the audience would find themselves captivated by the magnetism of the Führer. The eyes compelled their attention, the hand gestures controlled their response and the speaker's sense of timing was so masterly that he could compel everyone's rapt attention.

Moreover, the setting was right, for in the large gatherings at Nuremberg and elsewhere, enthusiasm would spread like wildfire. The skilful use of patriotic, stirring music – and the presence of SA/SS men at the door – added to the excitement of the occasion. Partly perhaps through fear, but more out of a sense of inspiration, those present at the rally fainted or lapsed into hysteria. It was the atmosphere, the performance and also the content which made the speech a success, for Hitler told his hearers what they wanted to hear, the message of a greater Germany which would gain revenge for its defeat in 1914–18.

Above all, as Enoch Powell has often pointed out, words are the politician's business, and the ability to communicate effectively by the spoken word is a skill which ideally every politician needs. Some have been particularly accomplished, and world leaders such as de Gaulle and Churchill were both gifted with the ability to use words to their best effect. Noted for their prose, they could both write clearly and impressively; on the public platform or via radio, they could enthuse their audience. De Gaulle was an outstanding orator who could use language skilfully. He was adept at exploiting the value of calculated ambiguity. When he told the Algerian settlers 'Je vous ai compris' (I understand you), it helped to identify him with those who were listening. But he never confided what it was he had understood, or what he intended to do about it.

Harold Wilson was also able to use words in a thoughtfully calculated way. He seemed to be straightforward when in fact the choice of language was made with great care. Pressed on how the abolition of the grammar schools would promote equality of opportunity, he responded that what he wanted to do was to extend a grammar-school education to everyone via the medium of the comprehensive school.

The age of great public-speaking has gone, and truly memorable feats of oratory have been rarely heard for many years. Churchill's 'blood, toil, tears and sweat' and Martin Luther King's 'I have a dream' speeches are striking examples of a genre now little displayed. Big personalities are out of fashion, and inspirational heroes emerge more in time of national peril. Moreover, great orators of the past often thrived on the spontaneity provided by a live audience. The age of television calls for a different style of communication, and it is the new medium with which we are particularly concerned.

## The election debate

In Britain, it is part of the ritual of a general election campaign for one or two of the contestants, normally the opposition leaders, to throw down the gauntlet and issue a challenge to the incumbent of Ten Downing Street to a television debate. It is a much tried and as often resisted formula, and one put forward by those who assume that they have more to gain from the experience. Thus in 1992 Neil Kinnock was confident that he would look and sound more impressive than John Major in any face-to-face confrontation. The side which rejects the match risks looking cowardly, but any storm soon passes. Such embarrassment could be considerably less damaging than agreeing to a format in which the candidate might perform badly.

The nearest Britain ever has to a debate between two rival speakers is the studio discussion, in which a speaker from either side of the political divide, and perhaps one from the third party, are chosen to debate a key issue. In the 1975 referendum campaign on Europe, it might be Benn versus Jenkins, or in an election it might be a Minister versus his shadow spokesperson, or in the regional/constituency level, one candidate versus another.

The television producer prefers a format in which there is a clear confrontation between two or three persons who take a markedly different standpoint. A Tory moderate and a Labour one may not make for an interesting confrontation, so that a right-wing Conservative is often placed against a more convinced socialist. It can go wrong if one of the politicians decides to agree with a substantial measure of what his opposite number says. This can derail the discussion, and make the politician seem reasonable. Such agreement is unusual, and more often the person in the chair is seen to be the reasonable man between two extremists.

The Americans have been more willing to use the televised debate, though party managers are only too aware of its potential damage. As with unscripted interviews and discussions, it can lay the candidate open to the possibility of committing a gaffe which could seriously damage credibility and standing. A weak performer risks being seriously mauled. Nonetheless, if one candidate is keen, the other has found it difficult to resist without appearing cowardly.

The Presidential and Vice-Presidential debates have been of varying quality, and the rules of engagement have differed from election to election. The one which has been endlessly quoted ever since is that held in 1960 between Kennedy and Nixon. The debate was broadcast on radio and television, and significantly, whereas polling showed that a majority of listeners thought that Nixon had emerged on top, a majority of viewers were in no doubt that Kennedy had won. When he did win, it was by the narrowest of margins (0.5 per cent of the popular vote) and it may well be that television swung the outcome.

Debates have almost certainly made a difference to the outcome of some elections, for in a close-run contest the importance of appearing steady and in control is supreme. If you cannot win, it is crucial to avoid mistakes. Errors have been made and some have been costly. Apart from the Nixon performance in 1960, when so much went wrong in the first meeting, the other famous or infamous gaffe was the moment in 1976 when Jimmy Carter benefited from a fatal howler committed by his opponent, Gerald Ford, then the Republican President. Ford said that Poland was not under Eastern European domination.

In 1980, Reagan easily outperformed Carter, but in 1984, in the Mondale versus Reagan encounters, the President was unconvincing in the first one. Attempts to provide him with detailed information had failed to work, for he had no mastery of detail and appeared faltering. Roger Ailes, a leading media consultant used by the Republicans, offered advice to the President, and this was to stick to broad themes rather than particular information. In responding to any question, it needed to be related to the themes. He also suggested that Reagan tackle head-on the single issue which was potentially the most harmful to him, that of age. Many voters were well-disposed to Reagan, but their doubt was his fitness to operate in such a demanding situation. When the inevitable question came up its impact was deflected by the use of a flash of Presidential humour: 'I want you to know that I will not make age an issue of this campaign. I am not going to exploit for political purposes my opponent's youth and inexperience'.

In the 1988 Vice-Presidential contest, the vulnerable Republican 'Veep', Dan Quayle received a classic put-down when he tried to identify himself with the Kennedy legend. His opponent, Lloyd Bentsen, responded tartly: 'Senator, I knew Jack Kennedy, Jack Kennedy was a friend of mine. Senator, you're no Jack Kennedy.' Quayle was outsmarted, and made to look foolish, and the damage was the greater in that it was that soundbite which was picked up by the media networks and replayed on all the major news bulletins.

Sometimes, the problem is a gaffe; at others it is dress or a an imprudent approach. In 1968, Hubert Humphrey, the American Democrat, did himself harm by answering one question for eleven minutes, and so appeared to be what in fact he was, a garrulous talker. Television demands greater brevity.

Good looks are also an asset, or at least it is necessary to compensate for physical deficiencies. Dukakis was placed on a dais behind the podium soapbox to conceal from the voters how short he was. The problems caused by inattention to detail had been brought home to the Democrats in the Reagan versus Mondale battle, for in one of the debates the lighting was set in such a way that Mondale appeared to have huge bags under his eyes. He had received expert make-up from a Hollywood artist and in frontal lighting would have appeared impressive and well-turned-out. He was made to look haggard and unimpressive.

The rules vary enormously from contest to contest, and party advisers are very concerned to avoid damage to their choice. The result can be to produce a wooden encounter, for there are so many checks built in to the rules to prevent an advantage for either side that the affair is sometimes lifeless and lacking in passion. In 1988, the sixteen-page document which set out the conditions negotiated by the party managers regulated not only the colour of the background, the distance between the candidates, but also laid down that neither candidate could address the other. The debate was really two parallel interviews, between one journalist and one candidate at a time. When Bentsen addressed Dan Quayle in the incident outlined above, he effectively broke the rules, though he did so with such efficacy that it was he who won the viewers' sympathy. The incident produced one of the few moments of drama in the series.

Any guidelines have to be carefully drawn up. There needs to be agreement on a chairman, and whether or not the person chosen should put questions on his or her own, or as part of a panel. Both formulae have been tried in the United States. Whatever the decision, the chairman needs to be effective, for the Keating–Howard debates in Australia (1995) were noted for weak chairmanship, and a failure to insist on a firm allocation of time for each speaker. Also, if Britain were to hold such debates, there would need to be a decision on which parties would be represented. Would it be a two-party contest, or would the Liberal Democrats (and even the Scottish Nationalists, north of the border) be allowed to participate? In the United States, in 1992, Ross Perot took part, but four years later the Americans excluded him and reverted to their standard format.

Debates are used in countries such as France, Germany, Italy and Canada, and they can succeed or fail in a different way, according to the viewpoint of those watching. The 1994 tussle between Silvio Berlusconi and Achille Occhetto degenerated into a slanging match which made for lively viewing, but generated little light. By contrast, Jacques Chirac and Lionel Jospin were almost excessively polite to each other in the French presidential election (1995), and this resulted in much less exciting exchanges, and poor spectator sport.

At their best, debates between the two contenders are a useful means of providing each candidate with an opportunity to reach a mass audience. The viewer can then make a choice between the merits of the rival candidates, and assess them for their effectiveness and sincerity. As in the political interview in Britain, once in the studio and under starter's orders they are effectively on their own. It is for this reason that Bruce argues that: 'Any incumbent who accepts the challenge of their opponent in this form needs their head examined. The latter has very little to lose and the former very little to gain.'[7]

## The televising of Parliament

Party conferences were until 1989 the nearest approximation to proceedings in the House. They are obviously not like Parliament, but they do have an intention – among others – to communicate with an audience at home, as well as at the centre where the gathering is being held. Coverage of them began in 1962, after prolonged negotiation, and soon became a matter of routine. So did the presence of television cameras at elections, unthinkable before the major breakthrough of 1959. But proceedings at Westminster itself were excluded from the screen.

### The experience of broadcasting radio

The BBC is required by its Licence to 'broadcast an impartial account day by day, prepared by professional reporters, of the proceedings of both Houses of Parliament'. This obligation was originally fulfilled by the use of reported speech, but since the 1970s by the use of actual extracts. The broadcasting of selected parliamentary debates, together with occasional Select Committee hearings, has taken place on the radio since 1975. At the time, this was hailed as a significant departure, but subsequently it seems modest enough.

Recordings of parliamentary proceedings are contained in short programmes such as *Today in Parliament*, a digest *The Week in Westminster*, broadcast on Saturday mornings and *In Committee*, broadcast on Sunday evenings. Occasionally debates are broadcast live – for example, the one on the Falklands War in 1982, and the one on Britain's relationship with the European Union in March 1995.

Sound recordings, often accompanied by a still photograph of the politician, were for several years used in television news, as were extracts from Question Time, which was broadcast in 1975 on an experimental basis, and then subsequently every Tuesday and Thursday. What the radio broadcasts showed was that Question Time is frequently noisy, and that some MPs were more concerned to make debating points than to add to the sum of public information. The audience was less than impressed to hear the baying and background comments which seemed to do little for the dignity of the House. So the coverage of debates has been a desirable antidote to what goes on in those sessions.

## Televising the House of Lords

The House of Lords had experimented with closed-circuit television in the 1960s and with sound broadcasting in 1977. In December 1983, Peers voted 3–1 in favour of admitting the cameras for a six-month experimental period, and in the following July the Select Committee on Sound Broadcasting duly issued its report, *Televising the House of Lords*, which made detailed recommendations on how to implement the experiment.

The rules were not too rigid, with matters of selection and of editorial control left to the broadcasting authorities, although ultimate control rested with the House. There was no obligation on the part of the television authorities to present a daily account of proceedings, coverage being conducted on a 'drive-in' basis, with cameramen and commentators coming and going as they wished. Generally, the cameras were to concentrate on the Peer who was speaking, but this rule was not a fixed one.

The experiment ran until the summer recess (1985), and the House voted to extend it until the Select Committee Report had been received. Opponents retained some of their original fears, many of which centred on matters of editorial control. They feared that a distorted impression of the House was being put out, primarily because the broadcasters had criteria of newsworthiness which did not match their own. Whereas the media-men tended to emphasise entertainment and spectacle, such Peers wanted the House to be seen as it really was.

When it emerged, the Report did not dwell on matters of editorial policy or on the balance of programmes, so that the Hansard research unit saw this as an area to explore. Its findings, as published in May 1986, found several positive effects. Although it suggested that the use of material in newscasts had not been a successful part of the experiment, it found that the late-night edited summaries and the ITN weekly programme had been 'a significant innovation'.[8]

Its researchers found that 'the style and format of presentation' were evolving in a way 'which is tailored to Parliamentary broadcasting and is not dominated by conventional news values'.[9] In particular, the extracts of individual Peers speaking had grown longer and more representative, the studio commentaries were more interpretative and the overall coverage of debates had increased. There was no evidence that Peers had significantly amended their behaviour as a result of the intrusion of the cameras into their proceedings, though speeches seemed to have become a little longer.

The use of film in newscasts and any associated commentary was one of the most criticised aspects, for some of the snippets selected were so short that the full flavour of the speech and therefore of the debate was missing. Too often, the main reason for choosing an item seemed to be that it tied in with some other news story, rather than the intrinsic importance or interest of the subject. Moreover, the approach of the newscasters and Parliamentary correspondents towards the House was almost 'sacerdotal': '[they] seemed to be going out of their way to ensure that the mystique and "specialness" of Parliament were preserved'.[10] This approach gradually gave way to a more lively coverage which, however, stressed the adversarial nature of debate, showing areas mainly of party conflict.

One of the main fears of Peers about allowing television into the Chamber was that it would provide an inadequate coverage of all types of work done by the House, but a comparison of the time allocated to the various aspects of the workload of the House and of the time actually spent by the House on such tasks showed that there was a broad correlation, as Table 10.1 indicates. Set-piece debates, as many Peers had anticipated, had greater coverage than the rest of the duties of the Chamber, perhaps because they were often dealing with leading issues of the day, perhaps because the better-known personalities tended to attend and speak in them.

Table 10.1. *The work of the Chamber as represented on television*[11]

| Type of work | Time spent by the Lords | Time allocated on TV |
| --- | --- | --- |
| Debates | | |
| General | 25 | 41 |
| Legislation | 42 | 39 |
| Select Committee Reports | 5 | 5 |
| Deleg. legislation | 6 | 2 |
| Ministerial statements | 4 | — |
| Starred questions | 6 | 5 |
| Unstarred questions | 8 | 4 |
| Other | 4 | 4 |
| | 100 | 100 |

In determining which areas of debate to cover, certain types of topic received more extensive coverage than others. Generally, matters concerning Government economic policy and areas of contention received greater attention than the time spent on them by Peers actually merited, whereas welfare issues such as housing and social security were relatively neglected (see Table 10.2).

Table 10.2. *Main subject-matter covered by television*

| Regularly covered | Infrequently covered |
|---|---|
| Relations of central/local government | Social security |
| Government economic policy/record | Health and welfare |
| Industry/trade/unemployment | Immigration |
| New technologies | Energy |
| Secondary education | Higher education |

Whereas an Interim Report (November 1985) had detected a bias against the Alliance and crossbenchers whose voice was heard less often than might have been expected, this imbalance had been corrected over the whole fifteen months of their research:

> Editors have succeeded in maintaining a rough balance between those who argue for a Motion or Amendment and those who argue against. Given the nature and membership of the House of Lords, this is a form of balance which is easier to maintain for any given debate than a simple balance between the parties.[12]

Peers decided to make the experiment permanent, in 1986. At that stage, 59 per cent wanted to see the experimental televising of the House continue, and 76 per cent wanted to see it made permanent. The general feeling was that the 'Lords had gained by the experiment, and members were seemingly disappointed when the lights were not switched on'.[13]

The generally favourable comment of the Hansard study has been endorsed in subsequent references. Television boosted the reputation of and interest in the Chamber, at a time when its hostility to some measures of the Thatcher Government was already provoking more comment about the House.

Peers seemed unworried by the presence of the cameras, and were less conscious than MPs were later to be of the need to impose restrictions on what might be shown. Initially, ITN cameramen were allowed to film from within the Chamber, and although there are now remotely-controlled cameras which operate from the basement of the Millbank building (as there are for the Lower House), the traditional rules under which shots are taken have tended to be interpreted loosely.

### A 1995 perspective

In the 1980s, before the televising of the House of Commons, there was more coverage of the Upper House; ITN showed *Their Lordships' House* and BBC *The Week in the Lords*. These have now disappeared, and material is now used (sparingly) in programmes on Parliament as a whole. Peers generally seem to be generally unaware of the coverage which is available of their work, but some have expressed disappointment that they have 'lost out' in the arrangements since 1989. Only viewers of *Sky News* currently have the chance to see a special weekly item on what they have been doing over the preceding few days, though the much smaller number of cable viewers are able to see the events of the previous day on the non-profit-making Parliamentary Channel.[14]

Peers seemed to like the innovation, their enthusiasm perhaps being all the greater because they get less coverage in papers and on news bulletins. The experiment was deemed a success, and this increased pressure on MPs to allow their own proceedings to be televised. Some people argued that in view of 'the anachronistic setting and leisurely pace . . . few useful conclusions could be drawn either way from the televising of their Lordships' deliberations',[15] but there was a feeling in the Lower House that they had stolen a march on the Commons and gained by the innovation. However, if Peers showed the House of Commons the way, the Lower House was slow to learn the lesson. Not until 21 November 1989 did the House of Commons appear on television, when it was shown debating the Queen's Speech.

The box below indicates the responses offered by Peers to a questionnaire (see Appendix) on their attitudes towards the televising of the Upper House.

---

**Responses to a 1995 questionnaire**

Of the twenty-two Peers who answered six questions (ten Conservative, nine Labour, two Liberal Democrat and one cross-bencher), the findings were as follows:

|  | Yes | No | Don't know |
|---|---|---|---|
| In favour after ten years | 18 | 2 | 2 |
| Believe Lords has had impact on: | | | |
| a. attendance | | 18 | 4 |
| b. behaviour | | 18 | 4 |
| c. frequency and length of speeches | | 18 | 4 |
| Find cameras intrusive | | 22 | |
| Believe editing and use of materials to be fair | 12 | 2 | 8 |
| Believe enough use made of recorded material | 4 | 10 | 8 |

What clearly emerged was an overwhelming acceptance of television in the House of Lords. Indeed, the only critic was Lord Stoddart of Swindon who argued that he had always opposed the idea, seeing it as 'merely a ploy to gain entry for the cameras to the House of Commons'; he disapproved strongly of the effects on the latter.

The reasons given for favouring television in the Chamber reflect the usual arguments given for televising either House, notably that 'Parliament belongs to the people; hence it should be open' (Lord Rodgers) and that it 'enables Parliament to benefit from the information channel most enjoyed by the public' (Lord Howe). In particular, it was seen as beneficial to the Lords because it made an unknown body more familiar to the public who, in the words of one prominent cross bencher, could recognise it as a 'courteous and civilised debating Chamber'. Lord Callaghan appreciated the importance of 'bringing to the attention of the public the work done by the Upper House which has not been recognised in the past'.

There was some regret that with the televising of the House of Commons there has been less interest in the proceedings of the House of Lords. In answer to Question 5, nearly half of the respondents felt that insufficient use was made of recorded material, even though the 'Lords could offer 'more substance than rhetoric (Lord Rodgers). Lord Howe felt that 'the media likes the more controversial debates in the 'Commons', and Lord Aberdare regretted the lack of coverage of 'major debates when eminent members with great experience take part'. Several Peers never watch the programmes which include recorded material, perhaps for the reason advanced by Lord Callaghan; as he works in Parliament, he has no reason 'to listen or to watch [its] proceedings'.

There were few complaints of unfairness in the editing and use of material. Several Peers felt unable to comment because they watched it so little, though Lord Stoddart had reservations and felt that there was 'no substitute for a continuous live broadcast of Parliament', if it has to be televised.

The overall view was that a decade after it began, the arrival of camera has had a negligible effect on the Upper House. No one found the cameras intrusive for the reason given by Lord Aberdare: 'We are all oblivious of the cameras, and it is more important to concentrate on a microphone.' Similarly, no one felt that there had been any significant change in the character of proceedings, either relating to attendance, behaviour, the length of speeches or to anything else, though a few were uncertain as to any impact there may have been.

The situation was summed up by Lord Gilmour: 'I don't think that television has had any effect on this place whatever.'[16] What did emerge was that some Peers had taken a close interest in the impact of television on the House of Commons. One argued that: 'The House of Lords is unaffected. The Commons has been seriously affected. The noise is worse and far more MPs want to speak than hitherto.' Lord Howe felt that 'Peers behaved exactly as though the cameras were not there. I suspect that the 'Commons – at least during Prime Minister's questions – has been rather more excited by their presence', and Lord Callaghan agreed that 'television has had more impact on the behaviour of the Commons than I expected when I originally voted for it'.

## Television and the House of Commons

The House of Commons has always been reluctant to allow the media in to report on its proceedings. In the eighteenth century, it resisted the intrusion of the press, it was reluctant to allow *Hansard* to cover its proceedings, and in 1923 a request for permission to transmit the King's Speech on radio was turned down by the Government.

The proposal to televise the House of Commons was debated in the 1960s and 1970s on several occasions. In the early votes, the proposal was usually heavily defeated, although in 1966 it was within one vote of being successful. By 1980, there were encouraging signs of a swing of opinion, and for the first time there was a majority in favour when the House supported a Ten Minute Rule Bill introduced by Austin Mitchell.

Mitchell believed that any technical problems could be resolved. Small, well-mounted cameras could be used which would not involve camera crews; the lighting in the Chamber would not have to be stronger than before; and finally, only the MP speaking needed to be filmed, so that there would be no shots of empty benches and sleeping backbenchers.

Three years later, the House voted for another such bill to allow coverage of select committee proceedings. In neither case did the legislation get any further, and in full debates many members of the House continued to exhibit their customary caution and fear. A number of Tory MPs tended to follow Mrs Thatcher's lead on the subject, and she was known to be hostile. She shared many of the usual fears about 'letting the public in', and was also concerned that television might undermine the strength of her Government's position in that it was a medium in which attacking speeches might tend to make a greater impact than those spoken by Ministers in defence of their briefs. She seemed to be overcoming her anxieties in 1985, but changed her mind at the last minute – as did the group of her party's MPs who were keen to vote in the same lobby as their leader.

However, finally, in February 1988, an experiment was agreed by a majority of fifty-four votes. An influx of new MPs in 1987 and the disappearance of some traditional opponents of televising the House had meant that a majority of members were keen to swim with the tide and bring the House into line with many other legislatures.

### The debate over admitting the cameras into the Commons

In the debates over televising the House, familiar arguments were regularly rehearsed, often with great conviction. Some were similar to the fears and forebodings which Peers had expressed prior to allowing the cameras in to the House of Lords. On the other side, those who argued for the innovation had similar considerations in mind to the ones which had motivated sympathetic Peers.

*The case in favour*

Those who supported the idea believed that it would make for 'intelligent communication between the House of Commons and the electorate as a whole' (Nye Bevan, in 1959), and give people more idea of what Parliament is about. It would perform an educative function, and hopefully improve public interest and information about the affairs it discusses. Bevan was the first significant MP to state the case for the innovation, and he saw it as a logical and necessary development of the democratic process:

> There is a lessening interest in our discussions. We are not reaching the country to the extent that we did . . . there do not exist at present in Britain the normal processes of democratic education that make the people aware of the problems which lie ahead of us, and of their own responsibilities . . . Would it not be an excellent thing if, instead of speeches being made in comparative obscurity, and, in fact, never heard at all except by the few members who assemble here to hear them, they were heard by their constituents?[17]

As television was so firmly established in our social life, it was often argued that it was unrealistic and wrong to deny it access to Westminster. It had become the foremost channel of communication available, the source of most people's political views, having replaced the press in its importance over the last thirty years. In these circumstances, the arguments and atmosphere could not be properly conveyed by reporters.

Also, at a time when many people resorted to direct action or thought of using the political strike weapon as a means of advancing their cause, it was hoped that televising its proceedings would help to restore the House as the focal point for democratic discussion, serving as a reminder of the need to work peacefully for reform through the traditional Parliamentary machinery.

It was hoped that television might stimulate Parliament to reform its procedures and make them more intelligible to an audience. It might encourage the House to be more efficient. It might promote improved attendance, as constituents would like to see their MP present. It might improve behaviour, for party dogfights, booing, cheap interruptions and rowdyism would be an off-putting and unedifying spectacle to many voters. A combination of television's intimacy and public criticism might combine to encourage an atmosphere of reason and persuasion.

To enthusiasts, the arguments against the proposal were invalid or unconvincing. Many of them were the same ones as had been used against the original proposals for the reporting of the House. It was argued that if this occurred it would change 'the character of the House'; if it were to do so, this would not matter and people would accept it in much the same way as they once came to accept newspaper reports.

## The case against

Critics suspected that there was little demand, judging by the small audience for radio coverage of politics. More significantly, they felt that television would mislead the public about the nature of Parliament. Front-bench 'stars' would dominate programmes, for producers would go for the edited highlights, the scenes at Question Time which were said to be untypical of the House at work. Backbenchers would be less often heard, but they might have to explain to their constituents why they were rarely to be seen on screen.

Ministers and backbenchers would play to the cameras and not address the House, for the temptation would be to speak to an impressionable mass audience rather than to fellow-MPs who were likely to vote according to the wishes of the party Whips and not act in an independent way. They would try to impress their electors by oratory and exhibitionism: 'It might make MPs nervous and show them giggling and behaving like schoolgirls', said the Labour Leader of the House, Herbert Bowden, back in 1963. The prospect 'frightened him'.[18]

Opponents also sometimes claimed that the presence of cameras would encourage outrageous behaviour by MPs in the knowledge that it would make good television. There were already occasional brawls and other undignified events. Television producers would be only too pleased, it was feared, to have the opportunity to display such scenes.

Foremost among the fears was that it would alter the character of the House and put an undesirable power into hands of the television producer in selecting what would be seen. There was the danger already mentioned of speeches being made to please constituents rather than to advance debate, and that telegenic MPs with interesting personalities would be featured at the expense of unattractive, duller ones. Would television thus trivialise proceedings, encourage people to think not in terms of issues and analysis, but of individuals? Rumbustious knockabout could be entertaining but detract from thoughtful coverage of the question.

Much would depend on the skill of the editors in selecting what would be shown and in summarising and elucidating the day's events. The presentation would have to be fair and not concentrate just on the exciting moments that might distort reality; one dissident speech might be more newsworthy than six supporting the party line. Television producers have a natural tendency to look for the exciting moments, and in particular the visually interesting ones. This might well make for distortion and sensation. A former newscaster who had become a Conservative MP, Tim Brinton, told the House that:

Inaccuracy was no slight to professional television and radio news editors. Television could never be truly real or truly truthful. The very nature of its work meant that it could not be anything else but selective, and selectivity had to mean, in the nicest way, a form of censorship.[19]

Others felt that television would destroy the intimate nature of the House. Members would be conscious that they were all the time on their air and this could have led to some jockeying for position at peak times, to try and catch the Speaker's eye, as members sought to address the nation at large.

Some of the arguments in favour were elevated ones about the nature of democracy. One of them, the freedom argument, was hard to resist – namely that once television exists it is an obnoxious restraint on the freedom of journalists to exclude it from the seat of democracy. As television is the major source of people's information about politics as well as everything else, surely it is anti-democratic to deny the viewers the first-hand sight of the place where the action is.

However, the arguments of politicians were sometimes tinged with a substantial degree of self-interest. Some saw the cameras as a way of rescuing them from the sink of public esteem into which politics as reported had cast them. Some on the opposition benches hoped that because television networks operate under statutory rules against bias, then the anti-government case would get a better hearing among the masses than it does in the newspapers. Considerations of party advantage were involved, and in another respect, namely that some key figures in government believed that the cameras would show their Leader to advantage over Mr Kinnock and exclude the third party from view in as much as Parliament relegates it to a peripheral role.

Some of the problems mentioned by opponents had already been overcome in radio summaries and in coverage of party conferences. But inevitably television would make a difference, for it would not just be a reporter but would influence what was being reported. For better or worse, the arrival of cameras would change the public perception about politics and therefore the quality of British democracy.

The nature of the Commons would be altered. The cameras could not be neutral, purely recording reality for the benefit of the wider public. They would subtly alter the reality of the occasion on which they were present. In this, they are quite unlike the press, so that there is no exact equivalence between the admission of reporters in the eighteenth century and the arrival of cameras 200 years later. Television has changed politics in other areas.

### Television and overseas legislatures

In January 1980 Austin Mitchell told the House that allowing television into the House would bring it into line with 'those European parliaments which allow coverage on television and with two score of legislatures around the world who have accepted television in the Chamber'.[20] He was certainly correct in his assertion that the medium had been widely accepted around the world.

For some while before the introduction of cameras into the Houses of Parliament, broadcasters and MPs were looking at other countries to see how they handled the relationship of television and their legislatures. A study by Holli Semetko for ITN found that twenty-six countries had TV coverage, varying from ceremonial proceedings such as formal openings, to full-scale live coverage of major debates and government committees.[21] Broadly the Commonwealth countries were slow to move towards coverage, so that Australia had covered formal openings of Parliament since 1956 but only experimented with live broadcasting in 1974.

France moved gradually to adapt its practice. In 1964 cameras were allowed into the National Assembly, though Minister's Question Time appeared on screen as recently as 1981. Live broadcasting of debates or edited versions still have to be authorised by the President of the National Assembly, as also happens in Austria.

On the matter of editorial control there is a wide spectrum of arrangements, ranging from almost total freedom at one extreme to firm political control at the other, as in France and Austria. Canada provides an interesting example of how fears about portraying a rowdy assembly can be handled. In 1977, when the cameras were first let in, the Whips insisted that the practice of banging desks during speeches, a Canadian equivalent of British barracking and jeering, should be halted as a precondition of the innovation. This did make proceedings more orderly. Another strict guideline laid down was that the cameramen should target only the speaker's head and shoulders.

It was borne in mind that attendance was sometimes sparse, and this avoided shots of an empty chamber. However, gaps were still exposed because of the shots over the shoulders, and so MPs were then encouraged to sit behind the speaker of the moment to create the impression of a busy and well-attended chamber; this was the practice known as 'doughnutting'. A 'flying quorum' of Members can, when orchestrated by the Whips, move to a different place to encircle whoever is speaking and give the false impression of a rapt and numerically significant audience. Without a wide shot of the chamber, the viewer has no other information.

Israel provides an example of a country which at first allowed relaxed rules concerning what could be broadcast. It began coverage of Knesset proceedings in 1969, and in the mid-1970s allowed the transmission of a live eight-hour debate continuously, on the only television channel available in Israeli households. Subsequently, more care was shown not to over-expose the population, but important debates are still covered and watched by almost the entire population. Acrimony in the chamber appeared to be good for television ratings.

*Guidelines under which the broadcasters operate*

Some advocates of television in the House would have liked to see continuous transmission of proceedings, as occurs in certain other countries. This might have been done by assigning the use of a special channel to political coverage. Inevitably, not every minute of the House's work is first-class entertainment, and although it would have given a more balanced picture of what Parliament is really like, it was felt that there would be insufficient interest to sustain an audience for very long on such a 'dedicated channel' as the main form of coverage (the Select Committee on Televising the Proceedings of the House did study the proposal for a dedicated channel, and eventually came down in favour of a tender from United Artists, which now runs the Parliamentary Channel as a non-profit enterprise on behalf of its owners, a group of UK cable operators. It began broadcasting in January 1992, using a signal delivered by satellite).

When the decision was made to go for an edited version, the House was keen to lay down rules on how broadcasters might go about their task. In what was said to be free reporting, curbs were quickly canvassed, such as no shots of MPs sleeping, no panning across empty benches, nothing except the talking heads. The broadcasters were dealing with politicians who were keen to be their own editors.

Bernard Ingham expressed his views in a meeting with the Prime Minister, John Wakeham and other senior Ministers:

> I think my view is accepted that the tighter the rules with which the experiment starts the better. The House can always relax them in the light of experience. It would be very difficult to tighten them during the experimental period unless the broadcasters were extraordinarily foolish.[22]

Many MPs, even of liberal disposition, shared his outlook, and the Select Committee laid down several restrictions in its report. It made detailed recommendations concerning the rules of coverage. The emphasis was on behaving in such a way that the dignity of the House and its proceedings would not be impaired, and that its function as a working body could be preserved; it was not primarily a place of entertainment.

Guidelines were given on the type of shot that could be used. Only the head and shoulders could be featured, and broadcasters were limited in that they could not show reaction shots and at times of 'grave disorder' (e.g. any rumpus in the Public Gallery) they were expected to focus on the dignified person of the Speaker. The strict rules under which television cameramen operated in the early stages meant that it was only the speaker's manner which mattered to the viewer, for there was little chance to see what else was going on in the Chamber.

In January 1990, some relaxation occurred; reaction shots of an MP clearly being referred to were allowed (though not in Question Time or Ministerial Statements) together with 'medium-range' shots of the Chamber some four rows behind the MP speaking or from the benches opposite; these group scenes were midway between the standard head and shoulders image and the wide-angle view. Zoom shots could depict a member in relation to colleagues in the vicinity. Yet in other ways the restrictions are still strict: 'the standard format for depicting the Member who has the floor should be a head and shoulders shot, not a close-up'.[23]

Many MPs are still wary of allowing more freedom to the cameramen for a reason given by Teresa Gorman: 'If the media were given the power to pan around then it would . . . change our behaviour. MPs would be constantly conscious of the camera and we'd have to sit there with plastered smiles on our faces all the time.' [24]

Channel 4 takes a contrary view, and reflects the frustration felt by some journalists who believe that they have free access in most television coverage and see no reason why it should be denied them in the House of Commons. For this reason, it shuns live coverage. Current Affairs editor, David Lloyd, sees the conditions as a denial of his journalists' freedom, and one which limits their capacity to fulfil their function: 'Broadcasters only have an interest in making an accurate account of what goes on.' [25]

Austin Mitchell has echoed such a view, noting that MPs have been unduly timid:

> the rules are over-indulgent to parliamentary dignity and inconsiderate of either television's needs or the viewer's interest . . . The needs of television as a medium and those of an electronic Hansard are different. Television needs to punctuate its coverage to add variety and interest by changes of shot; wide, close up, cutaway, reaction shot, change of angle to show context, move into close up etc. Yet from a Parliamentary point of view changes of shot are not televisual devices, but political statements. Cutaways to boredom detract from the speech. [26]

He forecasts that, in time, the House will relax the rules, once members become more accustomed to having the cameras in the House and learn to take them more for granted.

The Supervisor of Broadcasting, Margaret Douglas, accepts that 'the broadcasters would, in an ideal world, probably prefer that there were no such rules', but adds that 'there is general acceptance that [existing] coverage works reasonably well'.[27] She argues that total freedom, even if seemingly attractive, probably 'wouldn't actually look that different, even if we vested the broadcasters with that power'.[28] She recognises that for live broadcasts a variety of reaction and other shots might make for more interesting television, but notes that the same signal has to be acceptable 'for all extracts', including the edited ones which most people see. The point was elaborated by her predecessor, John Grist, when he mentioned the difficulty for a director who 'has to balance his/her cutaway shots politically . . . How can one balance a Labour yawn, a Conservative grimace or a Liberal attempt to intervene . . . free access to cutaways . . . puts the director . . . daily and hourly into making instantaneous political decisions.' [29]

The suspicions of MPs and their concern to preserve the dignity of the House explain why coverage is handled by a 'hybrid offspring of privatisation, retaining as much control as possible in the Commons, [whilst] foisting as much as possible of the expense on others'.[30]

### The situation today

Coverage falls into two main categories. There are the longer programmes which amount to the nearest thing so far to a televised *Hansard*. These include:

- **Westminster**, BBC2, a.m., 5–8 items, five days a week

- **The Parliament Programme**, C4, p.m., less formal, with interviews and previews of coming events, four days a week

- **A Week in Politics**, C4, a.m., highlights and interviews, Sunday only

- **Westminster Week**, BBC, p.m., survey of big issues

- **Westminster Live**, BBC, p.m., twice a week before, during and after Prime Minister's Question Time, plus coverage of other big events (e.g. Budget) and occasional debates (e.g. a Vote of Confidence).

- **Around Westminster**, regional reviews of the week on Sundays at 12 noon.

In addition there is the continuous unedited coverage provided by The Parliamentary Channel, via cable.

What most people know of the House comes from the shorter extracts. These are used in programmes such as *Channel 4 News* and *Newsnight*; for a wider audience, the BBC *Nine O'Clock News* and ITN's *News at Ten*, provide daily coverage of the bigger stories.

*The permanent arrangements for televising the House*

Permanent arrangements for the broadcasting of the House were finally approved in May 1991, and these covered both the Lords and the Commons, as well as committees. The service was to be run by an outside operator, on the basis of a public tender, with parliamentary control operating through a Supervisor of Broadcasting who would be responsible to the Select Committee which holds regular meetings.

The Parliamentary Broadcasting Unit Ltd, known as PARBUL, has fifteen directors, three drawn from each of the two Houses, plus the Supervisor, as well as seven from the broadcasting organisations and a Chairman appointed by the Speaker. The Company finances the staff and equipment for television coverage on the basis of shareholdings taken by the participating broadcasting organisations (BBC, ITV and Sky), and it supplies them with the 'clean feed'; the signal is contracted to CCT Productions Ltd.

Since 1992, the Parliamentary Recording Unit is charged with the task of providing MPs, Peers and broadcasters with video and audio material. This material is available to other bodies only by arrangement with the Select Committee on Broadcasting.

*The impact of television*

An early assessment of the impact of television was made by the Hansard Society in 1990.[31] The study was designed to examine the use of House of Commons material – from the Chamber and committees – in national broadcasting and in the regions. Concluding that the experiment had been a greater success than had seemed possible beforehand, it drew particular attention to:

1   An 80 per cent increase in the reporting of Commons affairs on national television, in spite of dramatic events occurring at the time in South Africa and Eastern Europe.

2   A substantial increase in Commons coverage in regional broadcasting, especially at the weekend, when backbench MPs were featured more than previously.

3   Less damage to the end-product than had been anticipated because of the restrictions on camera-use, especially after the easing of those limitations.

4   No increase in the frequency of 'disorder' in the House: on the four occasions when there was any disturbance, television was 'unlikely to have been the primary cause . . . all four came about because of genuine Commons concerns'.

5   A tendency for MPs to put down more questions for the daily ballot in the hope of their being seen on the screen.

6   A reasonable attempt at providing a 'fair spread' between ministers and backbenchers, national and regional interests, the Chamber and committees – though unavoidably, Ministers dominated the daily news.

7   The 'old story' of broadcasters to only take up those questions which the 'heavy' newspapers emphasise, and not to represent the wide range of matters discussed in the Commons.

8   A commendable attempt to achieve that political balance between the parties, which was a 'well-established practice' – though there were difficulties in regional broadcasting, for in some areas, such as that served by Anglia Television, there were fifty-nine Conservative MPs out of sixty, and this meant that the one exception seemed to be featured more than might have been expected; maverick Tories were used to ensure that critical views emerged, and 'outsiders' were brought into discussions to even up representation.

On the key question of increasing 'public interest and understanding of Commons affairs', there was a feeling among those in the study-group that the greater use of material concerning Westminster politics was an indication that broadcasters were convinced that there was a demand for such coverage. The report quoted the reactions of political pundits such as Glyn Mathias of ITN and John Cole of the BBC who had both sensed a better appreciation of what was happening in Parliament.

### An assessment

The effect of using edited headlights in news bulletins has inevitably been to concentrate attention on the main front-bench performers; only the amusing or hostile interventions of backbenchers receive the same treatment. Parliament is organised for gladiatorial contest, and much of the emphasis is inevitably upon questions and the responses to them. This makes the difficulty of being fair to everyone immediately apparent. Prime Minister's questions do not give an opportunity to anyone other than the Leader of the Opposition to follow up a point.

Question Time, with its swift repartee and varied subject-matter, is the stuff of good viewing, and all leaders in the period have been aware of the importance of making a good impression – hence the coaching in television techniques of which more is explained later in this section and on pp. 175–6. For the Conservatives, Mrs Thatcher was aware of the importance of 'getting it right' and viewers were conscious of a softer impression, whereas Mr Kinnock was anxious to be seen as responsible and statesmanlike.

Both performers in the Blair–Major duel are anxious to create a good image which could have a bearing on how the public perceives their suitability as prime-ministerial material at the next election. Advice has been sought from consultants about how to make the best use of their assets and minimise their deficiencies to enable them to put on their best show, for they know that television has raised the stakes of the weekly half-hour of banter across the despatch box.

Some politicians are critical of what they see as the farce of Question Time. Paddy Ashdown, the leader of the Liberal Democrats, has been scathing about 'the air of unreality, somewhere between farce and fantasy'[32] which is put on twice weekly, and Graham Allen, MP, similarly drew attention to a situation which has 'provided raucous sound-bites on the news and cult comedy for California'.[33] Others have echoed Alan Beith's forecast expressed back in 1985 that viewers 'would come to see this period as . . . a Punch and Judy show'.[34]

In giving evidence to the Procedure Committee in March 1995, Lord Callaghan, speaking with the authority of an ex-Prime Minister and elder statesman, was asked whether he thought television coverage had significantly affected the conduct of Question Time. He felt that the session had deteriorated, that 'the bludgeon had replaced the rapier' and claimed that 'in America, it is regarded as a comedy programme, and in Holland they view it with some contempt' – views from which his own opinion was not 'too far removed'.[35]

Sir Edward Heath, with similar qualifications and perhaps also a tendency to paint a picture of a golden age in the past when there was a greater courtesy between the combatants, agreed. He denounced the 'hideous shouting match', and added: 'I do not think that members on their feet screaming at each other can possibly have any idea what effect they are having.' [36] In as much as this decline has occurred, it may have had more to do with the lack of personal rapport and mutual respect between Neil Kinnock and Margaret Thatcher, who differed markedly in background, attitudes and values, and whose encounters were particularly abusive.

Other than at Question Time, the lively moments in the House, ones which yield memorable headlines because of the bang-crash-wallop of confrontation, do inevitably get more prime-time coverage than extracts from the hours of patient debate in which MPs often courteously argue with, and give way to, each other, or deliver often rather dull but informative speeches. Such debates would often be seen as rather tedious, the more so given the sanitised approach imposed upon the broadcasters by the Commons committee.

Understandably enough, the public like to hear and see excitement, and it is the dramatic occasions such as Mrs Thatcher's final performance which arouse interest and even fascination. The truth is that radio and television are not so interested in the substance of debates but in atmosphere and mood, in confrontation and the higher moments of drama. This is why the only regular live broadcast is Question Time, which takes up just half an hour a week out of a total sitting time of around forty hours.

The noise and organised barracking of some speakers, as Tory backbenchers sought to throw Mr Kinnock or indeed 'to get Mr Blair', have attracted adverse comment, but such features were there before the cameras arrived. In the Westland debate in 1986, Mr Kinnock was discomfited by the behaviour of the Tory heavy crew, 'the bovver boys', as their Deputy Chairman, John Maples, called them in December 1994. Maples was only too anxious that a telegenic Mr Blair should get a rough ride to tarnish his attractive image.

It would be difficult to sustain any suggestion that things have got seriously worse since television has arrived, even if the public perception of politicians has sunk in recent years. This has more to do with factors about the way in which they conduct themselves outside the House, than how they behave inside. The most dire forecasts of what might happen to MPs' behaviour have not materialised. If anything, the worst excesses have been tempered, as MPs know that it would damage their reputation if they were seen to be behaving in an unseemly manner. Some have done their image good by their skilful interventions and performances in debate.

Indeed, there is little evidence of a change in the way in which MPs address the House. There are occasional verbal pyrotechnics unrelated to the main themes of the debate, from some members who nurture the hope that their performance may get transmitted, but most MPs appear to realise that if they go in for the rhetorical flourish at the expense of any worthwhile comment, their efforts would lack credibility. Some may try and hog the cameras by spurious points of order or procedural gimmicks after Question Time when they think that the viewers might still be able to see what is going on, but such stunts are easily spotted and are likely to incur the hostility of other MPs and be irksome to the public. Inasmuch as they are exhibitionist and do behave badly, there is no reason why they should be able to protect themselves against public hostility by closing the windows on their squabbles.

Some MPs are keen to be in on the picture, and have a tendency to place themselves in a prominent position behind the Prime Minister at Question Time – like the Canadian 'doughnutting' to which we have referred. From such a vantage-point, they can be seen by the electorate, more especially by their constituents who know they are in attendance. Others are conscious of how they appear when the camera is in their direction, but any change of habits in this regard is small-fry. A few continue to behave in a way hardly calculated to enhance their image, and those who called out or lost their temper before have usually been the people who do so now.

Shrewd performers have been conscious of the need to adjust their language to make it intelligible to the voters. References to complex issues have been simplified, the classic example being the suggestion of a more retributive, perhaps even vindictive approach to issues of justice by Teresa Gorman. Speaking in a debate on crime and punishment, she urged that rapists should be disabled from repeating their offence. Her justification suggests her appreciation of the need to speak in accessible terms:

> When I complained that rapists should be castrated, if I'd said it in that way it wouldn't have got a fraction of the attention that it did; by saying that I thought we should cut off their goolies, the whole House roared and every pub across the land was talking about it that night. But how would I as a backbencher have ever got that amount of attention?[37]

No official advice was issued by the House authorities to MPs with regard to adapting to the requirements of the camera. Advice may have been issued by individual political parties to their members, and rumours that MPs had been approached by various image consultants were soon spreading around Westminster and in the press – but it was a matter for the firms and individuals concerned. In moving the loyal address on the Queen's Speech on 21 November 1989, Ian Gow (who was the first member to be televised under the new arrangements) commented on such stories at the beginning of his speech, referring to a circular he had received from one such consultant: 'The impression you make on television depends mainly on your image, 55 per cent with your voice, and body language accounting for 38 per cent of your impact. Only 7 per cent depends on what you are actually saying.' He went on to quote a part of the letter which appeared to be an extravagant claim as far as he was concerned: 'We can guarantee to improve your appearance through a personal and confidential image consultation. You will learn if you need a new hair style – and where to get it – and the type of glasses to suit your face.' He considered himself beyond redemption on both counts!

Barbara Follett is the style guru said to have convinced Labour MPs of the importance of looking good on television. Most of the Front Bench are said to have been 'Follettised'. She is credited with persuading the red-headed Robin Cook to slip into autumnal colours, browns and oysters. Harriet Harman is one of those Labour frontbenchers who has received the treatment and become what one Conservative MP referred to as 'tarted-up Labour women'; [38] she was transformed, in the words of a *Guardian* writer, 'from mumsy housewife into metropolitan sophisticate'.

## The reactions of politicians to the arrival of the cameras

Mrs Thatcher was quoted in *The Times* on 24 November 1989 as saying, 'It is going to be a different House of Commons.' [39] Having confessed that her first experience was that it was an ordeal even without television, but 'if you are not careful, you freeze'. David Amess (Con MP, Basildon) felt that the cameras had 'trivialised our proceedings and we have spoilt that very special atmosphere we had here'.[40] Always an opponent of the idea of letting the cameras in, he is contemptuous of the way in which some MPs have changed the way they behave and their appearance to suit the electronic media. He has drawn particular attention to a change in the appearance of Labour women, and notes, 'Socialists used to be scruffy, now they look smarter than Tories.' By December 1993, Michael Portillo regretted his vote in favour and later claimed in a controversial speech that television was undermining the reputation of Parliament; it encouraged the public to sneer at politicians and contributed to a mood of cynicism about our institutions.[41]

Such views are not typical of those of many MPs who have come to accept the age of television, and see benefits in its introduction. Many would disagree with Portillo and argue that any increased cynicism derives from other factors. They might point to better attendance at Question Time, and to the increased coverage which Parliament now gets in the media.

Television has done something to halt the decline of Parliament as an institution, and for many voters has given the political process new meaning; they can see and hear what is going on. In the past, MPs were only able to get a sounding-board for their ideas by getting an interview on the *Today* programme or on *Newsnight*, a freedom inevitably denied to the majority of them. Now the opportunity to be seen on television is available to all of them, though not necessarily at the time of their choosing.

They can be seen performing the hitherto unglamorous tasks of Select Committee investigation, for the profile of such work has been increased by television. The wish to be seen to be informed and conscientious is one that encourages MPs to devote time to their committee duties.

Ironically, at the very time when they can be seen about their work it remains the fact that some MPs seem ever more keen to seize the chance to grace the television shows or to give an interview on the College Green opposite the Palace of Westminster, and are less concerned about being active in the Chamber itself.

### The impact on style and appearance

When the House was televised for the first time, British politicians became more conscious of their appearance and manner. Attention was inevitably on the main performers, and Mrs Thatcher in particular. She had not shown much interest in the media and never usually watched herself on television; according to Bernard Ingham, she gave out the order 'Turn it off', whenever she came up on a set.[42] Yet she made an exception in preparing for the autumn experiment in 1989, and according to the Press Secretary 'spent some time looking at videos of the experimental coverage before the signal went out over public television'. Her experience brought two principal concerns – the danger, because of the angle of the camera, that the viewer would only see the top of her head if she read a speech, and the consequent need to inject greater bodily movement into her delivery. Ingham anticipated that 'her presence, her authority and her command' would prove an asset, and felt that her profound scepticism about the wisdom of televising Parliament was unwarranted, for she could only benefit from the innovation.

Of course performers of her reputation had long polished their performances in the rehearsal studios of BBC and ITV, and were tempered in the fire of live interviews. When the House went on air, several other less-schooled politicians – some of whom had opposed the experiment and thought it would damage the House's reputation – felt a need to check their profile.

Those who worried about the coming of the cameras wondered whether a certain understandable preening and practising would be carried to such an extent that it would change the nature of the House, and the public perception of it. The viewers were going to judge whether they wanted to listen largely on the basis of what they saw, and MPs were likely to be over-conscious of this.

Performing in the House is very different from performing in a studio. It is easier in that they can have a script in their minds if not in their hands, and will not be interrupted by an interviewer. Yet it is more difficult in that MPs cannot be seen to be playing or playing up for the benefit of the cameras; passion must be convincing.

The nearest approximation to Parliamentary television technique is speaking at party conferences, though here the attention is not just on the speaker's behaviour and posture, for the camera is free to keep a check on the Leader's reaction to colleagues' speeches or to roam among the ranks of listeners. Politicians at conferences have to appear to be holding the attention of the assembled mass, at the same time as making their mark in the viewer's living-room. They have to try to impress leaders without offending constituents. Above all, they have to appear to say what they mean and mean what they say. Some politicians believe that sincerity is the most important weapon, for the public will soon discern any who lack it.

Presence and body language are important too. Different politicians have adopted, consciously or unconsciously, different mannerisms, ranging from the Kinnock head-butt to Thatcher's goose-peck. Using the head and shoulders to effect is the more important in the House as that is what the viewer will normally see. Much of the overall impression is due to physical appearance, and viewers will form an initial reaction on the basis of what they see before a word has been uttered. The manner of delivery is also important and all these considerations impact before content can be viewed. The speaker has to make it possible for people to listen to what is said, without irritating distractions. The voice needs to be interesting and not monotonous.

In other words, it is vital for politicians to be able to get their message across within the limitations of the medium in which they work. They need advice on so doing, and this is where the various media gurus can be of obvious assistance – as we saw in the previous section.

## The reactions of MPs: a questionnaire

In an attempt to find out the views of a selection of MPs about the impact of television, the author devised a questionnaire and contacted Members to ascertain their attitude to 'letting the cameras in' (see Appendices). Of the fifty who replied, more than half were unwilling to complete the survey. Some were unprepared to give 'simple responses to questions which merited a detailed and lengthy answer', whilst others explained – often at some length – that constraints of time, in particular the demands of their constituents – prevented them from doing the task justice. Twenty-four others recognised that a brief answer (or merely a tick without a comment) would suffice and be of use in helping me to develop an overall assessment of Members' reactions.

The detailed findings are included in the Appendices, but the conclusions can be seen in the box on p. 172.

## Conclusion

Political discourse is made for television, in the sense that the drama of the big occasion or the confrontationalism of QuestionTime make good spectacle. It is, of course, not a show put on for the benefit of the television journalists, but it is the place where democratic debate by elected representatives occurs. If the public enjoys the drama of the occasion, then that is something to which they are entitled. Parliament is televised partly as entertainment, but more a public service to inform people about what is happening.

For big occasions, there is a substantial audience and issues such as the debate on VAT on fuel in December 1994 have aroused considerable public interest. Many debates are inevitably less appealing, and there are occasions when proceedings are tedious and pedestrian, but there is usually something worth televising, be it only Question Time, a Minister's statement followed

**Responses to a 1995 questionnaire**

Of the fifty MPs approached, twenty-four MPs agreed to answer the questions asked. Although the persons contacted represented a balance of the party membership in 1995, this was not true of the replies. A majority of these were from the Labour benches, though a few Conservatives but no Liberal Democrats provided a response; one SNP and one Plaid Cymru member also gave their opinions. Similarly, although some declared opponents of televising the House were approached, they were not among the respondents.

The findings were as follows:

| | Yes | No | Don't know |
|---|---|---|---|
| A supporter of the experiment | 24 | | |
| Preferred a dedicated channel | 18 | 4 | 2 |
| Coverage fair to: | | | |
|   a. all parties | 22 | 2 | |
|   b. backbenchers | 10 | 14 | |
| Too much emphasis on QT | 22 | 2 | |
| Value of QT deteriorated | 10 | 12 | 2 |
| Reputation of House suffered because of broadcasting QT | 7 | 14 | 2 |
| Television beneficial because it: | | | |
|   a. promotes greater awareness | 24 | | |
|   b. brings Parliament closer | 18 | | |
|   c. restores importance of Westminster | 8 | | |
|   d. stimulates better attendance | 2 | | |
|   e. promotes better behaviour | | | |
|   f. helps bring about modernisation of Parliament | 10 | | |
|   g. other considerations | 2 | | |
| Possible adverse effects: | | | |
|   a. encourages MPs to speak to constituents rather than fellow MPs | 6 | 12 | |
|   b. destroys intimacy of House | 2 | 18 | |
|   c. emphasises gladiatorial aspect | 20 | 4 | |
|   d. lighting/cameras intrusive | | 20 | |
| Rules too restrictive | 16 | 4 | 4 |
| Other doubts | 4 | 20 | |
| Any impact on personal manner/behaviour | 2 | 22 | |
| 'Follettised'? | | 24 | |

by subsequent Opposition protests. What gets the attention are the moments of great Parliamentary drama and clashes of principle, but people are entitled to see it as it is, whether the extracts of the day are exciting or less stimulating. As Robin Day put it in 1963, 'Television would let Parliament be seen for what it is; most of the time a workshop, and some of the time a theatre.'[43]

Parliament must work with the tools of the age, and television of its proceedings has established what Bevan meant by 'intelligent communication between the House of Commons and the electorate as a whole'. To shut itself off from the prime medium of communication was to diminish its importance. By allowing the cameras in, Parliament has emphasised its importance as the prime forum for political debate.

At some stage, the televising of Parliament was inevitable, the more so once the radio microphones were allowed in and the Lords opened its doors. Now that it has happened it is difficult to see what all the fuss was about, and it is accepted as natural by most viewers. The arguments against seem as arcane and futile as were the debates about whether to allow the press in to report about Parliament. Television producers are no less responsible than the average newspaper executive, and no less concerned to protect the status of Parliament,

There is no evidence that the democratic process has been harmed. Some would say that it has been enhanced, for Parliament is better known and understood by the nation at large, and the public is more aware of what goes on inside Westminster. If that means that they know more of the defects of the system, then that is a by-product, arguably a desirable one. It is up to the party managers in the House to put its procedures in order, and to ensure that MPs behave or perform their duties in a manner pleasing to the electorate.

## The political interview

In the age of television, political interviews have become one of the most significant means of political communication. Not only are they a means of establishing facts, probing motives and holding politicians to account for their attitudes and behaviour; they are also influential in establishing their reputations. Hence, the [over-stated] comment of Bruce that: 'Interviews are not about the search for knowledge, they are about performance'.[44]

In spite of their importance, the genre has been generally neglected by writers and commentators on the political scene.[45]

### The development of the political interview

If interviewing was slow to develop in election coverage, it had been used to cross-examine politicians at other times for some years. Some of the first lengthy sessions had been conducted back in the 1950s, and those in *Face to*

*Face* were particularly probing. That series did not use politicians, but the idea of the in-depth study was becoming accepted. ITN arranged some lengthy interviews by Robin Day of President Nasser and Harold Macmillan later in the decade, and thereafter they were used regularly to question party leaders and other figures during the lifetime of a Parliament.

Early BBC interviews were scripted, and questions were submitted to politicians in advance, but ITN did not go in for this less demanding arrangement. *Election Forum* involved three interviewers, who firstly sifted through some 11,000 postcards sent in by the general public, and then asked Mr Heath and Mr Wilson a selection of their enquiries. No questions were composed by the journalists involved.

In the 1970s, the procedure developed during election campaigns, and in 1979 *Panorama* used a different format by which the questioner, Robin Day, had two MPs from the previous Parliament on either side of him. They then interviewed a leading Tory spokesman, and vice versa. By then the habit of the 'star interview' had become familiar over more than a decade, a format in which a skilled professional sought to pin down a leading political figure.

Since the 1960s, the practice of interviewing politicians has become well established as a widely accepted part of the political scene. Interviews have become more incisive and penetrating, and in response the politicians have had to rise to the challenge. Public figures are questioned in greater depth, and the 'supplementaries' of a resourceful interviewer can elicit useful information and sometimes trap politicians into revealing more of their true thinking than they intended to do. At its best, the interview can stimulate the performer and entertain the public.

As the popularity of the genre developed, changes began to appear. Not only did the number of such interviews and interviewers increase, but styles changed as well. Some questioners are offensive and harassing, others are seemingly gentler and more exploratory in their technique. Many sessions, such as those by Brian Walden or Jonathan Dimbleby, are now lengthy, sometimes lasting for approaching an hour.

As the set-piece confrontation developed, so its importance has been recognised, not only by the politicians and those who organise their appearances. Newspaper editors often seize upon their content for the next morning's editorial, and any striking observation – or even worse, any slip – can make a headline on an evening news bulletin.

In 1992, there were many formal extended interviews, and on *Panorama*, *Walden*, *Newsnight*, *This Week* and other such programmes, the party leaders were exposed to scrutiny, in short interviews or in more lengthy encounters. Today, particularly at the weekend, television and radio political programmes abound. If one of the frequent criticisms of television coverage of politics is that it is preoccupied with soundbites, that complex issues are too often relegated to three-minute slots between other items in the news, then the Sunday interview is the antidote to this. Moreover, these shows appear to survive in the audience market, otherwise producers would not sanction additional lunchtime sessions. As coverage of political issues in the press appears to have diminished, so interrogators have siezed the baton of political reporting.

## The need for a good performance

### Coaching the candidate

Political parties, via their campaign managers, have realised the importance of television, and spend much effort on coaching their standard-bearers in media technique. Candidates and their advisers are only too aware of the need to react spontaneously to the different style of questioning on offer. The interview is potentially a disaster area, for a slip-up could be highly costly to the chances of personal or party electoral success. Senator Edward Kennedy's failure to offer a coherent response to a question on why he wanted to run for the Presidency in 1983 much discredited him in the eyes of his mass audience, and dealt a serious blow to his chances of appealing to a wide sector of the American public. Hence the need for assistance to be given to politicians over how to conduct themselves.

An interesting example of the effectiveness of teaching a candidate about how he should react concerns the experience of the Republican, George Bush, in the 1988 Presidential election campaign. He was confronted by an experienced CBS reporter, Dan Rather, and Roger Ailes (who was serving as the political consultant) requested that the interview be live 'down the line', with Bush at his office in Washington, and Rather at studios in New York. The advantage was that Bush could be prompted by Ailes throughout the interview, and when difficult questions were asked about the candidate's role in the Arms for Hostages controversy, he could hold up key words to assist the candidate in his response.

The confrontation made good television, even if it added little to the sum of information known beforehand. Given the necessary prompting, Bush was able to react aggressively, at one point turning the tables on Rather and putting him on the spot. By so doing, Bush's image as a 'wimp' was made to look unreal, and it was he rather than Rather who seemed to be in control.

In *You are the Message* (Doubleday: New York, 1988), Ailes describes how he and his team have a formula on how a candidate should respond, $Q = A+1$. If Q is the question, then A is the concise answer which should be given before the interviewee adds on any key points they wish to make from their own agenda (the +1 factor). Using this formula, the candidate conveys the impression which they wish to leave. They are also advised to admit to an occasional error, the more so if it is one which seems to indicate their basic goodness, if slight naivety, when faced with people much worse than them. An admission of guilt can defuse a hostile line of questioning, though the technique bears little repetition lest it convey the image of an error-prone politician.

Another technique is to ensure that the candidate adjusts their mood to that of the interrogator. If the tone is hostile, then the candidate needs to be relaxed and calm, for this conveys the impression that candidates are the master of their emotions, however aggressive and threatening the situation. Some consultants suggest that what is said is less important than how it is said, and they teach candidates how to improve their non-verbal communication. Glen Berlin, President of Berlin Training and Development, stresses the value of ensuring that the overt message is in tune with the subliminal one; otherwise doubt is cast on sincerity.[46] He attaches importance to the way in which a tutee stands or sits, and to the gestures which he gives. Jabbing a finger can look aggressive, whereas standing with hands held together in front of you can look as if you're defensive (the 'fig-leaf' posture). Similarly, he stresses that his students should not invade the space of the interviewer, by leaning forward too far.

Emphasising the crucial significance of non-verbal communication, he remarks that: 'Smart candidates will make sure that their non-verbal messages are congruent with the verbal messages, thereby dramatically increasing the probability of being understood, believed and elected.'[47]

There are differences between the American and British experience. In the US, consultants exercise more control over the way in which interviews are conducted, and the straight British-style approach, in which interviewers ask unscripted questions, is less frequently employed.

### The reactions of interviewees

Of late, doubt has been cast on the value of these interviews, some of which are seen to be undemanding and predictable. Moreover, skilled performers have become effective in parrying the line of questioning, so that answers fail to illuminate key issues or indeed make good television. Although there is always the prospect that there might be a slip, most politicians have been so well prepared for the encounter that they avoid the possible pitfalls.

Butler and Kavanagh quote an editor of the *Today* programme as speculating on whether these interviews retained a value in their current form. He asked: 'Did people actually learn anything from them? Did they tell us anything new?'[48] He wondered whether it was time to take another look at them, and cast doubt on whether they have a future. This theme has been taken up by Sir Robin Day.

Day has argued that although there is now more time allocated to interviews, and that there are more of them, the method has of late lost some of its value.[49] In a symposium meeting to discuss the coverage of the 1987 election, he observed that in the days of Macmillan, Heath and Wilson, it was possible to extract more information than is available from politicians today. Although such figures answered questions in their own style and on occasion could be evasive, they did generally address the question which was being asked.

He believes that, in more recent times, politicians have become more adept at ignoring the question altogether:

> The significance, value and appeal of the big television interview has de-clined. For different reasons, but with similar results, Margaret Thatcher and Neil Kinnock developed a technique which devalued the interview as an instrument of democratic scrutiny. They were both determined to make the television interview a platform of their own. The interviewer's questions, or attempts at questions, were treated as tiresome interruptions to the statistical hammering of Thatcher or the repetitious rhetoric of Kinnock. To prevent the monotony of a monologue, the interviewer was forced to butt in when he could, if he could.[50]

Mr Kinnock and Mrs Thatcher were in his mind prime examples of politicians who took the view 'to hell with the television interviewer, we are going to say what we want to say'. As a source of information, therefore, interviews with them had less impact than they once would have done. They came carefully prepared, with their mind full of particular items from the party programme which they wished to impart, having been coached by their media advisers on how to respond. They steam-rollered interviewers with their preconceived answers.

They evaded answering the question by adopting different techniques. Whereas Mrs Thatcher was forceful and sometimes hectoring, often rounding on the interviewer and questioning his (most are male) assumptions, Mr Kinnock sometimes did the same, although he also used a technique employed by John Major. This involved the admission that he either did not know or was unprepared to give the answer: 'I'm not going to say what you're asking me to.' It risks conveying the image of being ill-informed or unhelpful, but it can also come across as being straightforward. In the case of Neil Kinnock, he also answered at greater length, and although this could suggest that he was informed, at worst it could make him seem like the 'Welsh windbag' that his critics discerned.

Two lecturers at York University, Peter Bull and Kate Mayer, have analysed the techniques used by Kinnock, Thatcher and Major, and having pointed to the differences, have found that the common factor was that for at least half the time they did not answer the questions asked.[51] In the case of Kinnock, he spoke for 74 per cent of the interview, compared with 64.5 per cent for John Major. The research provided a number of examples of the methods adopted to evade answering. It provides an illuminating typology of non-re-plies, dividing techniques for avoidance into eleven categories:

1  Ignoring the question.

2  Acknowledging the question without answering it.

3  Questioning the question.

4  Attacking the question (e.g. that it is based on a false premise or is factually inaccurate).

5  Attacking the interviewer.

6  Declining to answer.

7  Making a political point.

8  Giving an incomplete answer.

9  Repeating an answer to a previous question.

10  Stating or implying that the question has already been answered.

11  Apologising.

Making political points was by far the most frequent approach adopted by both Margaret Thatcher and Neil Kinnock. After this, came attacking the question. Unique to the former was a tendency to attack the interviewer, as in this extract.[52] Sir Robin asked the Prime Minister which was, in her view, the greater evil as an outcome to the 1987 election; a coalition between Thatcherism and the Alliance and other minority parties, or letting in a Kinnock minority government committed to socialism and unilateral disarmament. Mrs Thatcher replied: 'Nothing you say will trap me into answering what I do not believe will happen or trap me into saying . . . er . . . precisely how we would react to that circumstances you know I might indeed I would consult my Cabinet colleagues the very thing you've accused me of not doing'. Sir Robin responded: 'I didn't accuse you of anything, Prime Minister, you keep on accusing me of accusing you of things.' The authors of the study note that the example was entirely consistent with the aggressive strategies so often adopted, 'in which Thatcher was found to wrong-foot interviewers and put them on the defensive by making frequent objections to interruptions, by personalising issues and by taking questions and criticisms as accusations'.[53]

Of course those who are interviewed are entitled to use the tactics which enable them to cope with what for many of them, under the heat and glare of the lighting, is something of an ordeal. They know that reputations can be won and lost, and that a serious slip can damage their standing, and there may not be a chance to correct any error which anyway may not be realised at the time. The situation is a tense one, and the temptation to argue a point and become involved in an altercation is sometimes difficult to resist – though such disputation can seem petty and off putting to the listener.

Day's argument is open to dispute, for in seeming to suggest a golden age when interviewees answered the question one comes up against the experience of Heath and Wilson. Others in the symposium were less convinced about the ease of interviewing Heath, and many observers would conclude that Harold Wilson was very adept at dealing with those who sought to elicit information. He was capable of being most evasive, and had discovered a useful ploy to play for time. Having received a difficult question, he would appear to preoccupy himself with lighting his pipe, and the pause involved served to take the sting out of the situation. It also made him seem relaxed and unperturbed by the question. Gerald Kaufman, who served as his parliamentary press officer, saw a different side to Robin Day:

> He didn't go to the studio to answer questions; the questions were an irrelevance which had to be listened to. He went there to say something. He decided what he wanted to say – the message he wanted to communicate to the people who were watching and then, regardless of the questions that were put to him, he said what he meant to say.[54]

The use of particular phrases such as 'Let me tell you why I disagree with that', 'The best way I can answer that' or 'That's an important point, but more important is the fact that . . .' can defuse the intensity of the occasion.

Politicians are defensive about their performance and tend to blame the interviewer for rarely letting them develop their view. They feel that too often, as they are developing a key point, they are cut off and pressed on some aspect – the whole being designed to expose some disagreement or disunity within the party. Tony Benn has articulated this point, suggesting that 'politics, as conveyed by television, is largely confined to the tense, urgent contest of the studio interview', which at best can be illuminating and instructive: 'At their worst, they can be humiliating and degrading'.[55]

He laments the inability of the politician to develop his views at length, for the professional broadcaster is so aware of what makes good television that the tendency is to cut in and cut off the response. He particularly objects to the fact that the person who is doing the interview is not a person who has ever been elected to anything himself, and that broadcasters often have an inflated view of their own importance. Like other politicians, he is very aware that the public can form an impression of the character of politicians as a result of the way they respond under fire. Any fudge or flannelling will be spotted by the more discerning listener, and interruptions designed to bring the interviewee to the point can be embarrassing and dent credibility.

Broadcasters tend to see the lengthy answer as an excuse to meander away from the subject, and make statements of little relevance to what is being asked. Hence Day's observation that:

> I have interviewed politicians for 50 minutes at length and still at the end of that they haven't answered the question in a reasonable way. At the last election after one 40-minute interview, my taxi-driver the next morning would say, 'Very interesting, last night! Yes. Did you understand a bloody word 'e said? Never answers the question does 'e'?[56]

The gist of his remarks is that the big interview has been taken over by the politicians, and that it has lost much of its value. 'You don't have a dialogue with these political leaders. You don't really achieve anything very much.'

The television interview ought to be one of the voter's few defences against what David Butler would see as the advent of 'professionalism' in elections. This is a surprising comment for a skilled interviewer, and it may reflect Day's own difficulties in coping with the forceful personality of Mrs Thatcher. In any case, if it was true that the main party leaders of the 1980s tried to hijack the interview, then the performances of John Major and others since her time have been less less successful in dominating the agenda.

There have always been politicians who don't answer questions, and Glyn Mathias of ITN disagreed at the 1987 symposium on the success of interviewing Ted Heath. From his experience of eliciting only an oft-repeated set-piece answer, he concluded that attempts to take over and evade the issue were not such a recent phenomenon. He described Enoch Powell as a difficult person to interview, for he was adroit in sidestepping the question, for 'if he was really in a corner [he] would quote to you in Latin! . . . and if he thought the interviewer was likely to understand, he would quote in Greek'.[57]

Some big interviews can be particularly revealing, and Peter Riddell felt that whereas Mrs Thatcher's speeches were carefully crafted by her advisers in interviews she was liable to say something more interesting. Before she became Prime Minister she talked of the danger of the country being swamped by immigrants, and similarly her views on Victorian values and the Welfare State were often more clearly revealed on those occasions. She often revealed more than she perhaps originally intended.

## The position of the interviewer

Interviews are live in one of two ways. They can be in the sense that they are conducted at the time of transmission, sometimes in difficult circumstances, when the setting is noisy, the atmosphere dramatic, and the politician in a hurry to get away – as across the road from the Palace of Westminster, on The Green. If not, they are live, in that once recorded as live, they go out without any editing. From the interviewer, they require a high degree of skill and an ability to think 'on the spot'. They are conducted in the presence of the great and the mighty who govern us, some of whom are star performers in stage-managing their performance. The interview is being watched by millions of people, some of them experts in the field under discussion, be they economists, businessmen, diplomats or world leaders. The party managers will also be keeping a keen eye out for any signs of distortion or bias.

Interviewers must be aware of the background against which they operate. They wish to advance their own career and therefore need to win the approval of those who run their organisations. This imposes pressures upon them to deliver a strong performance, for example they are likely to be aware of the fact that the person they are questioning could possibly be at some time now or in the future in a position of authority over them. He or she might be a member of a government which has to make key decisions on the future of the medium, such as deciding on the survival of the licence fee. It may be that in that capacity he or she will have the power of appointment to a senior position in their hands. If the interviewer 'roughs the interviewee up', then this could provoke revenge.

Prior to the interview itself, some politicians have been known to be difficult over what topics they will or will not answer questions on. Warnings can be given of complaints to the Director-General if the line of cross-examination seems unduly hostile, and the hierarchy of the BBC, for instance, will be anxious not to offend senior politicians currently in power. In early 1994, John Humphrys was accused by Lord Tebbit of being unfair in an interview about the Westminster Council 'scandal'. He threatened Humphrys with his solicitor. Because of such constraints, the interviewer has to consider carefully the 'rules of engagement' prior to the event actually being recorded.

In the difficult sets of circumstances under which they may be expected to operate, interviewers must be lucid and cogent, and ask short and direct questions, whether they be prepared or asked off the cuff. They must choose their words with care to avoid committing any libel, for there is no legal filter to check observations. In addition, they must be tenacious; the viewer is expecting them to press the case with some force, discontinuing any line of questioning which is proving unproductive, but asking penetrating supplementaries whenever the answer is difficult to extract.

The questioner needs to be knowledgeable about the subject, and the expert performer will spend time in the House observing what goes on and how politicians react, to decide how they should best be handled. Interviews by chat-show hosts or personalities are unlikely to be so demanding or informed, and are more concerned with getting to know a person better rather than drawing out information and pinning down particular views.

Interviewing also involves the capacity to make quick decisions at the precise moment, for as we have seen most interviewers are functioning under the critical gaze of the audience, although in recent years some encounters in the studio have been conducted whilst instructions are dictated by the producer through an earpiece. Such prompting is not used by the 'big names' and is anyway impossible in live interviews conducted in unusual situations.

## Interviewers and their techniques

Much depends on the resourcefulness of the interviewer, and his grasp of the arguments. Experience derived from listening to politicians in the House can be very useful, and even if they lack expertise in economics they can still conduct an effective interrogation. The styles and techniques of the different interviewers are in marked contrast to each other; for instance, Bruce has noted that David Dimbleby, like David Frost, has 'a kind of insouciant self-confidence which sustains him during an interview', and is fond of the 'past words and present contradictions' and the 'differences with colleagues' ploys.[58]

The approach can vary according to who is being interviewed. Some questioners are rude and aggressive, a criticism once made of Robin Day who, however, came to be regarded as almost too pro-Establishment in his handling of big names, with whom he seemed to be on friendly terms. In the relaxed atmosphere of the *Breakfast with Frost* programme, several guests have committed themselves in a way they might regret, their remarks then being picked up by all the news broadcasts for the rest of the day and pored over in the Sunday newspapers. Frost adopts a looser style of questioning, which politicians tend to like in that it enables them to convey their message. Rather than detailed and precise examination, he goes in for the more general approach before zoning in on issues which may be of interest and wider appeal. However, he can interrupt effectively when someone needs to be brought to answer the main point.

John Humphrys admits to being considered aggressive in his approach and has had difficulties or 'run-ins' with some politicians.[59] He prefers a different term: 'I'd say persistent. We should not allow politicians just to get their message across.' [60] He has been compared to a terrier rather than a rottweiler, one 'who regards the interviewee like a bone to cling on and chew . . . "He catches on extremely quickly and can instantly find a hole in a weak argument. He then loves to exploit it." Unlike most presenters, Humphrys is not bothered about ending an interview at peace with the interviewee.' His co-presenter of the *Today* programme, John Naughtie, has also had rows with leading figures, notably when Neil Kinnock made it clear that he was not going to be 'bloody kebabed' by him. Generally, however, the Naughtie style is a less argumentative or confrontational one, though inevitably the technique varies with the interviewee.

Among the most searching interviews were those conducted on the *Walden* programme, on which Brian Walden perfected a forensic style of questioning, in which he persistently probed at a particular theme, asking almost the same question in a slightly different way several times, then summing up what was said to that stage in a way which meant that the politician had committed himself more than he or she realised. It was a logical process of analysis, which could only be handled by a very canny, professional politician, such as as John Smith or Cecil Parkinson.

On such occasions, the manner is argumentative more than merely interrogative, and the questioner seeks to have a discourse with the interviewer. Questions are not so much questions, more propositions and opinions to which a reaction is invited. As such, encounters can be a fine intellectual exercise for the connoisseur, 'as the best intellectual conversation can be'. In prime-time interviews, such an approach would be less viable, for the viewer is waiting to see how the politician reacts under scrutiny, and is not expecting to see an opinionated, self-indulgent questioner. He is there as an aid to prompt the politician rather than as a star performer in his or her own right.

The style of *Walden* and *On the Record* is not popular with all politicians for it can ruthlessly unmask a lack of logic or rigidity in their thinking. Whereas some relish exposing themselves to this type of scrutiny, others are more wary. Among the critics of this technique, one media guru outlined a familiar objection: 'A very precise line of attack with subsidiary questions rehearsed for each answer means that the interviewer spends 20 minutes or more fruitlessly trying to get the interviewee to accept a highly damaging proposition.'[61] Many politicians dislike this, knowing the most they can hope for is to avoid producing a gaffe for the Monday papers. But the programme is respected for its academic approach and most Cabinet Ministers accept they must do it occasionally, he conceded.

## The responses of the politicians

For any politician, the ability to deal spontaneously with difficult questions from a range of interviewers is important, though each has his or her own favourite, and there are those whom they seek to avoid. Mrs Thatcher was noted as someone who 'elevated interviews into a quasi-Royal event, in which the lucky recipient of an audience may petition for a few moments of her time. Those who refuse to play the forelocking footman go on an "enemies' list" kept by her Press Secretary.' Brian Walden was her favourite for the very serious encounter, but she was keen to appear on the Radio 2 *Jimmy Young Show*, where she felt she could convey her message without being probed too awkwardly. Under examination from someone like the Dimbleby brothers, she could be more exposed.

In 1987, questioned by David Dimbleby, she let slip an ill-chosen phrase when she spoke of people who showed concern about the level of poverty and provision for the needy, as those who 'just drool and drivel they care' – an unwise choice of phrase, as she quickly realised and for which she apologised on three occasions. (The incident interestingly illustrates the desire of the BBC not to cause even greater offence to the Government than it was often then doing. Recorded in the morning for evening showing, the extract could have been revealed on news bulletins at any time throughout the day, as Central Office feared might happen. In fact, it was not shown in any bulletin until after transmission of the interview, and then only as the last item in a fifty-minute programme – too late for it to be exploited by the opposition parties or journalists, as this was the last day of the campaign.)

Denis Healey, in *The Time of My Life*, has written of his liking for the tough interview as his preferred means of influencing public opinion. For him, Robin Day was the supreme example of a professional who had done his homework properly,

> remorseless, but always fair in his pursuit of a straight answer. Thanks to a first-rate research team, Brian Walden was an effective expositor, but he used to irritate me by summing up my argument so as to suit his own case rather than to remind the viewer of what I had actually said. Peter Jay . . .

had the most powerful mind of all; but he was sometimes more anxious to demonstrate that fact than to explore my views.[62]

*Viewer involvement*

An innovation of recent years has been the way in which members of the public have been able to put questions directly to leading politicians. Sometimes this is done on radio phone-in programmes during the lifetime of a Parliament, but elections provide a particularly good opportunity. Things have come a long way since the original *Election Forum*, for now people ask their own questions and can – allowing for the constraints of time – be more insistent on getting their questions answered.

The advantage here is that whereas (as Day suggests) some politicians have become so adroit in avoiding or ignoring the nub of the challenge that the big interview has lost some of its value, they are under a very different form of scrutiny from voters whom they cannot treat with disdain. Using the public also avoids the danger of what Sir Robin has recognised as 'a little Establishment sword play. Ordinary people talk a little more uncouthly and more freshly.'[63] In *On The Record*, there is a studio of animated members of the public who reveal a deep grassroots interest in the question of the day. Ministers tend to be wary of studio audiences, for the questions are less predictable than those of professional interviewers, and they can be tougher and asked with evident conviction.

In recent election campaigns, the technique of voters challenging politicians directly has been used extensively. It was in 1983 that Mrs Thatcher was famously grilled by a caller, Diana Gould, who questioned her view of the sinking of the *Belgrano* in the Falklands War. Whereas on occasion interviewers have to sit back and accept some stick when the interviewee rounds on them, the lady in question was not versed in the traditional codes and proceeded to challenge the Prime Minister's 'unreason' with her own. It was a bruising and unsettling episode, which made the party a little more wary about about exposing its leader to such a dialogue in the following election.

Much depends on how informed and persistent the questioner is. On *Election Call* in 1987, Mrs Thatcher was able to sidestep one caller with agility. When a nurse asked an awkward question about the Health Service, he was in turn asked 'Where is your hospital?' On hearing that it was 'Mold in North Wales', the Prime Minister replied 'Yes, I know. I was there the other day, you've got a very good hospital with five new dialysis machines', and fourteen this, that and the other.'[64]

In 1987 there were several formats designed to promote such participatory discussion, with electors able to challenge politicians – sometimes on the basis of greater acquaintance with the facts, sometimes based upon their own personal experiences of the situation, be it unemployment or health. Butler and Kavanagh record how in 1992 Neil Kinnock was confronted with a trade unionist who on the basis of her experience of the introduction of equal pay was certain that Labour's policy of a statutory minimum wage would damage prospects for employment, a topic on which Tony Blair also found himself challenged.

Michael Heseltine was similarly wrong-footed by a questioner who wondered how the public could ever trust a man such as he, for by challenging Mrs Thatcher in 1990 he had effectively 'stabbed her in the back'. Other such encounters took place not just on national programmes such as *Election Call* and *The Granada 500*, but in the regions where, for instance, ITV's *Central Choice* arranged similar opportunities.

## The television interview: an assessment

Television interviews have developed into something of an art form. At their best, they are a reasoned dialogue, and although different interviewers and politicians have different techniques, the result is a productive contribution to political debate. Politicians are on the spot and what can develop is a conversation, with questions answered in a reasonable, direct way. At other times, the outcome can be a relentless grilling, in which the politician seeks shelter in evasion.

As the ability of the politicians to cope with questioners becomes more professional, then this requires new techniques on the part of the interviewer. Some answers can be prepared or scripted or learnt by heart, but not all. The answers cannot be on a teleprompter as for a speech to camera. The spin-doctors, the image-makers, the PR wizards and others can advise on voice, on posture and on manner. Politicians can be professionally coached about what to say and how to say it, but once the interview has started the politician is alone. An interview on television is one public act which is not wholly in the hands of the ad-men, the propagandists or the marketing men.

Of course, sometimes the questions can be anticipated, and before an interview usually some guidelines are established about what they can be asked. Hence the touchiness of politicians when on the *Today* programme, having been called in to answer on one subject, they sometimes find themselves answering on another. But even if the topic is predictable, the actual question cannot always be guessed, nor can the way in which the interviewer chooses to develop the line of argument.

Some people regard interviews with some scepticism and see them as having more to do with the vanities of all involved. In the professional journal, *Broadcast*, a current affairs producer expressed this refrain, in his observation that:

A presenter – relaxed, charismatic, incisive questioner – meets politician, confident and well-trained in deflecting even minor questions. And so it goes, each understanding the other's strategy, but rarely being politically significant or revealing; more of a psychological gameshow than current affairs.[65]

Others claim that the days of star interviewing are over, that as a political device the performers are now too used to dealing with media men. Too often, interviews become something of a fencing match, in which the politician parries the thrust, and ducks and weaves to avoid the next rapier thrust.

For all of the deficiencies of the method, in particular the difficulties of interviewing politicians and getting answers which the viewer wants, the interview has great value. It is a means of securing the accountability of politicians for their own and their party's behaviour. The right to question those in authority is an essential one in a democratic society, and the question and answer format is an established way of conducting an argument and imparting facts and opinions.

At its best, conducted by an able person with knowledge and style, a television interview is not only good television but a way of cross-examining a politician and illuminating problems. It is also an opportunity for the audience to form a view of the character and honesty of the public figure being interrogated. Their strength is that they are not based on whispered conversations with spin-doctors but benefit from visibility and accountability. They are the viewer's defence against the professional, against the manipulation of the media. A Cabinet Minister interviewed live on television cannot declare his or her opposition to the single currency, and then subsequently ask not to be identified. It's not just a coincidence that one of the Sunday shows is called *On the Record*.

As Robin Day has put it:

> Television interviews are one way by which political leaders can be genuinely open to questioning of a critical, informed and challenging nature. When a politician is interrogated on television, it is one of the rare occasions outside Parliament where his or her performance cannot be completely manipulated or packed or artificially hyped.[66]

Today, interviews are an established part of political communication, and politicians who as a breed were once suspicious of the medium and unwilling to submit themselves to its demands, now seek out with some enthusiasm an opportunity to get on the air. Their managers seek to book appointments in advance, and Bernard Ingham has recorded that it was one of his prime duties to book appearances. In an age when the viewer could not see them in their natural setting in the House, it became a desirable practice 'to get on the box'.[67] Some of them become familiar, established star performers by this method.

One of the difficulties is that not all politicians have such access to the studios. Some are regular performers, and inevitably the concentration is on the leading names which the public wants to see. This was an argument advanced many years ago by Nye Bevan for letting the cameras into the House:

Recently, and not only recently but for many years now, there has grown up what I consider a most humiliating state of affairs in which Members of the House are picked out to take part in television broadcasts at the *ipse dixit* of the bureaucracy at Broadcasting House. In fact, there has been nothing more humiliating than to see Members of Parliament in responsible positions selected by unrepresentative persons to have an opportunity of appearing on the radio or television . . . Also, what is almost worse, political alternatives are not placed before the people in a realistic fashion because of the selection of speakers that takes place.[68]

Inevitably, there are many MPs who rarely if ever are asked to appear, for the producer is influenced by considerations of experience, authority and standing, and television expertise; sometimes the party demands that only an acceptable spokesperson should appear. Television of the House answers one of these difficulties, and gives access to all. Now a party leader can be questioned by those who have been themselves elected. But this does not detract from the value of the probing interview by an incisive interrogator, and particularly in the election campaign when the House is not sitting, interviews provide an invaluable opportunity for the public to see those who aspire to lead them under conditions of detailed scrutiny. How they respond can do much to affect their standing in the community, and be influential in helping the undecided to make up their minds.

It may be desirable to broaden the number of interviewers to avoid problems of familiarity and predictability, hence the advantage of members of the public sometimes being used to put politicians on the spot. But the skilled professional does have the techniques to enable him or her to seek out the truth, and ordinary people can see their concerns being aired and pushed with some forcefulness if the interviewee is proving difficult to pin down. They might see the interviewer as being on their side, asking the questions about unemployment or the Health Service or other matters on which they would like to get an explanation of what is being offered by Government or Opposition parties.

There is a danger of the interview being seen primarily as entertainment, a spectacle in which the persistent interrogator takes on the great and the mighty in a kind of gladiatorial contest. This feeling has been aired in recent discussion of the value and form of the medium of investigation. Within the BBC there is a debate being conducted on whether the existing format is the best available, and it concerns the way in which some star performers can become self-obsessed prima donnas.

The Director-General, John Birt, sparked off controversy in a lecture given in 1995, in which he analysed the relationship of politicians and the media.[69] He has condemned the way in which some interviewers tend to sneer at their victims, and seemed particularly uneasy about the hard-hitting Paxman-style interviews. He appeared to suggest that some of his star interviewers were acquiring inflated egos, and stated that some broadcasters were excessively 'overbearing and disdainful'. He singled out interviews for criticism as part of a general analysis of current affairs coverage, and criticised the 'ritualistic encounter – which is little more than a brief opportunity to bicker' – and noted that elected politicians have 'a higher claim to speak for the people than journalists . . . We . . . should beware of interviewers who fell more self-important than the subject matter.' His comments were thought to refer more to reporters and interviewers who used the brief few-minute interview, than to the more in-depth extended format.

In the discussion which followed, a producer of the *Walden* programme conceded that he had regularly framed 'a disorientating opening question' calculated to trigger 'broadcast argy-bargy', the concern being with what made good television rather than to allow politicians to explain their position.[70] His desire for drama in the encounter, and the politicians' wish to use the contest to confuse and deceive their audience, led to a situation in which 'the whole business no longer serves much purpose'.

Others find the manner of interviewers to be too gentle and gentlemanly, bearing in mind the failure of politicians to answer questions, and their use of prepared platitudes and irrelevant statistics. Hence the comment of one respondent in the *Guardian*:

> in an ideal world, populated by great and visionary politicians, if we had a Gladstone and a Disraeli, a Nye Bevan and a Churchill, what Mr Birt says might be all very well. But he must realise that journalists have to deal nowadays with many politicians who will say anything to get elected, and, once elected, anything to stay in power. If such people will change their opinions for political advantage, cover up sleaze or incompetence, and meet justified criticism by saying it's all a 'dark plot' by the media or people on the *Today* programme, to unsettle the Government, isn't a small sneer pardonable?[71]

In private polling conducted for the BBC, viewers and listeners were asked to rate their top six interviewers. Only 3 per cent were critical of Humphrys who was the preferred choice of respondents, and although Jeremy Paxman was seen as the 'rudest' he was also rated as 'outstandingly good'. Nearly four out of five were satisfied that interviewers were both fair and polite, and more than two-thirds were impressed by the way in which they judged how and when to move on to the next question.

Some journalists and broadcasters who commented on the period following the Birt speech were irritated by the way in which the remarks had made their job more difficult. They claimed that when they asked hostile questions of a politician, they were liable to receive a query about whether the Director-General favoured such tough questioning. They made the point that in arranging interviews they are often subject to much arm-twisting by politicians who are adept at manipulation.

The gravamen of the Birtean indictment was that too much time is spent in discussing the 'tedious Westminster manoeuvring which was all we had to talk to them about'. Birt, who had once famously condemned a 'bias against understanding' in much current affairs coverage, wanted to see more analytical discussion of matters which really did concern the public – crime, homelessness, social breakdown and the state of the environment, 'the events and forces that most shape our lives', and less of a preoccupation with disputation with those who rule or who aspire to do so.

Interviews, and other forms of political analysis and discussion on television, are under review, and it may well be that changes will be made in the near future to the way in which discussions are conducted and to the number of such set-piece occasions. Journalists are likely to resist such an inroad, for interviews provide a fine opportunity for them to develop and enhance their personal image. Politicians are also likely to wish to defend this use of airtime, for the chosen performers value the chance to have a platform from which they can convey their opinions.

## Politicians and broadcasters: a reflection

The relationship between politicians and the media is often an uneasy one. They need each other, but tend to be mutually suspicious. Broadcasters need the politicians both in order that they fulfil their statutory obligation to provide balanced coverage, and to give them interesting programmes about politics and current affairs. On behalf of the public, they can offer the viewing public an opportunity to call our political representatives to account. Politicians need the media to enable them to get their message across to the voters in their homes. A constant battle rages between them over the terms of contract, and each side tends to believe that it could do the job of the other side better than the present incumbent.

Some broadcasters give politicians a hard time, for by doing so they see themselves as fulfilling a public duty as watchdogs of our democratic system. They feel that without their interruptions in interviews and their probing questioning of those who rule, the elected representatives would seek the chance to air their views at great length and present a purely partisan picture of events. Politicians feel that they are the people whom the public have elected, and that it is they (not the appointed interviewers and television journalists) whom people wish to see and hear.

Politicians have become more adept at using the media for their own advantage, and they have many ways of manipulating it to get their view across. Chapter 8 illustrates some of the ways in which government Ministers achieve their aims, and crude political arm-twisting has its place. Michael Cockerell has demonstrated how conscious Prime Ministers have been of the power of television and have sought both to influence those who run broadcasting and to reinvent themselves in such a way as to improve the impression they created.[72]

Several have been wary of the media, and Macmillan spoke of its 'hot, pitiless probing eye'. Churchill saw the BBC as 'honeycombed with socialists'; Eden similarly feared that the Corporation was riddled with left-wingers, some of whom were intent on shining the light in his eyes to ruin his broadcasts, and Harold Wilson had similar fears about the technicians whose use of the lights could, he feared, make him seem shifty. Tony Benn has written of Harold Wilson's method of dealing with the BBC: 'If there was anything he did not like on the BBC, he would threaten them with not putting up the licence fee – it was as simple as that.'

Manipulation is not confined to those in office. The majority of MPs have a highly developed awareness of the power of television, and many of them seek to enhance their image and convey their views by exploiting its potential.

'Image advice' is a growth industry, and we have seen how Sir Gordon Reece was able to help Mrs Thatcher to improve her image by lowering and softening her voice and by 'power-dressing'. An army of other media advisers and advertising men remade her for the television age, refashioning her whole manner and style. Others, ranging from Neil Kinnock to Tony Blair, have been concerned with ensuring that they look and sound 'good on television'. Television demands this of them, for the annihilation of Michael Foot in 1983 showed what could happen to a leader who shunned the medium. Peter Mandelson has stressed the importance of 'getting it right', for 'TV does more to make or break a politician than any other medium. It is the voter's key source for forming impressions of politicians. They are looking for good judgement, for warmth, for an understanding of people's concerns. That can only be demonstrated on television.'[73]

'Soundbiting' is another means of manipulating the medium, and the speeches are several politicians are so crafted that the key points are summarised in pithy phrases appropriate for use in news headlines. 'Photo opportunities' are yet another way of obtaining favourable coverage, for as Sir Harvey Thomas has explained: 'You try to put the television companies in a position where the very best television comes in the 90 seconds you want to go out . . . [it is] manipulation with a small 'm' and a nice smile.'[74]

Andrew Rawnsley has vividly described the lengths to which politicians will go to get the right pictures on the screen. As he put it:

What they love is what Clive James called the 'fake candid'. Those bogus, sanitised events are full of smiling voters and smirking politicians and empty of any politics.

'No words here', Neil Kinnock's press minders would tell accompanying journalists during the last election, as his campaign became one extended photo-opportunity. At times, half the nation's babies seemed to have been snatched by Walworth Road for the impress of the Labour leader's lips. Anything he could do, she [Mrs Thatcher] could do better . . . she inaugurated a new softer image with a charge down a Cornish beach with a borrowed

King Charles spaniel: 'I would love a dog', breathed the Prime Minister, 'but my job won't allow it.'[75]

Television editors and journalists go along with this for they want good pictures. They provide a saturation coverage of political events, particularly at election time. They cannot show everything, and they attempt to select those areas which look to be of potential interest. The minders who look after candidates know that it is up to them to ensure that plenty of good copy and favourable images of their candidate are available at the right time and in the right place.

As Rawnsley remarked, in pursuit of such images, Mrs Thatcher ate fish and chips, coated chocolates, examined dead lobsters with forensic interest, climbed cranes, disappeared down pits, and had the condition of her heart tested:

> The most bizarre event of all set the Prime Minister in a field crushing a new-born calf to her iron bosom. 'If we are not careful', said Denis, as her grip tightened around its neck, 'we will have a dead calf on our hands'. What his wife was actually strangling was something rather more precious – political debate.[76]

To some extent, television has trivialised and personalised politics, though not all programmes could be said to have abetted this process and this trivialisation is not the sum of its contribution to political understanding. Probably more people than ever before are fairly informed about political matters, even if the level of overall knowledge which is retained is disappointingly small.

Many politicians are concerned with creating the right image to please the marginal voters and some then complain when their own over-simplifications trivialise politics. More thoughtful ones would like to get their message across at greater length, and to develop their argument. Some editors and journalists would like to see more serious discussion of politics in depth. But the constraints of time, and the need to keep programmes sufficiently appealing for a mass audience, do limit the opportunity for more worthwhile discussion.

More and more, in the battle for ratings and economic survival, the emphasis of many programmes is on the need to be 'entertaining'. Issues which cannot be presented in the form of conflict, or do not lend themselves to exciting visual illustration, tend to be ignored. Much of current coverage is confined to the studio interview or the party political broadcast. Arguably, there is too little exploration of political ideas or of opinion outside Westminster.

Both sides, broadcasters and politicians, have connived at the situation as it has developed. Some of those who now complain of the quality of media coverage are those whose views were once rather different. In 1959, it was the young Tony Benn who sent a memo to Hugh Gaitskell, the Labour leader, suggesting that rather than concentrate on the issues, party propaganda needed to appeal to the viewer's interest, with suitable pictures, music and personalities: 'Suppose we decide our theme is to be 'the land and the people'. Then the opening film sequence should be an atomic power station under construction, seen across fields of waving corn. And our music should be Jerusalem, sung by a Welsh choir.' [77] The wheel has come full circle, and the party which so notably cut itself off from media hype in the early 1980s, has now adopted techniques which the Conservatives have long seen as inevitable in the television age. Without such concessions, television can seriously damage a politician, and however much they distrust the media professionals, politicians know that they need their services if they are to reach their target, the electorate.

## Notes

1   D. Kavanagh, 'Their Masters' Voice', *Contemporary Record*, vol. 3, no. 4 (April 1990), p. 25.
2   *Ibid.*, p. 26.
3   Catherine Bennett, 'Trust me, trust my vows', *Guardian*, 2 October 1996.
4   M. Lawson, 'Great political speeches', *Guardian*, 18 September 1996.
5   P. Bull, 'The Use of Hand Gesture in Political Speeches', *Journal of Language and Social Psychology*, vol. 5, no. 2 (1986).
6   J. Atkinson, especially *Our Master's Voice: The Language and Body Language of Politics* (Methuen: London, 1984).
7   B. Bruce, *Images of Power* (Kogan Page: London, 1992), p. 171.
8   R. Stradling and E. Bennett, 'Televising the House of Lords', Report no. 2 (Hansard Society, London, 1986).
9   *Ibid.*
10  *Ibid.*
11  Adapted from information in *ibid.*
12  Adapted from information in *ibid.*
13  *Ibid.*
14  *Ibid.*
15  The Parliamentary Channel currently broadcasts on Tuesdays, Thursdays, Fridays and Saturdays.
16  R. Stradling and E. Bennett, 'Televising the House of Lords'.
17  A. Bevan, House of Commons debate, November 1959.
18  H. Bowden as quoted in R. Day, *The Case for Televising Parliament* (Hansard Society: London, 1963), p. 15.
19  Sir T. Brinton, House of Commons debate, 20 November 1985.
20  A. Mitchell, *Talking Politics, The Politics Association*, vol. 3, no. 2, 1990.
21  Holli Semetko, ITN survey, 1991.
22  Sir B. Ingham, *Kill the Messenger* (Harper Collins: London, 1991), p. 219.
23  BBC Guidelines.
24  T. Gorman, MP, quoted in S. Franks and A. Vandermart, 'Televising Parliament: Five Years On', *Parliamentary Affairs* (Spring 1995).
25  D. Lloyd, as quoted in *ibid.*

26  A. Mitchell, *Talking Politics*.
27  M. Douglas, Letter to author.
28  S. Franks and A. Vandermart, 'Televising Parliament: Five Years On'.
29  J. Grist, 'Televising the Commons', *Intermedia* (January/Febuary 1993).
30  Sir T. Brinton, House of Commons debate, 20 November 1985.
31  A. Hetherington, K. Weaver and M. Ryle, *Cameras in the Commons* (Hansard Society: London, 1990).
32  P. Ashdown MP, as quoted in S. Franks and A. Vandermart, 'Televising Parliament: Five Years On'.
33  G. Allen MP, as quoted in *ibid*.
34  A. Beith MP, House of Commons debate, 20 November 1985.
35  Evidence to House of Commons Committee on Procedure, March 1995.
36  *Ibid.*
37  T. Gorman, as quoted in S. Franks and A. Vandermart, 'Televising Parliament: Five Years On'.
38  D. Amess MP, as quoted by J. Moir, *Guardian*, 4 October 1994.
39  M. Thatcher MP, quoted in *The Times*, 24 November 1989.
40  D. Amess, House of Commons debate, 19 July 1990.
41  M. Portillo MP, speech to Conservative Way Forward Group, January 1994.
42  Sir B. Ingham, *Kill the Messenger*, p. 170.
43  R. Day, *The Case for Televising Parliament*, p. 22.
44  B. Bruce, *Images of Power*, p. 156.
45  But see *Politicians and the TV Interview* (Parliamentary Affairs, Hansard/Oxford University Press: Oxford, 1993), for a useful and thorough analysis.
46  G. Berlin, *Campaigns and Elections Magazine*, December 1991.
47  *Ibid.*
48  *Ariel* magazine, 25 May 1992, quoted in D. Butler and D. Kavanagh, *The British General Election of 1992* (St Martin's Press: London, 1992).
49  Sir R. Day, *But With Respect, Sir* (Weidenfeld and Nicolson: London, 1993), pp. 1–8, 92.
50  *Ibid.*
51  P. Bull and K. Mayer, 'How Not to Answer Questions in Political Interviews', *Political Psychology*, Vol.4, No.4 (1993).
52  *Ibid.*
53  *Ibid.*
54  G. Kaufman, as quoted in L. Rees, *Selling Politics* (BBC Books: London, 1992), p. 152.
55  A. Benn MP, public speech, October 1968.
56  Sir R. Day, *But With Respect, Sir*.
57  G. Mathias, in I. Crewe and M. Harrop (eds), *Political Communications: The General Election of 1987* (Cambridge University Press: Cambridge, 1989).
58  B. Bruce, *Images of Power*, p. 165.
59  J. Humphrys, *Observer*, 20 February 1994.
60  *Ibid.*
61  S. Brooke, *Media Guardian*, 23 January 1995.
62  D. Healey, *The Time of My Life* (Penguin: London, 1993), p. 443.
63  R. Day, in I. Crewe and M. Harrop (eds), *Political Communications: The General Election of 1987*.

64  Quoted in D. Butler and D. Kavanagh, *The British General Election of 1987* (Macmillan: London, 1988).
65  Writer in *Broadcast*, June 1992, as quoted in Sir R. Day, *But With Respect, Sir*, p. 5.
66  Sir R. Day, *But With Respect, Sir*, p. 5.
67  Sir B. Ingham, *Kill the Messenger*, p. 347.
68  A. Bevan MP, quoted in *The Case for Televising Parliament*,
69  J. Birt, Dublin Lecture, April 1995.
70  D. Cox, *Media Guardian*, 13 February 1995.
71  John Mortimer, *Guardian*, 8 February 1995.
72  M. Cockerell, *Live From Number 10* (Faber: London, 1988).
73  P. Mandelson MP, as quoted in L. Rees, *Selling Politics*, pp. 45–6.
74  Sir H. Thomas, quoted in B. Bruce, *Images of Power*, p. 118.
75  A. Rawnsley, 'Box of Political Tricks', *Guardian*, 9 September 1988.
76  *Ibid.*
77  As quoted in *ibid.*

Part III

# The media, democracy and the future

# 11

# The media and democracy

Democracy implies the existence of certain basic freedoms, among which the right to express and listen to opinions is fundamental; the media must therefore be free to expound a variety of viewpoints. Traditionally liberal democracies are associated with the idea of a free press and, in more recent years, with broadcasting services which operate in a climate in which radio and television editors and journalists are able to gather and use information as seems appropriate for their programming.

The absence of state control over the media is, then, an acid test for any country which aspires to be regarded as democratic. At first sight, Britain fulfils the criteria effectively. The BBC and ITC enjoy a substantial measure of independence and are committed to ensuring balance and impartiality in their output. Newspapers, though biased in their presentation of the news and current affairs, are allowed to print most of what they wish to say without fear of reprisal or falling foul of the law. Political debate can be conducted throughout the media with much vigour, and although considerations of national security inevitably inhibit what can be broadcast or written, this is not a barrier to the expression of a broad range of views on a wide variety of subjects. There is a constant diet of political controversy which is freely conducted in a range of publications and programmes.

The media would appear to be a living example of democracy in action, but whilst many people would claim that their contribution is positively beneficial to the democratic process there is another view which regards the structure and behaviour of the media as inimical to the operation of a free society. Hence the observation of one writer that:

> Occasionally, the media expose some aspect of the decline of the democratic spirit, but in many ways they are accomplices and a catalyst to it. The activities of the tabloid press have been a disgrace to liberal democracy for a number of years . . . [of television] one effect of the media has been to trivialise politics, to concentrate upon the personalities . . . and to express complex issues in a shorthand form which is so abbreviated that all depth is excluded in pursuit of a marketable soundbite.[1]

## The main means of communication today

Today, we rely heavily upon the media as a means of conducting our political communication. In ancient Greece, Athenian democracy was practised in a small city-state in which all of the free people could directly have a say in the running of the community, and in which politicians could address them directly. After the development of the mass franchise in Britain and elsewhere in the nineteenth and twentieth centuries, there was still that direct link between politicians and the voters, even though many people had little opportunity to take an active part in the process. The mass meetings addressed by Joseph Chamberlain and Gladstone over a hundred years ago and by many politicians since then provided an opportunity to inform some of the electors at first hand.

The various media are needed to educate the electorate by presenting the arguments on issues of current controversy. The factors which influence their output and the quality of their output are matters of concern to all who cherish democratic values.

### The advantages and disadvantages of the media

The mass media allow the public to become better informed about the issues of the day. They seek to ferret out facts which may be of interest to their viewers, listeners and readers. In that television conveys political material in an interesting, palatable and digestible manner, then this could be said to raise the profile of people's understanding of the body politic. It is an important function, and inasmuch as the media help to disseminate ideas and information, organise debate and take up issues of public concern their role enhances democracy. As Robins puts it, they 'play a crucial role in structuring and widening political debate in Britain, so that issues such as the environment, industrial relations or the "poll tax" receive attention until the problems are addressed by the government'.[2]

Moreover, sometimes this is material which the government would prefer to keep to itself, or in the hands of a privileged elite. Papers and television programmes have been active in exposing issues, whether in helping to establish the innocence of the Birmingham Six or in exposing the dubious dealings of Westminster Council and its alleged manipulation of housing policy in the interests of the local Tory Party. They have enquired into the funding of the same party by businessemen and groups such as Aims for Freedom and Enterprise, and into the activities of financiers such as Azil Nadir.

As governments tend to construct a wall of secrecy around such embarrassing revelations, the more active journalists on radio and television, as well as in the papers, find out what the public might like to know and place the information in the public domain. In defending public liberties (as in the Spycatcher case) and in exposing injustice or sleaze, the press can be especially and effectively vigilant.

Journalists are much more timid across the Channel, for in France newspapers are relatively bland compared to the British experience. Editors and reporters there connive with politicians in order to keep things quiet. They distinguish between financial and sexual affairs, and as their slowness in making revelations about President Mitterrand and the existence of his daughter indicates, they tread with much discretion in dealing with sexual peccadilloes and preferences. Neither have they been forceful in exposing money scandals in recent years, and they have been accused of toadying to those who are prominent in public life. In postwar France, the notion of investigative journalism, based on careful accumulation of the factual evidence, has often been ignored. Often the French press accepts what it is given and recycles it.

Of course, if there is much which is beneficial in British journalism at its best, there is the other side of the coin. It is also notably active on more personal issues, and is open to the charge of scandal-mongering and hypocrisy. This may be in the public interest, if dubious financial dealings are brought to the reader's attention, but in other cases newspapers are purely salacious in intent. At its worst, one can see the tabloid excesses of papers such as the *Sun* with some of its tasteless and lurid headlines. Reporting can easily become sensational in the interests of stoking up circulation or winning the ratings war, and investigations into private lives often have little to do with the way in which well-known figures conduct their public roles.

People often look in vain for in-depth, serious and balanced coverage of issues. In the press, the treatment meted out by the tabloids is shamelessly biased, and in 1987 and 1992 there were many examples of gross anti-Labour partisanship. Accurate reporting may yield to the demands of the arresting phrase, and on television (as we have seen) it is often the case that interviewers have sought to dramatise situations, going for lively confrontation and personalising issues between rival sides in an argument.

Austin Mitchell, MP, is critical of the media's performance, and he seeks to demonstrate that the public is saturated with

> gossip . . . personalisation, all the trivia of a tabloid world, rather than being satiated on hard information or educated by explanation and analysis. The media's preoccupations are never sustained. Education is not seen as one of its responsibilities. The public neither gets, nor is helped, to understand alternative strategies . . . The media demand instant answers . . . Sensationalism sells newspapers and wins viewers. Explanation and understanding are boring. Politicians are pushed into vacuities and every action is criticised. The bland lead the blind . . . Media democracy is perpetual populism and the endless clamour for easy answers.[3]

### Democracy and the media: the views of the theorists

We have seen that the various media have a role of fundamental importance in imparting an array of information and thereby helping to increase the understanding of the electorate. They also express a variety of opinions, even if some receive greater emphasis or fairer treatment than others. The effectiveness of their performance in fulfilling these tasks is viewed differently by those who are Pluralists and those who adhere to the manipulative school of thought.

Critics who adopt the manipulative model as a means of understanding the media see them as a way via which members of the ruling elite can perpetuate their position and influence. They see the media as a conservative force in society. They argue that in various ways the media are a threat to democracy in that they are controlled and operated by a narrow range of people who, non-elected as they are, have the power to control the dissemination of information and opinion, and thereby manipulate or at least influence the electorate.

Because of this the views expressed in the media are insufficiently diverse, and the ideas of those who wish to question the way society is run receive perfunctory and inadequate coverage. Often, they are presented as extremists, and the ideas of strikers, black and gay activists and Greenham women get less than a fair hearing. Rather, it is the voice of the most powerful groups in society which are regularly given an airing. They tend to encourage conformist behaviour. Early discussion of Aids tended to warn people from deviant lifestyles and encouraged support for monogamy and heterosexuality; Aids was portrayed as primarily a homosexual affliction. Discussion of strikes and obedience to the law again tends to emphasise conforming to the core values of society.

Because of the outlook of those who inhabit the world of the media, certain values regularly emerge, and these help to shape the agenda for discussion, and the way in which issues are handled. In the case of the press, there is an overt bias in its reporting. Within broadcasting, there is still a lack of objectivity but the slant is a more subtle one. It is editors and journalists on television and in newspapers who choose what is to be reported and how the material is presented. In these ways, those who work in the media are not merely a mirror of popular opinions; they are helping to mould what the public thinks and how it reacts. People's opinions can only derive from what they see and hear. Much of their information comes from the media so that the power of the media is immense and is actually or potentially harmful to democracy.

Such an approach as that outlined above broadly endorses the viewpoint of those who believe in the hegemonic or manipulative models which we have earlier explored. Other writers take a more sanguine approach to questions of ownership, bias and influence, and in any defence of the media they would be seen, in spite of all their deficiencies and disadvantages, as beneficial rather than inimical to our democratic way of life – this is the pluralist perspective.

Defenders of the media point to the lack of state control and the absence of the type of censorship which prevails in totalitarian countries. Free speech is broadly protected, except for reasons of national security, and subject to certain legal restrictions editors and journalists can report on any issue and publish or voice a range of comments, as freely as editors/programme-makers allow.

Because of the statutory obligation to be impartial, broadcasters at least display a degree of objectivity which is the envy of many other countries. This independence and freedom from government control means that the BBC and commercial television and radio authorities can express a range of opinions, and in the case of the press private ownership allows journalists to tackle any issue which the editor (or in some cases the proprietor) thinks appropriate. For all of the lapses of the tabloid press, at their best newspaper reporters can provide excellent examples of investigative journalism – taking up issues the government would prefer to see covered up, unearthing scandals and embarrassing information and in a general way acting as a vigilant watchdog of the community.

In this way, Ministers are kept on their toes and open to public scrutiny, and are made aware of public anxiety about the effects of their actions or inactions. The media therefore reflect and transmit public concern, and in this pluralist view, rather than manufacture opinions, they reproduce and reinforce ones which are already there. People only watch and listen to what they want to see and hear, and only read those papers they like. They will recall only what confirms their outlook and ignore evidence to the contrary.

## Moulding or reflecting opinion?

The media act as a window on public opinion and as a shaper of it. Broadcasters and newspapermen can articulate half-formed moods and actively seek to persuade people about the necessity of a certain course. Good journalists examine issues critically and help inform citizens by disseminating facts and arguments; they can also reflect public concern to the government, via the leader column and in the selection of letters (especially those from informed and eminent writers) in newspapers and in phone-in programmes and in interviews for radio and television.

Newspaper barons of the past were very powerful, and the press was feared and courted by politicians. Northcliffe, and later Rothermere and Beaverbrook, were keen to exercise power and influence over the Conservative Party and its governments, though they did not always get the result which they wanted. Even Northcliffe remarked that his aim was 'not to direct the ordinary man's opinion but to reflect it'. Beaverbrook had no such inhibitions, telling a Royal Commission on the Press that he ran papers 'purely for the purposes of making propaganda'.

The *Mirror* has often combined the two roles, generally reflecting its readers' opinions but on occasion crusading for a particular course. However, no paper wishes to get out of step with the outlook and aspirations of its readership, for they wish to retain their allegiance; excessive campaigning for a party or cause might backfire. As we have seen, the *Mirror* initially opposed the belligerent policy of the Prime Minister over Suez, but found that its circulation dropped – and so it then abandoned its role as a crusader and became the reflector of opinion. The attitude of any wise editor of a popular newspaper is likely to be:

'you have to give the public what it wants, otherwise you go out of business'. A commercial press exists to make a profit and the political leaning must not be allowed to get in the way of that preoccupation.

Many journalists claim that they are providing what the public wants, what one commentator expressed as 'the classic trichotomy – blood, money and the female organ of sex'.[4] Murdoch's *Sun* has opted for the latter approach, and its readers are probably more interested in the contents of page three and the popular stories and sports coverage than they are in the editor's political line.

Similarly with television. Is it driven by public opinion or does it lead it? Who is in the driving-seat, the viewer or the broadcaster? The fact that politicians are so sensitive to alleged bias on television suggests that they assume that there is the likelihood of influence – otherwise there would be less point to their protest.

No one can easily establish whether readers are impervious to blatant or more subtle propagandising or are influenced by it, and academic debate largely depends upon the school of thought to which those involved in the argument adhere.

### A free press?

The existence of a free press is widely regarded as one of the main criteria of a democratic system. Various arguments have been advanced in favour of the idea. Censorship stifles the freedom of the individual to analyse issues for him or herself, in that it denies people the necessary information from which they can reach their own conclusions. Writers from John Locke onwards have interpreted press freedom as basic to the right of the individual to get at the truth; for John Keane, it 'is a guarantee of freedom from political coxcombs, Parliamentary hoodwinking and governmental slavery. It ensures good government, based on the natural rights of rational individuals'.[5]

Jeremy Bentham argued strongly for press freedom in his letters *On the Liberty of the Press and Public Discussion* (1820–21), in which he urged that state censorship of public opinion was a licence for authoritarian rule, because governments are ruled by self-interest and 'Such is the nature of man when clothed with power . . . that . . . whatever mischief has not yet been actually done by him today, he is sure to be meditating today, and unless restrained by the fear of what the public may think and do, it may actually be done by him tomorrow.' Newspapers have an essential role in checking despotism and inefficient rule, for without their information and exposures elections could not be considered as a genuine expression of what the voters really think. As Keane summarises Bentham's position, 'a free press increases the probability of prudent decisions by making publicly available comprehensive information about the world. And a free press casts a watchful eye over the bureaucracy, thus preventing the outbreak of nepotism between legislators and administrators.'[6]

For John Stuart Mill, there was more to press freedom than utility, the likelihood that it would produce better government. It was primarily a matter of reaching the truth about any situation, for it is only by hearing different sides of the argument and balancing conflicting opinions that an accurate picture of events can emerge: 'When there are persons to be found, who form an exception to the apparent unanimity of the world on any subject, even if the world is in the right, it is always probable that dissentients have something worth hearing to say for themselves, and that truth would lose something by their silence.' [7]

In the modern world, in non-democratic countries, the value of the press as a counterweight to despotic government is much appreciated by those who wish to protect the rights of individuals and groups who are the victims of repression. In regimes such as the former white regime in South Africa, when apartheid was at its peak, censorship of the press was a regular feature, and papers often appeared with columns unprinted – the censor had forbidden publication of some article considered damaging to the reputation of the government, perhaps a feature exposing some instance of tyranny or cruelty.

Stoffel Botha, the Minister of Home Affairs and Communications in the late 1980s, often used his draconian emergency powers to prevent publication; after 1950, the authorities were allowed to close down any newspaper. He earned the dubious distinction of contributing a new phrase to South Africa's political vocabulary, 'to stoffel', meaning 'to stifle'.

Against such a background of censorship, in countries ranging from Soviet Russia to other authoritarian regimes around the world, the freedom of the British press can be further considered. The British publishing industry is free in the sense that newspapers are not owned or controlled by the government or one of its agencies.

There are restrictions on what material the editors can use, but these restrictions are laws which aimed to prevent such things as defamation, racial incitement or other behaviour which could be harmful to the interests of individuals or groups. The Official Secrets Act (OSA) imposes limitations on the use of 'intelligence' material, and the press usually abides by self-censorship in its acceptance of D-notice restrictions which are designed to stem the flow of 'sensitive' material.

By the standards acceptable in a liberal democracy, however, there is no major threat to press freedom in Britain from legislative controls. In John Whale's book (*The Politics of the Media*), he emphasises this concept of the Western democratic ideal, and in the absence of state control he argues that the public are able to determine what they choose to read. According to this 'pluralist' view, there are sufficient papers and other publications owned by a private proprietors to allow the spread of a wide range of views, sufficient to ensure that the democratic process can operate effectively.

Some academics and writers on the left take a different view, and see the threat to freedom as a more serious one; from their perspective, the danger in Britain comes not from governmental interference but from the concentration of ownership and the resultant limitations on the diversity of views available. They stress that ownership of newspapers has increasingly passed into the hands of multinational groupings such as that of Rupert Murdoch, and the fact that some newspapers have disappeared and that those remaining tend to have a strong anti-left-wing bias means that consumers do not have access to a wide range of viewpoints.

## Recent trends in the coverage of politics in the media

As well as a free exchange of views and opinions, democracy thrives on a reasoned and informed outlook; there are many barriers to the achievement of this desirable goal. Anxieties about the declining quality of coverage in the tabloid press and of the diminishing quantity of analysis in the broadsheets are well-founded and have already been explored (see p. 82). With regard to television, there are also legitimate grounds for concern. The tendency today is to presidentialise our election coverage and do less than justice to the issues involved, for as Negrine observes, there is an 'infatuation with personalities and, in particular, political leaders'.[8]

The way in which the broadcasters set the agenda at election time is another cause for concern. In 1992, television coverage was much criticised by the politicians for its preoccupation with Jennifer's ailing ear and, in the last week of the campaign, with the likelihood of Labour taking up proportional representation and cooperating with the Liberal Democrats in a 'hung Parliament'. Politicians are democratically elected and broadcasters are not, hence the frustration of critics such as Tony Benn with the way in which major issues get less than a full discussion because they are not the ones which broadcasters choose to highlight. The resentment was shared by several politicians in 1992, and it was Michael Heseltine who urged the media, 'on behalf of all political parties . . . to give us a chance to get on with the issues . . . We depend on you. There is no other way we can get over what we want to say.'[9]

Benn's oft-stated view that the media trivialise political discussion (see p. 70) is also relevant to our discussion. Trivialisation may be seen as a by-product of the television age, but when the press portray a partisan and often sensationalist image it is all the more important that high-quality television coverage of political events should be available, if the educative role of the media is to be fulfilled. This leads us on to explore more fully the way in which television has changed the political scene, as politicians have become aware of the potency of the medium as a means of conveying their ideas and selling their personalities to the voters.

## Packaging politicians on both sides of the Atlantic

In our section on selling politicians, we have seen that television is not simply a neutral reporter of the political scene, for it can actually change the way in which political issues are presented and discussed. Rather than being a medium which transmits thoughts and ideas, a role so necessary in any democratic society, it actually changes the way we communicate and the way in which we arrive at our ideas. Some writers would argue that recent trends in television coverage of politics are inimical to democracy which prides itself on the values of a full and free discussion of information.

Such is the power of television that those politicians who could once thrive because of their intelligence and experience, may today not get elected because they are insufficiently telegenic. The abilities they possess might not be the ones which are desirable and necessary for television success.

We live in an era when new techniques of political campaigning are in vogue, and we are at the mercy of media specialists who seek to influence our views by an array of staged media events and through advertising. These are the days of the negative campaign, saying something critical or abusive about an opponent rather than something positive about the issues. Political abuse is no new phenomenon, but television gives any 'slagging-off' of the opposition a higher profile. American habits of concentrating on the unsuitability for office of a rival candidate have become part of the political scene, though the absence in Britain of thirty-second commercials denies those who trade in insults an obvious outlet for their message.

Whereas Gladstone set out to convince his audience by a reasoned statement of his views, the emphasis is now upon emotion rather than rational debate; soundbites have replaced genuine discourse. Today, meetings are revivalist gatherings, staged occasions such as the Sheffield Rally, to which entrance is carefully controlled and in which everything is done to make it a media success. Emotional broadcasts are another part of the picture. Of course there have always been negative tactics and the emotionally-charged outbursts of great orators such as Gladstone or Lloyd George could whip people into a frenzy of excitement in which their reason was lost. But we have moved far beyond this, and in the type of media hype which we now witness some observers have discerned more similarity with the mass rallies of Germany in the 1930s.

Like the cinema, television is a medium of entertainment so politicians (and in particular their advisers) have seen the need to attune performances to the demands of the medium. They have to be entertaining if they are to compete with the rest of the output on the screen, which is so dominated by allegedly amusing programmes and highly professional advertising.

Today, therefore, instead of the politician speaking on the stump about those issues with which he feels the public should be concerned, we live at a time where the politician needs to know what the voters think are matters of concern. Their views are assessed in market research, and the issues which trouble or excite them are highlighted. The political consultant and other gurus then devise ways of ensuring that they address those anxieties or demands.

We have then a situation in which political discourse is now conducted in a way which suits the needs of television, and in which the form of debate is more influenced than ever before by the efforts of the professional persuaders. Fitness for office is not so much about personal qualities but about being seen to be acceptable to the eye and ear. The trend is an accepted part of the American scene and the politicians chosen in recent years have often been people adept at handling television; Bill Clinton has at times used the medium most effectively to stage a comeback when experiencing a bad patch.

In Britain, we lag a few years behind in American techniques of persuasion, but the pattern of the postwar era is that what happens across the Atlantic soon arrives here and becomes a part of the political scene. For instance, the autocue, used by President Reagan and viewed with envy by senior British politicians, soon made its way into this country.

There is an obvious danger, at a time when personality counts for more than in the past, that mastery of television might enable a charlatan to get elected, and that once elected the advisers and consultants could protect the successful candidate from embarrassing challenges. The British in-depth interview does provide a kind of antidote to this danger, for those personal qualities come under heavy scrutiny and in the 'Walden' type of programme policy deficiencies can be much exposed. But most people do not watch this kind of gruelling encounter, and the likelihood is that those people who use television the most to obtain their information may be the very people who are least discerning and able to come to a reasonable conclusion based on knowledge. They probably don't read other sources and therefore what they see has a potent effect on the least sophisticated electors.

In America, the closest the voter gets to learning of the issues is in many cases the Presidential debate with all its limitations, for the advertisements do nothing to impart worthwhile information and the number who view Congressional proceedings on television is necessarily limited. In Britain, we can also now see our representatives in action in the House of Commons, and Question Time at least is an institution which shows those in power being forced to defend their position, even if it does little to inform people of the issues. The interviews conducted in the election in *Election Call* are a reminder of how leading figures can be put on the spot by skilful members of the public who can unsettle their composure.

Britain has in many ways learnt from the American experience, and whilst some Americans feel that they can incorporate something from our system about the accountability of politicians at Question Time, much of the learning has been in the other direction. In recent years, there has been an increasing British obsession with walkabouts, photo opportunities and other pseudo-events created for the media. In 1992, there were again several examples of the Americanisation of politics at work, not least the style of the two broadcasts we have covered in Chapter 9 (the 'Back to Roots' broadcast of John Major and the Labour one concerning Jennifer's ear), and in the

Sheffield Rally, a triumphalist occasion which in presentation was very reminiscent of the American convention.

Party broadcasts, free airtime, vigilant journalists and politicians more prepared to answer questions about their proposals, help to differentiate us from US experience in certain respects, and are some kind of safeguard against our adopting the worst aspects of American electioneering methods into Britain. Yet as we have seen, the PPBs and PEBs themselves have to some degree 'gone American' in style and form.

Perhaps such thoughts are too alarmist, for negative and emotional campaigning have long been part of the British scene, and if it is true that politicians have often been chosen because they are likeable then the public might be deemed capable of spotting someone who is patently insincere and not to be trusted. Yet McGinnis's study of the 1968 Presidential election showed that even Richard Nixon could be packaged and marketed, and his version of events is, in the words of Alistair Cooke, 'a short and terrifying account of what happens to a presidential candidate in an age which regards the advertising man as an important and natural ally of the politician'.[10]

It may be that on this side of the Atlantic we are less susceptible to the excesses of emotionalism and negative campaigning that beset American politics. We have already said that television is more often viewed as a reinforcing medium than one which changes people's basic beliefs, and if this is the case a candidate who lacks appeal and a party with an unpopular policy cannot get themselves elected. Jennifer's ear and the Sheffield Rally could be said to have backfired, and they may even mark the time when British politics diverted from the path pursued on the American scene, or at least held back from its worst excesses.

In America, as we have seen, party matters less and ideology has never been a strong feature of the party system. In Britain there are more evident differences, and parties have a stronger commitment to certain ideals and attitudes. Voters might respond to negative poster advertisements as used effectively by the Conservatives in recent elections, but the point is that the message they contained, on defence policy in 1987 and taxation in 1992, coincided with real concerns which many people felt. The one on taxation in particular rammed home a theme which was in harmony with many electors' own perceptions of their economic self-interest.

## Turnout and finance at election time

In the United States, American methods could be seen as inimical to democracy in other ways. The methods of propaganda have done little to stimulate interest in the political process, if the turnout in presidential elections is a criterion. Negative advertising has been a destructive force in that it has undermined people's view of politicians and their trustworthiness. Progressively over the last thirty years the voters have decided that they have been so disillusioned with the political process that they have shunned the ballot box, and after the peak year of 1960 (over 63 per cent) turnout has dropped by more than 10 per cent.

Rees quotes Senator Darnforth in 1990 who told his colleagues that:

> political campaigns turn the stomach of the average voter. Most people, by the time election day occurs, are sick of the whole process. I don't know what academics have concluded, but I know what I have concluded just on the basis of talking to my own constituents. They are sick about modern politics and they are particularly sick about what they see on television.[11]

Others agree in finding the new style of politics distasteful. For Professor Postman, it 'degrades us. It keeps people cynical about and indifferent to the voting process'.[12]

Of course, it could be misleading to equate a low turnout with negative campaigning, which has long been a feature of the political scene. There are other factors involved. Rather than voter-cynicism deriving from the endless negative images, it could be that people are more critical about what politicians do once they have attained power; they feel let down by the result of their past choices. In Britain, there has been no such continuous decline in turnout, and the number who do vote has varied more according to people's perception of their own prospects and fears, than because of the effects of advertising. It is difficult to establish any causal relationship between recent trends in electioneering and the scale of turnout.

The growing costs of elections is another area for democratic concern. In America money is crucial and the cost of recent presidential and congressional campaigns has in certain states been phenomenal. Television space is costly to buy, and for any would-be presidential candidate there must be hours of spadework in working out a programme of fundraising, and some candidates have withdrawn when that has proved impossible.

In Britain, electioneering has also become expensive, but the fact that our parties are allocated five- or ten-minute political broadcasts may provide difficulties for the media gurus who seek to fill the time effectively, but it does mean that there is not the same costly competition for advertising space. Money is important and the Conservatives have in the past been regularly able to outspend the other parties in such things as hiring poster-sites, but the limits on expenditure at constituency level, if not of the national campaign, do help to mitigate the effects. Calls by the recent Select Committee for limitations on political donations would help to control the less edifying features of fundraising.

The media have a central role in British democracy, both as a means of helping to form and represent opinions. Our survey indicates that there is no room for complacency about their performance in carrying out this task. The tabloid press has deserved its low reputation of recent years, and television, whilst at its best a medium for conveying information in an interesting and stimulating manner, can too often trivialise and personalise issues, and fail to provide the depth of analysis which a healthy democracy needs to sustain it.

## Notes

1 J. Keane, *The Media and Democracy* (Polity Press: Oxford, 1961).
2 L. Robins, *Contemporary British Politics* (Macmillan: London, 1994).
3 A. Mitchell MP, 'The Media', *Wroxton Papers* (Phillip Charles Media: Barnstaple, 1990), p. 20.
4 I. Gilmour, *The Body Politic* (Hutchinson: London, 1969), p. 392.
5 J. Keane, *The Media and Democracy*, ch. 1.
6 *Ibid*, pp. 15–77.
7 *Ibid*, pp. 18–19.
8 R. Negrine, *Politics and the Mass Media in Britain* (Routledge: London, 1994), p. 167.
9 As quoted in D. Butler and D. Kavanagh, *The British General Election of 1992* (Macmillan: London, 1992), p. 164.
10 A. Cooke, as quoted on dust-cover of Joe McGinnis, *The Selling of the President* (André Deutsch: London, 1970).
11 L. Rees, *Selling Politics* (BBC Books: London, 1992), p. 174.
12 N. Postman, *Amusing Ourselves to Death* (Viking Penguin: New York, 1985).

# Future trends

Government policy has in the past been primarily concerned with the structure and organisational arrangements through which the media operate. The preference has been for self-regulation, as is the case with the advertising industry and the press, rather than state intervention. Where control has been considered necessary, the tendency has been to establish bodies with modest powers of regulation.

Nonetheless, any government must be concerned with the future of the media, particularly broadcasting. Not only is it the most powerful medium, it also requires decision-taking on a series of often-related issues. As new technologies emerge, there is no option to continue merely as we have done before. Innovations such as the development of cable and satellite television have repercussions for terrestrial transmission, though as they are global matters Britain inevitably finds itself responding to issues over which it has limited control. However, even with terrestrial broadcasting, there are still many decisions to be taken. Some are regular causes of contention, such as the fate of the licence fee, whilst others have been in the air for several years, a fifth television channel, advertising on the BBC and indeed the future of the Corporation.

That the situation is a fluid one has largely been acknowledged, for the 1994 White Paper, *The Future of the BBC*, attempts to chart a future for broadcasting in general and the BBC in particular. There is inevitably much dispute about the centrality of the Corporation in any coming developments, for there are those who feel that its continued existence along present lines is undesirable and impractical.

## The future of the BBC

The BBC has a traditional commitment to high standards of programming, and those who wish to see this preserved fear that the development of commercial pressures might result in quality being driven downwards. The issue is of great importance to those who are anxious about the scheduling of current affairs programmes at times of the evening when they can expect a sizeable audience.

The BBC is especially renowned for its position as a public service broadcasting authority, but that concept has been under threat in Britain and elsewhere. Governments have been keen to introduce market discipline and competition, and their interest has been made easier to fulfil because of the arrival of the new technologies of which we have spoken. These changes in the pattern of communication have brought new providers into the arena, but although this can mean a more diverse array of channels there are real grounds for concern that it may involve a deterioration in quality of output.

As yet, even a Conservative government well-disposed to the free market has rejected the privatisation of the BBC and, following the advice of the Peacock Committee, any ideas of advertising on television as well. But although recent changes as outlined have ensured its survival as a publicly-funded and publicly-owned institution until 2007, that status cannot be guaranteed indefinitely.

Indeed, there are already moves towards pursuing a more commercial agenda. The White Paper suggests that the Corporation should be allowed to operate with greater commercial freedom, via a separate company, BBC Worldwide Ltd. Such ventures cannot be financed via the licence fee (i.e. by cross-subsidising of BBC operations), for this would place competitors in a disadvantageous position.

A change which has been suggested is that the Governors of the BBC should be elected, their deliberations and decisions made more public and their role clarified. The point is that, in the light of inevitable attempts at undue political influence, particularly by the government of the day, the Corporation should be placed on more sure foundations.

Such suggestions reflect a concern that the continued acceptance of the BBC as a public service broadcaster cannot be taken for granted. The White Paper reaffirmed its support for this traditional function, but there are voices from within the Conservative Party which have questioned the alleged timidity of the Government's proposals, and who would like to see the BBC either broken up and/or privatised.

In the past, the predominance of the BBC in the broadcasting field was taken for granted, for only a narrow range of channels was possible. In the 1990s this is no longer the case, for the revolution in communications has created a situation in which there is a multiplicity of channels available via satellite and cable, so that different channels can cater for specialist interests. Already, in the United States, apart from the three main terrestrial networks, there is a multi-channel cable network available, with forty-six channels nationwide.

In many of these channels, paid for by subscription, viewers will only be billed for the programmes they actually watch. So the audience will be free to choose the programmes it requires from a vast array of providers, and pay only for what they select. The impact of these channels might for the foreseeable future only affect a limited number of people, but the communications revolution which began in 1982 when Sky began its operations is set to continue at a quicker pace. Since then, the number of satellite channels in Europe has increased (from 4 to more than 130) and the schedules of Sky have been significantly extended. Moreover, cable companies are spending over £66 million in creating the basis for their UK network. American experience has shown that the impact of new technologies is to supplement rather than to replace traditional terrestrial services, but new innovations are slowly taking root.

In the development of the mass media, new technologies have not usually rendered existing ones unnecessary. Newspapers survived the advent of wireless broadcasting, the radio and cinema survived the arrival of television, and the cinema has recovered from the original onslaught, and now operates successfully alongside video. In each case, the original form made the necessary adaptations and by concentrating on what it does best, has been able to flourish still.

Terrestrial television and the BBC in particular will probably do the same, for many viewers will appreciate the fact that through its scheduling it makes the choice of programme for them, instead of their having to decide from a lengthy list of possibilities. Moreover, such will be the hours of broadcasting material available in the future that an organisation like the BBC could have a key role in the production of programmes. The value of its production capacity will grow, as demand for programmes rises faster than the commercial broadcasters' ability to make them.

Public ownership may be distrusted on the right of the Conservative Party, but a publicly-financed BBC can, at its best, provide a better guarantee of quality and diversity than a more commercially-oriented organisation which needs to make a substantial profit for the proprietors and shareholders. Their existence might be a guarantee of greater choice, if not of real diversity of programme type, but they are less obviously a guarantor of good taste and cultural standards. The BBC provides a quality benchmark to which others might aspire.

The prospects of the licence fee surviving its allotted span are uncertain. There are many critics who point out that the BBC does not even dominate the viewing habits of those who only use the terrestrial channels. In homes with Sky, the BBC annual share is less than a third, and in the long term likely to fall considerably further as satellite and cable extend their hold. The conclusion is that when the audience falls below a certain level, then it would be indefensible to allow further financing of the Corporation by the licence fee.

Of course, the licence fee is not intended to be a subscription fee in the way that pay-television is. It is effectively a tax, and just as non-motorists pay for the road network via general taxation even if they make little use of it, so the public pay a hypothecated tax for broadcasting, irrespective of whether they use the particular service on offer. As a recent study of the financial arrangements put it: 'Just as parents of children in fee-paying schools are required to pay for state education and patients in private hospitals to fund the National Health Service, so those who opt out of the BBC still have a duty to pay for it.'[1] Moreover, if the BBC does offer programmes of a traditionally high standard, then the licence fee can be said to be worth paying, in that its continuation helps to raise standards overall.

There are problems with the licence fee. It is a regressive tax, paid by everyone who owns a television irrespective of their ability to pay or of their use of the BBC. Moreover, as it is set by the government of the day, it does provide Ministers with a means of exercising undue influence over the Corporation. Also, they keep increases to the level of inflation, but broadcasting costs are if anything rising more rapidly than the general rate of prices – hence, a squeeze on broadcasting revenues. If paid for out of general taxation, however, the squeeze could be even greater, as the search for economies in expenditure seeks out ever-new targets.

The alternatives are also problematic. Advertising would change the character of the Corporation and subscription would be no guarantee of the continuation of quality programming. Few people are enamoured of the licence fee, but few can think of a better solution. Hence the conclusion of the National Heritage Select Committee (1994) that it is the 'least worst' method available to preserve the independence of the BBC.

### New forms of communications

We have seen that new technology has already had considerable impact on the media over the last decade, and developments are already occurring which are likely not only to create new forms of communications but, in doing so, also to impact on our ideas of democracy. What is happening is that new services such as electronic mail are becoming available, for which the consumer only needs a telephone, a personal computer and some software. He or she will then be able to access the Internet system, the backbone of the information highway, and have the means of extracting a mass of information, political or otherwise.

Computer-literate American politicians, ranging from Al Gore to Newt Gingrich, have embraced the new technology. The Vice-President has spoken of his wish to create a global information infrastructure, believing that the information superhighway can be used 'to promote, to protect and to preserve freedom and democracy',[2] and Gingrich envisages a situation where power is transferred electronically 'towards the citizens out of the Washington beltway'.

In the United States, the system is now being used by pressure groups, most notably the American gun lobby, as a means of lobbying Congressmen. In the short term, this type of use is the most likely political development, for activists in various interests now have an easy means available of placing pressure on those who are elected to represent them. Via the Internet, information can be obtained on all members of the House of Representatives and the Senate, and on many who serve in state and local legislatures. Their backgrounds and voting records can be explored, their vulnerability to pressure assessed.

The most dramatic breakthrough is the way in which interactive contact can now be made between the citizen and the White House, an indication of how widely its use is spreading. But in addition to enabling the voter to pass information to those elected to public office, the 'Net' is available as a means for members of the public to contact others who are accessed to the medium. They can communicate with a person down the road, or someone across the world if that person is linked by the system.

In Britain, the system of interactive communications is only in its infancy, although some MPs are seeing its potential as a means of contacting their constituents in 'live' surgeries. At present, few of them are geared to the new technology, but it is likely that the network of users will be greatly extended over the coming years, enabling electors to state their problems and express their views to their elected representatives.

What are the implications for democracy of this growth in electronic mail? The scope for the use of e-mail is enormous, most obviously as a means of transmitting opinions and exerting pressure on those in office. Such technology empowers voters, and provides new means for them to be more actively involved in political dialogue. It opens up the possibility that millions of them across the world will be able to pass information to one another, so that the overall level of knowledge of the citizenry will increase.

Voters will wish to use these new developments to their advantage, and those elected to public positions will need to be more conscious of those whose vote placed them there. This does not mean that they have to be subservient to public pressure, but certainly their performances will be more effectively monitored.

Of course, those who use the Internet are not representative of the whole electorate. Indeed, at present, although there are some 50 million people linked by the system throughout the world, in Britain it is inevitably only a very small proportion which has this facility. Any elected member must remember that he or she is at Westminster to represent the whole constituency, not just those who have an electronic voice. For this reason, some are wary, and stress the importance of ensuring that more people can use the 'Net', otherwise it gives power to an elite and leaves out the information-poor. Gore constantly reminds his American audiences that the real democratic potential of the Internet depends on universal access.

In the longer term, however, the prospect exists that people could take part in a kind of referendum via the 'Net', and this would give the elector a greater significance than ever before. MPs and Congressmen would need to listen to carefully to public demands, and Kevin Kelly of *Wired* magazine has suggested that 'the Internet revives Thomas Jefferson's 200-year-old dream of thinking individuals self-actualising a democracy'.[3] Gore and Gingrich share similar views, and believe that the superhighway could transform the culture of democratic politics. However, the dangers of 'electronic populism' and 'mobocracy' have been recognised even by some of those most closely involved in the area of information technology.

New inventions open up new possibilities both in the near future and into the far distance. As with all the other forms of the media which we have explored, there is a need to watch developments closely and see what regulation is appropriate. The question of ownership by powerful media multi-nationals arises, as does the possibility that the network could be used to disseminate racist propaganda or pornographic material. The difficulty is that with the internationalisation of the media, it is more difficult to achieve effective control.

## Notes

1 R. Collins and J. Purnell, *The Future of the BBC* (Institute for Public Policy Research: London, 1995), p. 13.
2 Al Gore, quoted in 'All Power to the Cybernauts', *Guardian*, 22 February 1995.
3 K. Kelly, *Wired* magazine, quoted in *ibid*.

# Appendices

# A questionnaire on the House of Lords

Please complete the questionnaire as fully as possible.

1　After 10 years of televised proceedings, do you regard television in the House of Lords as a good thing? Please give reasons, if time permits.

2　In either case (whether you favour the advent of the cameras or disapprove of the innovation), do you think it has had an effect on:

　a.　attendance levels?

　b.　Do you think it has had an effect on the behaviour of Peers? For example, is there a tendency to speak to the cameras rather than to fellow peers? Has television introduced a more heated tone to the proceedings?

　c.　Do you think television has had an effect on the frequency and length of speeches?

3　Do you find the presence of the cameras intrusive, or indeed off-putting? If so, in what way?

4　Do you regard the editing and use of televised materials by the broadcasting authorities as fair?

5　Do you think enough use is made of the available film from the House of Lords now that there is an abundance of material available on the House of Commons?

6　Has the arrival of television in the House changed its character in any ways other than already referred to?

Name _____

Party affiliation _____

Are you prepared to be quoted, or would you prefer your views to remain anonymous?

# A questionnaire on the House of Commons

Please answer as fully as you are able, and give reasons where they are appropriate.

1 Were you a supporter of the experiment to televise the House of Commons?

2 Would you have preferred a 'dedicated channel' providing continuous broadcast material from the House to the present arrangement of using edited extracts?

3 Do you think that television coverage has been fair to:

   a. all parties;

   b. to backbenchers?

4 a. Is there too much emphasis on using extracts from Question Time?

   b. Do you think that the value of Question Time has deteriorated since the introduction of the cameras?

   c. Do you think that the reputation of the House of Commons has suffered as a result of the broadcasting of Question Time?

5 a. If you favour televising the House, would you please indicate which of these considerations ranks most highly in your view?

     i. Helps promote greater awareness of what goes on at Westminster.

     ii. Helps bring parliament closer to the people.

     iii. Restores the importance of Westminster in national life.

     iv. Helps to stimulate better attendance in the Commons.

     v. Helps to promote better behaviour in the Commons.

     vi. Helps stimulate the campaign to modernise the procedures of the House.

     vii. Any other consideration.

   b. If you feel that the cameras should not be allowed in the House, please explain why.

6 Many people feared that allowing the cameras in would have one or more of these effects. Can you please indicate if any of these have happened:

     i. Encourages MPs to speak to to their constituents rather than to those present in the Chamber.

     ii. Destroys the intimacy and conversational style of the House.

iii. Emphasises the gladiatorial contest of the Front Bench speakers, and therefore gives a false impression of the overall work of the House.

iv. The lighting/cameras might prove intrusive.

7 Are the rules under which those who control the cameras operate still too restrictive?

8 Have you any regrets about letting in the cameras, which have not already emerged?

9 Has the arrival of the cameras in the House had any impact on your behaviour/appearance in the House – e.g. dress, manner of speech, seating position, etc.?

10 Have you felt the need to seek professional advice and be 'groomed' for television – e.g. 'Folletised' by any agency?

Name _____

Party affiliation _____

Are you willing for your views to be attributed in any written material?

# Responses to the 1995 Questionnaire

Despite the reluctance of the House to admit the cameras, it was impossible to find an MP who opposed their admission. Most would have preferred a dedicated channel providing continuous coverage as well as the present arrangement, though a common view was that this would be fine in principle, 'but not realistic' (Clare Short).

The overwhelming view was that television has been fair to all parties, though significantly a representative of a small party, Plaid Cymru, felt otherwise. Many respondents felt that backbenchers had been ill-catered-for, though others were less certain; the point was made by one of them that she did not 'get much opportunity to see it', and was therefore unable to offer a judgement.

Although Robin Corbett liked the emphasis on Question Time, because it 'gives a good spread of members on the Back Benches', the overwhelming view was that Question Time – especially Prime Minister's Questions received too much attention, though this was seen as 'inevitable' (Clare Short). The majority did not feel that the value of Question Time had deteriorated, nor that the reputation of the House had suffered because the public can now see it live or in extracts used in the news. Indeed, the point was made that television meant that 'more people now better understand how we work' (Robin Corbett). Some were more concerned that Question Time did contribute to the low view many people hold of Parliament, and that its value had declined, 'but I don't think the cameras are the reason'. The point was made by Margaret Ewing that Question Time 'has always been the party political hustings of the House of Commons'.

Of the reasons given for televising the House, most MPs believed that it helped provide greater awareness of what goes on at Westminster, and helps keep the House in touch with the public. None felt that the presence of the cameras has encouraged better behaviour ('Definitely, No!', Michael Fabricant), and only two believed that it encouraged better attendance, but nearly half felt that it assisted in the campaign for a modernisation of Commons proceedings. The onlt additional argument advanced in favour of television in the House was that it was essentially democratic in that it 'supposes the answerability of government and of MPs' (Dafydd Wigley)

Of the possible effects of allowing the cameras in, no one found the lighting of cameras intrusive. A few MPs believed that they 'encourage [Members] to speak to their constituents rather than to those present in the Chamber', but many felt that they do not 'destroy the intimacy and conversational style of the House', for the reason given by Jeff Rooker; 'No, because most times we forget the cameras.' In line with the feeling that Question Time received too much coverage, there was a widespread feeling that television 'emphasises the gladiatorial contest of the Front Bench', though it was pointed out that the nature of the House is 'confrontational' (Bob Ainsworth). Most MPs felt that the rules under which TV operates are too restrictive, though 'there have to be safeguards, particularly if live feed is allowed' (Dafydd Wigley).

Few expressed any other regrets about the impact of the cameras, but the Plaid Cymru representative felt that in the run-up to the 1992 election the Government acted unfairly by 'concocting statements at 3.30 on Tuesdays and Thursdays', presumably to gain publicity for the electorally popular announcements, and Michael Fabricant has concluded that 'coverage trivialises the House of Commons'.

With regard to the personal impact, as opposed to any impact on the House and its repuattion, only Jeff Rooker chose to comment. Having now seen himself on film, he feels the 'need to keep still at the Despatch Box'. None admitted to having sought professional advice on grooming/manner/ deportment/voice projection. It would seem that though some frontbench spokespersons are candidates for the Follett treatment, backbenchers who lack the attention of the camera's roving eye are less convinced of the need to seek advice. The decision to do so, it was pointed out, is a purely individual matter.

# Further reading

This book has explored a number of areas which most books on the mass media refer to only briefly. Nonetheless, there are many works worthy of reference, several of which are alluded to in the script or in the footnotes.

In particular, Ralph Negrine's volume on *Politics and the Mass Media* (second edition, Routledge: London, 1994) is a comprehensive introduction to the role of the mass media at all levels, and it explores the relationship of politics and broadcasting effectively and thoroughly. It also has a very lengthy series of reference notes which mention many valuable sources.

John Keane's *The Media and Democracy* (Polity Press: Oxford, 1991) is – as its name implies – concerned with the importance of the media to a democracy, and tackles areas of debate on topics such as the liberty of the press.

Bill Miller's study of *Media and Voters* (Clarendon Press: Oxford, 1991) is an analysis of the content and influence of the media in the 1987 election, and David Denver's *Elections and Voting Behaviour in Britain* (second edition, Harvester Wheatsheaf: Hemel Hempstead, 1994), both offer penetrating observations on the impact of the media on voting behaviour, and are certainly worthy of further exploration.

The Butler and Kavanagh studies of recent elections (in particular those on the British general elections of 1987 and 1992), published by Macmillan (London), contain valuable chapters on the role of the media in specific elections. They survey the way in which the media handled the campaigns, and the reactions of the politicians to that coverage. Studies on particular campaigns are often helpful in illustrating how the media operate, and *The Selling of the Prime Minister*, by Rodney Tyler (Grafton Books: London, 1987), gives an interesting account of the last election fought by Margaret Thatcher as Prime Minister.

The survey of Joe McGinnis, *The Selling of the President* (André Deutsch: London, 1970), provides an illuminating study of the way in which new techniques of marketing were used to sell Richard Nixon, a candidate not immediately seen as lovable by the American electorate. Laurence Rees's *Selling Politics* (BBC Books: London, 1992) and Brendan Bruce's *Images of Power* (Kogan Page: London, 1992) are both worth consulting. They deal with the world of the image-makers, the advisers and consultants whose task it is to market parties and politicians.

The BBC Handbooks and Yearbooks provide up-to-date information and an up-to-date bibliography, and the Corporation's *The BBC: Seventy Years of*

*Broadcasting* (London, 1992), written by John Cain, is a helpful introduction to the development of the organisation and to the relationship of politicians and the broadcasters. The writing of some of those who have worked in the media is stimulating, if not always objective; in such a category falls Bernard Ingham's *Kill the Messenger* (Harper Collins: London, 1991).

Shortly before the final version of this work was completed, Routledge produced a new volume by Brian McNair, *An Introduction to Political Communication* (London). Unfortunately it arrived on the scene too late to influence the content or judgements of my own study. It is written more for candidates pursuing courses in Sociology or Media Studies, whereas it is hoped that this more lengthy review will be of interest to those students but is primarily targeted at students of Government and Politics.

Around the same time, Dennis Kavanagh's *Election Campaigning: The New Marketing of Politics* was published by Blackwell (Oxford). As its name implies, it is also concerned with the selling of politicians and the 'Americanisation' of British electioneering. It explores some of the ground included within this survey, although it allows little space for a number of my own interests – such as the political interview. On an initial reading, its analysis and conclusions do not appear to conflict with those in this book, in any significant way. It is a very useful addition to the literature on the subject.

# Index